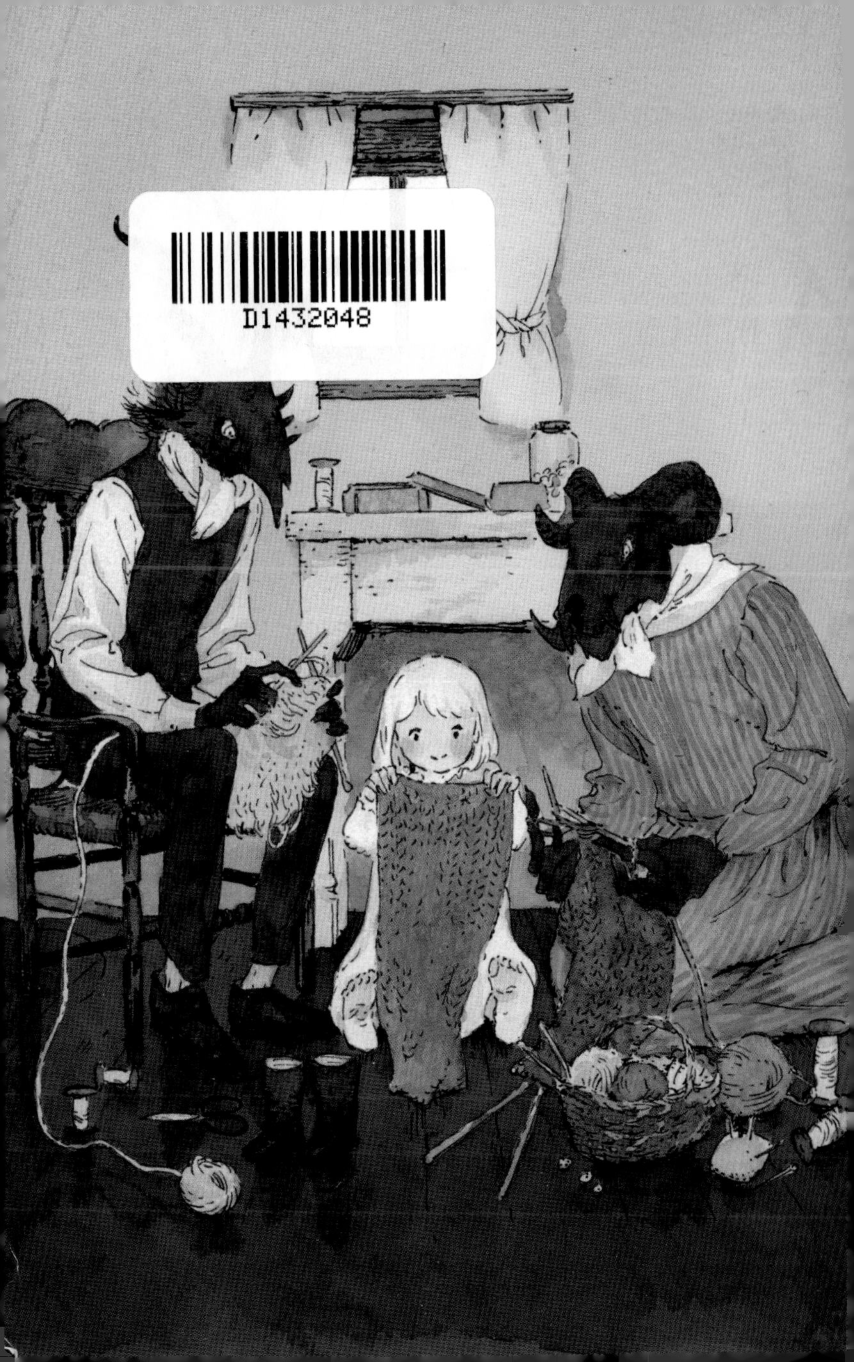

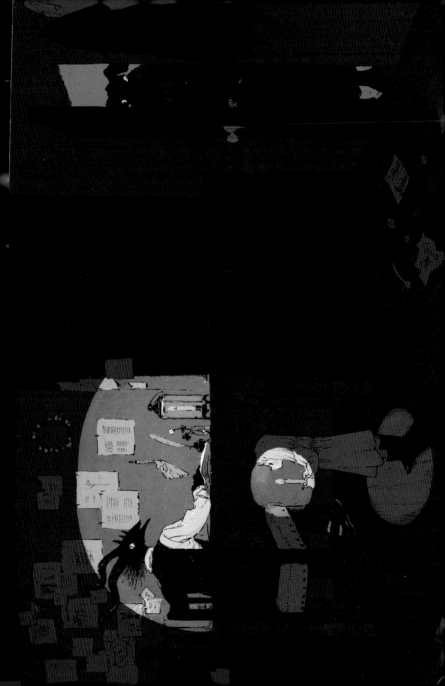

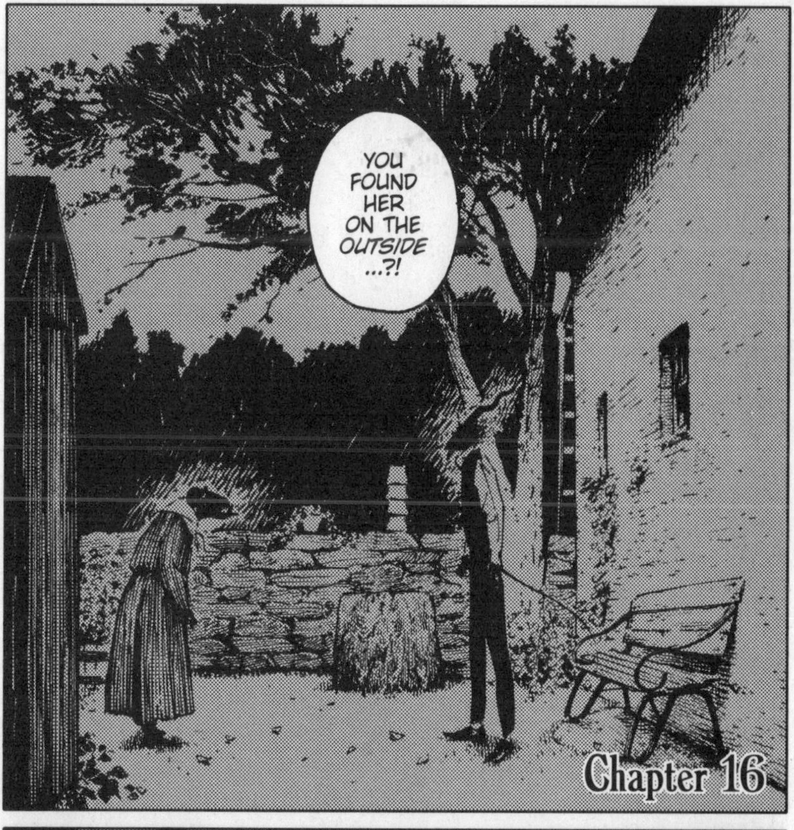
YOU FOUND HER ON THE OUTSIDE ...?!
Chapter 16
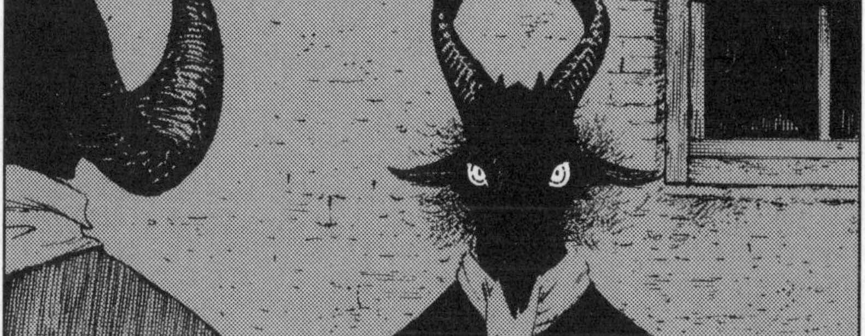

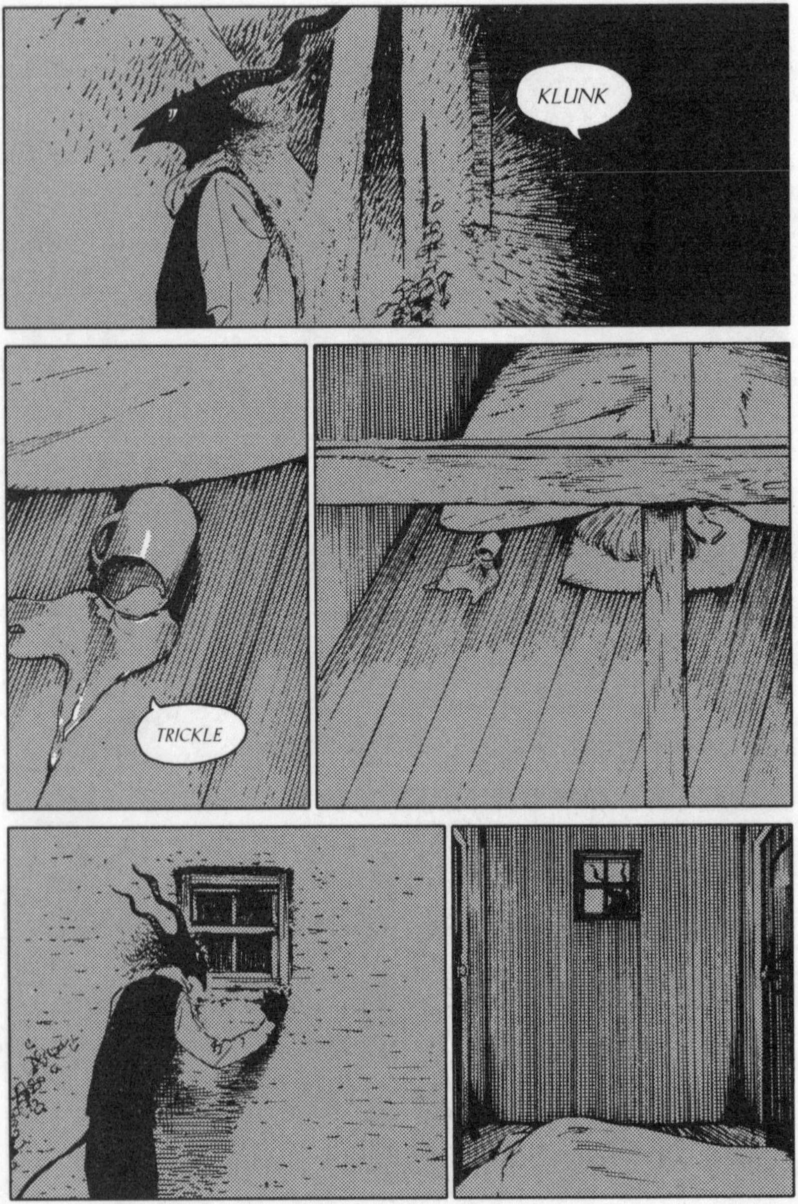
KLUNK
TRICKLE

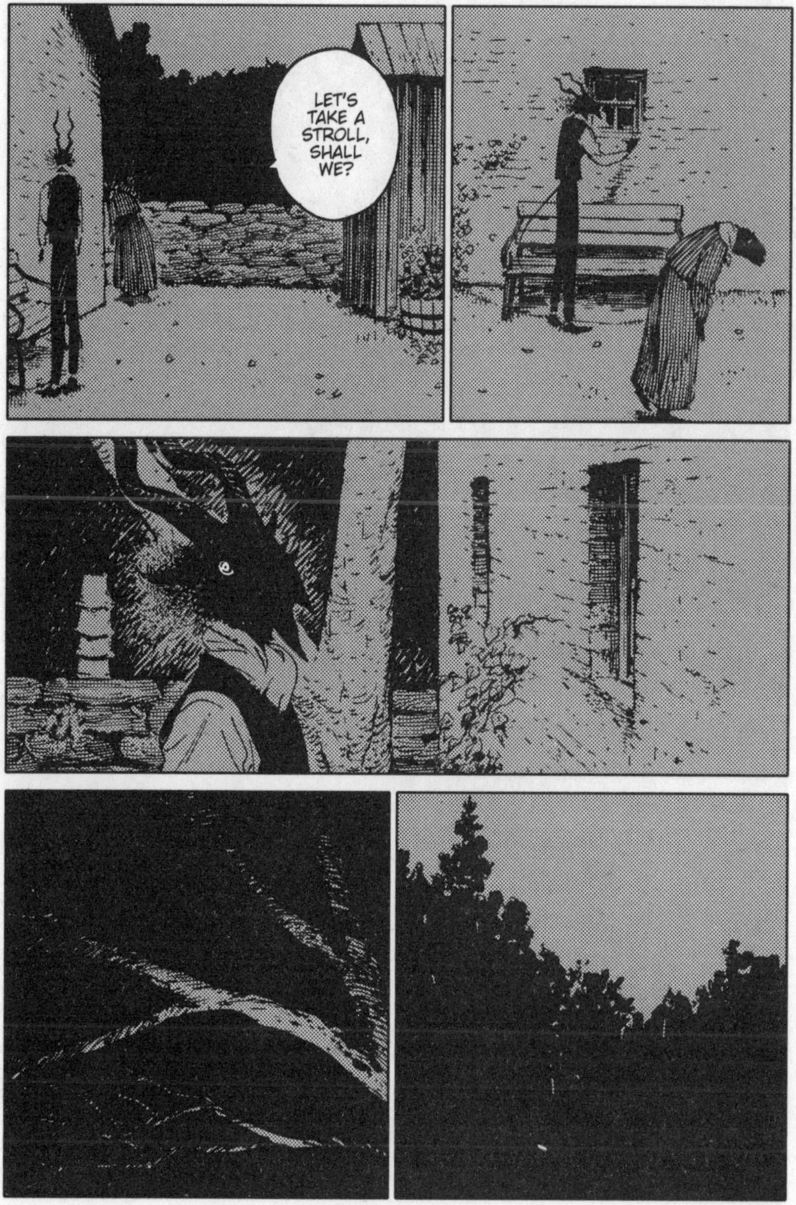
LET'S TAKE A STROLL, SHALL WE?

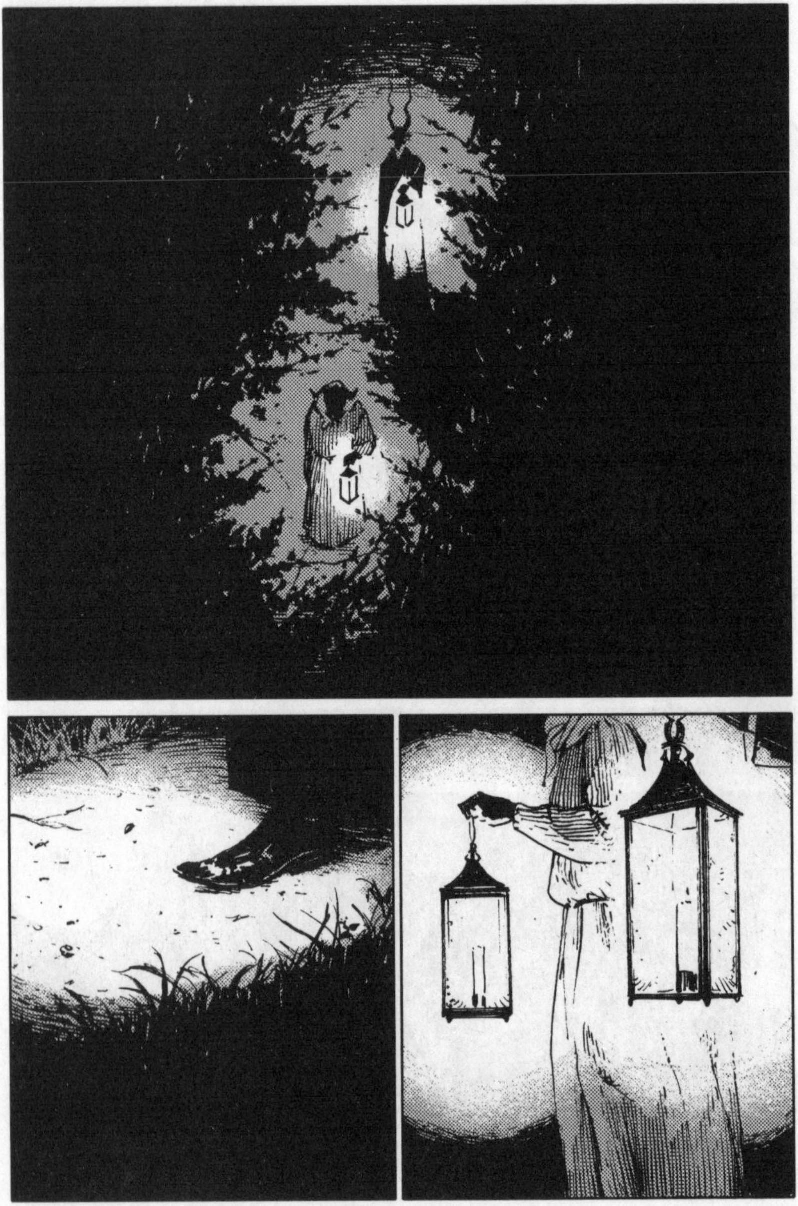

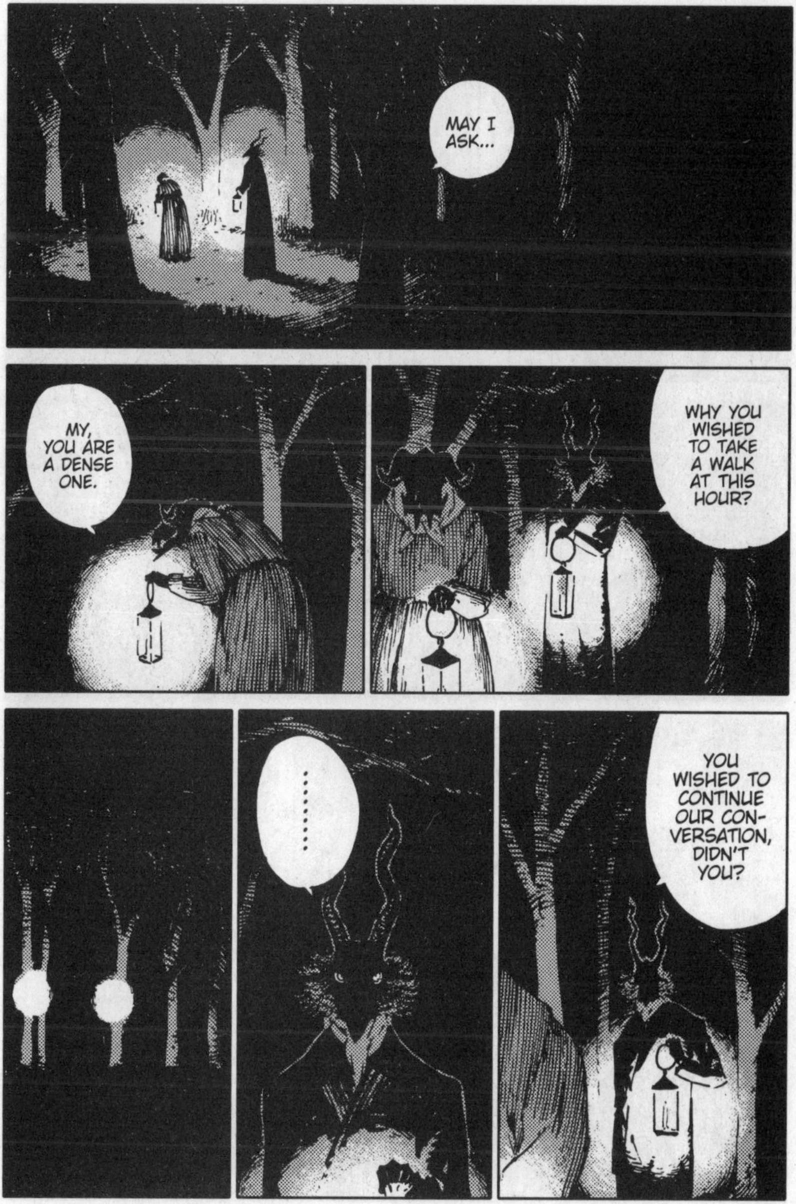
MAY I ASK...
WHY YOU WISHED TO TAKE A WALK AT THIS HOUR?
MY, YOU ARE A DENSE ONE.
YOU WISHED TO CONTINUE OUR CON-VERSATION, DIDN'T YOU?
......

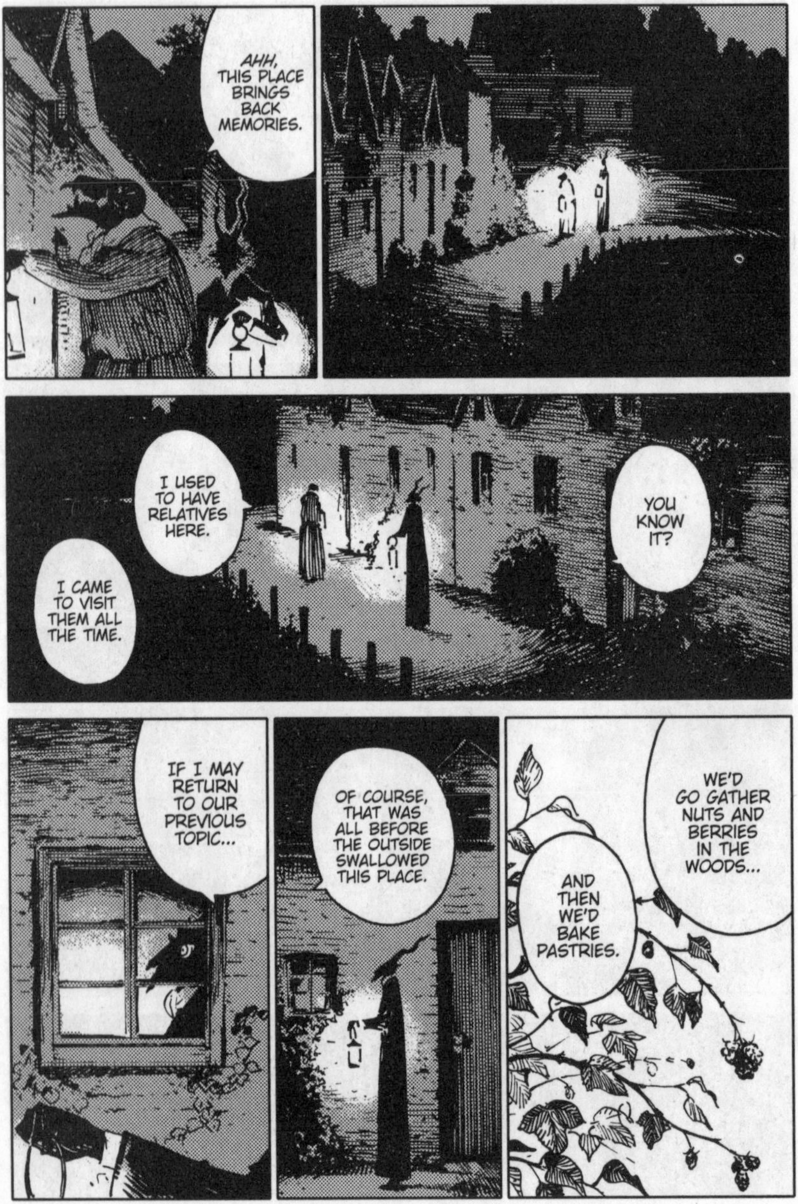
AHH, THIS PLACE BRINGS BACK MEMORIES.
YOU KNOW IT?
I USED TO HAVE RELATIVES HERE.
I CAME TO VISIT THEM ALL THE TIME.
WE'D GO GATHER NUTS AND BERRIES IN THE WOODS...
AND THEN WE'D BAKE PASTRIES.
OF COURSE, THAT WAS ALL BEFORE THE OUTSIDE SWALLOWED THIS PLACE.
IF I MAY RETURN TO OUR PREVIOUS TOPIC...

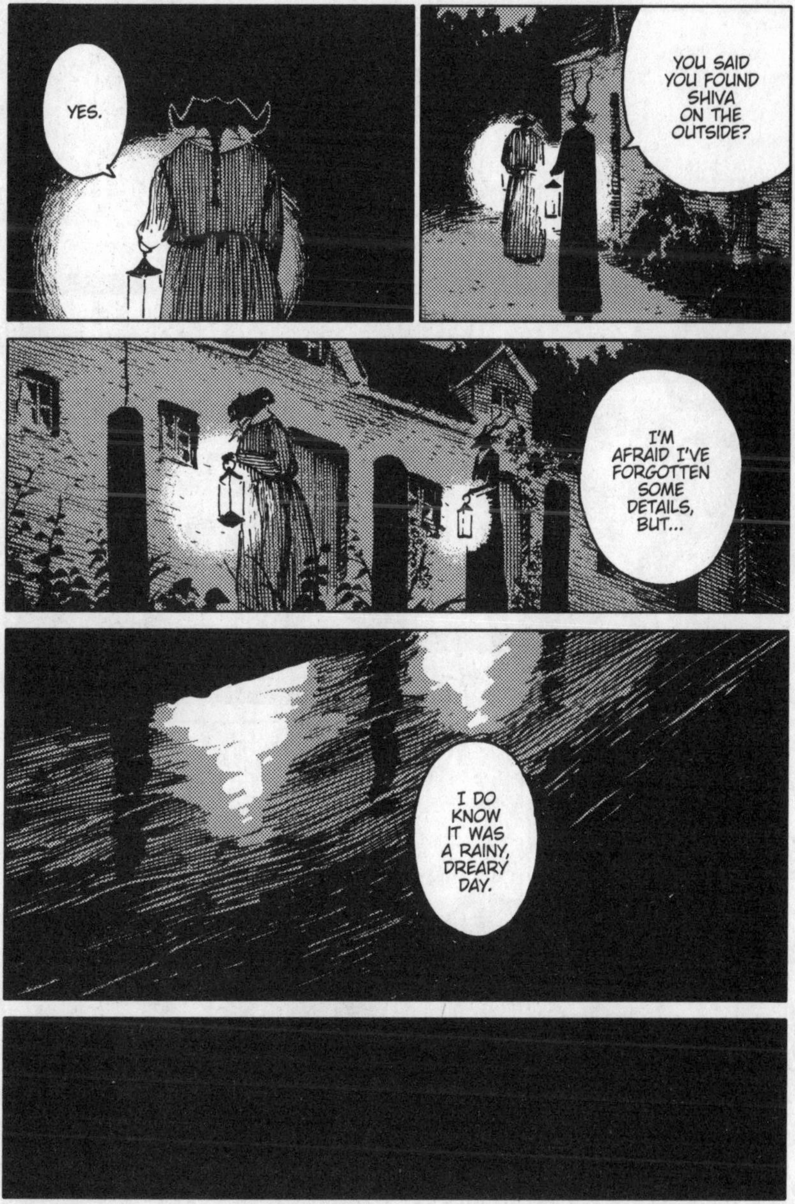
YOU SAID YOU FOUND SHIVA ON THE OUTSIDE?
YES.
I'M AFRAID I'VE FORGOTTEN SOME DETAILS, BUT...
I DO KNOW IT WAS A RAINY, DREARY DAY.

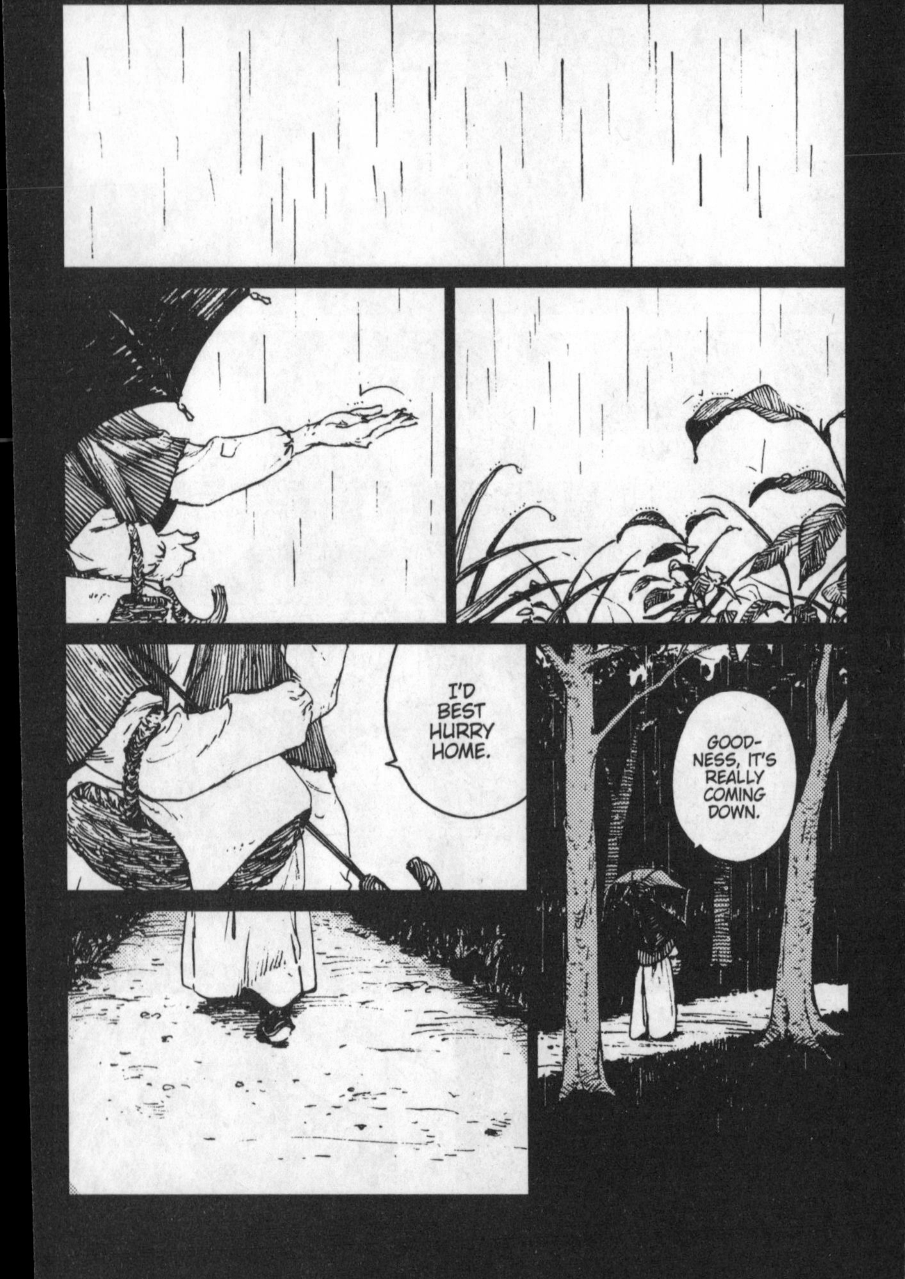
I'D BEST HURRY HOME.
GOOD-NESS, IT'S REALLY COMING DOWN.

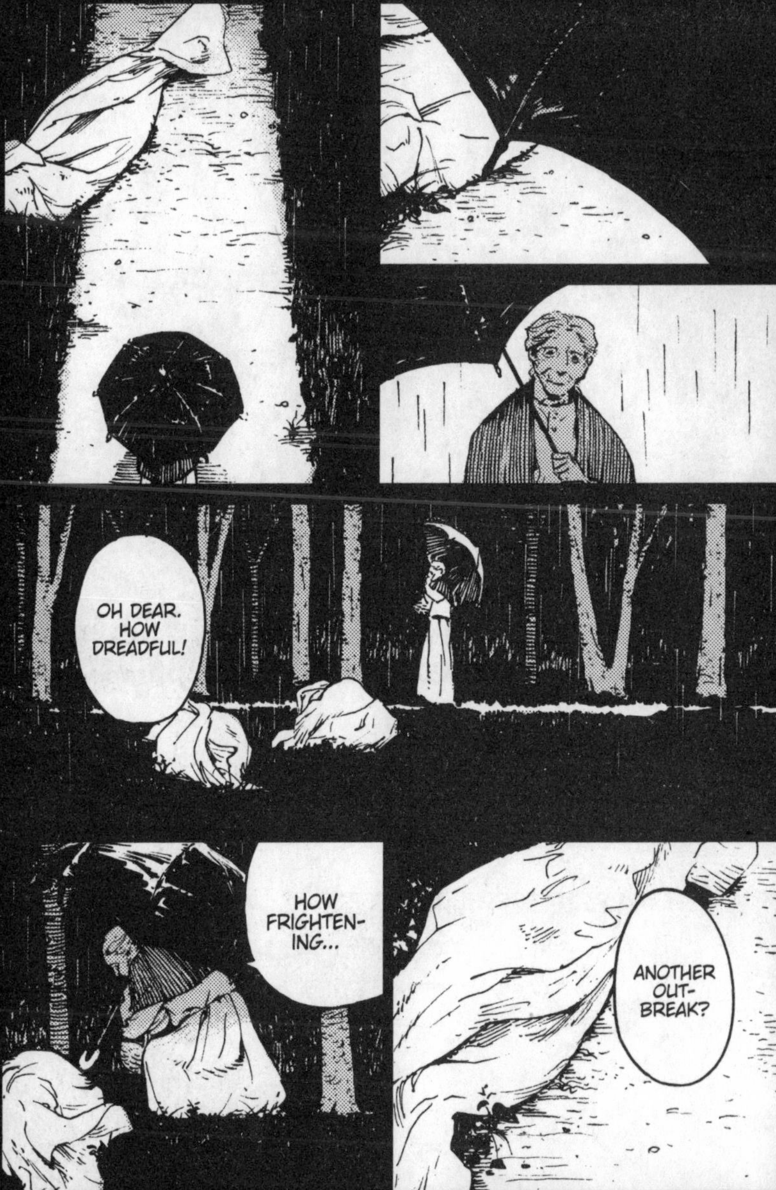
OH DEAR. HOW DREADFUL!
HOW FRIGHTEN-ING...
ANOTHER OUT-BREAK?

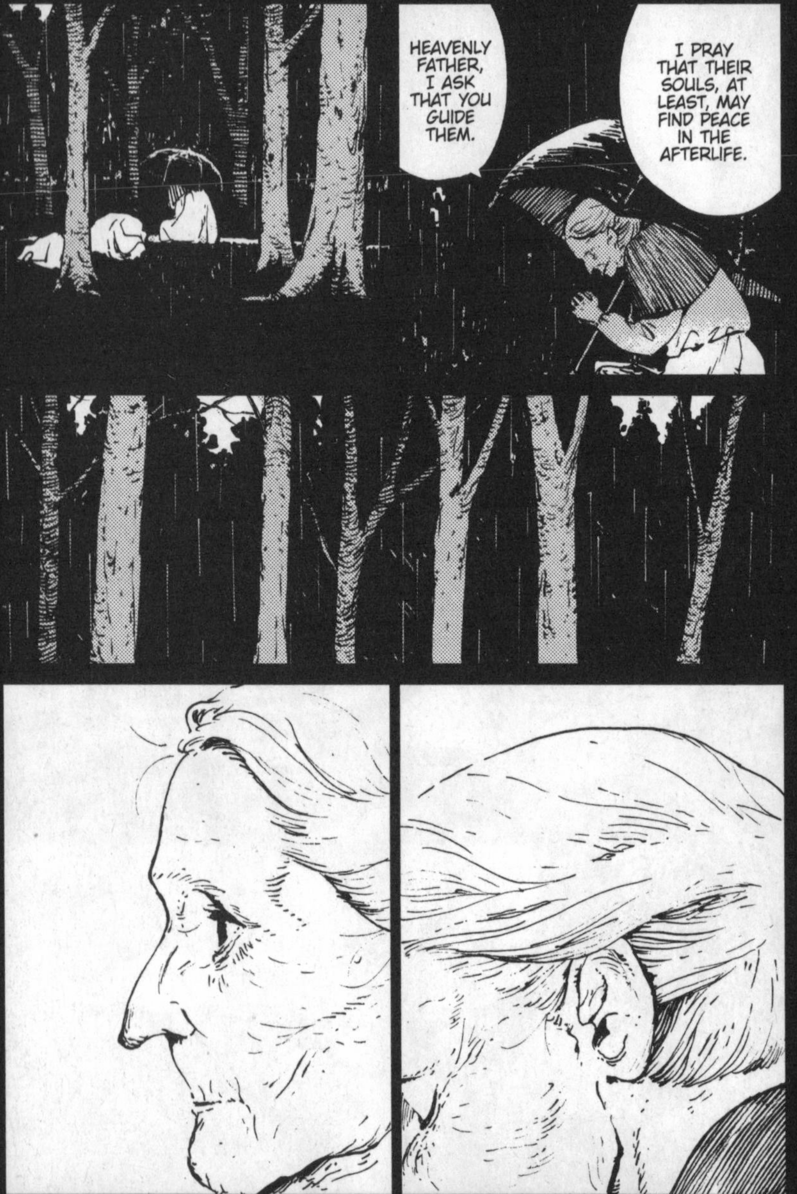
HEAVENLY FATHER, I ASK THAT YOU GUIDE THEM.
I PRAY THAT THEIR SOULS, AT LEAST, MAY FIND PEACE IN THE AFTERLIFE.

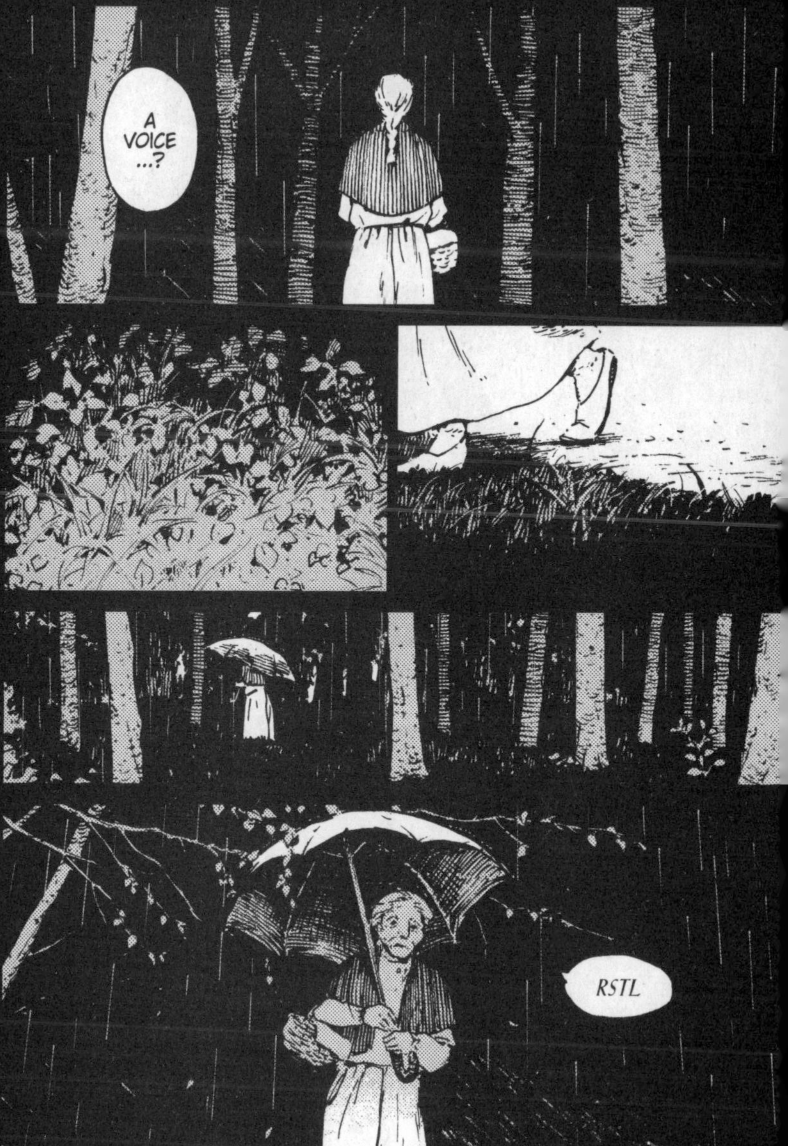
A VOICE ...?
RSTL

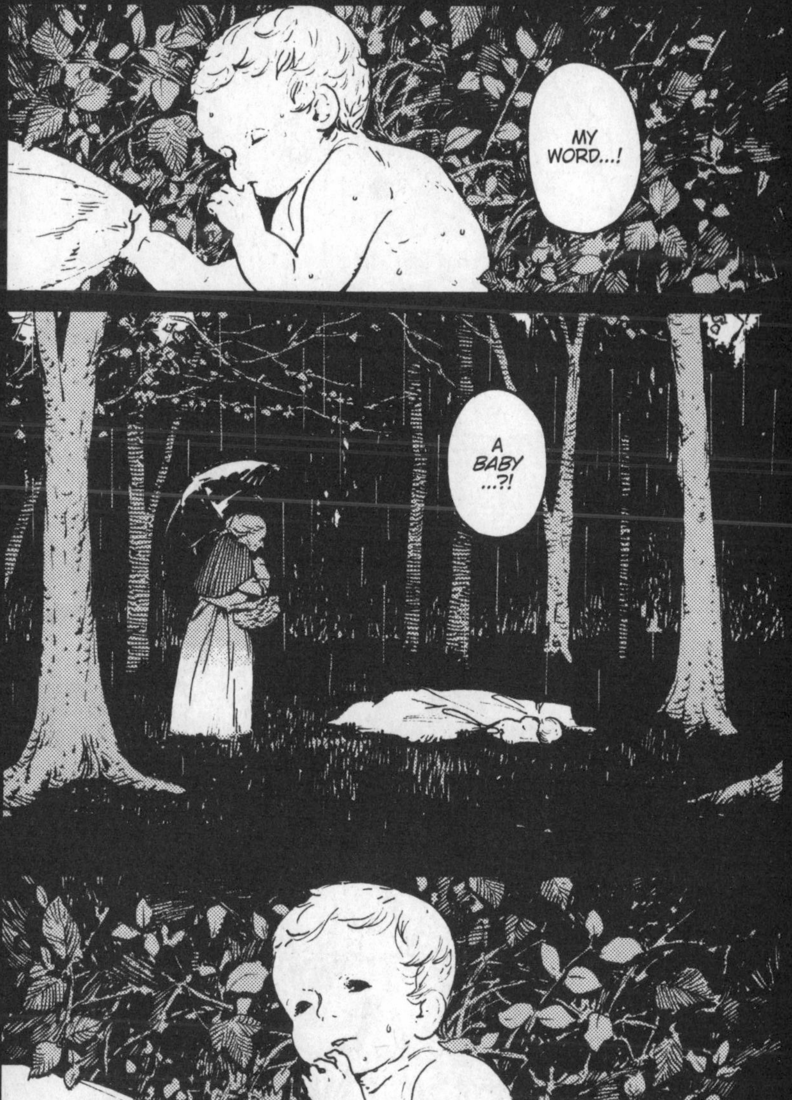
MY WORD...!
A BABY ...?!

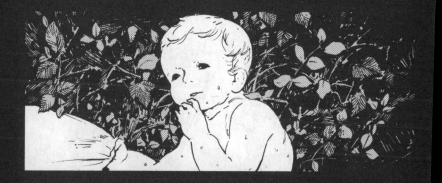

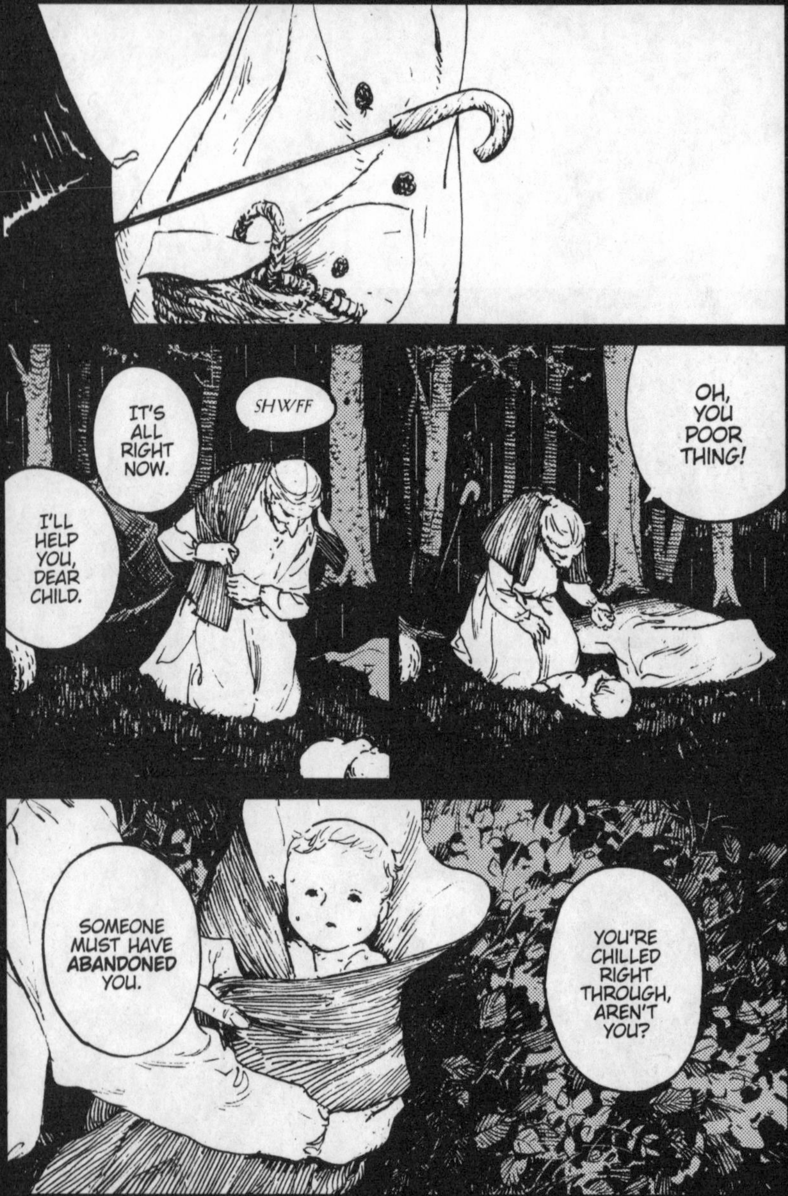
OH, YOU POOR THING!
SHWFF
IT'S ALL RIGHT NOW.
I'LL HELP YOU, DEAR CHILD.
YOU'RE CHILLED RIGHT THROUGH, AREN'T YOU?
SOMEONE MUST HAVE ABANDONED YOU.

HOW
CRUEL...!

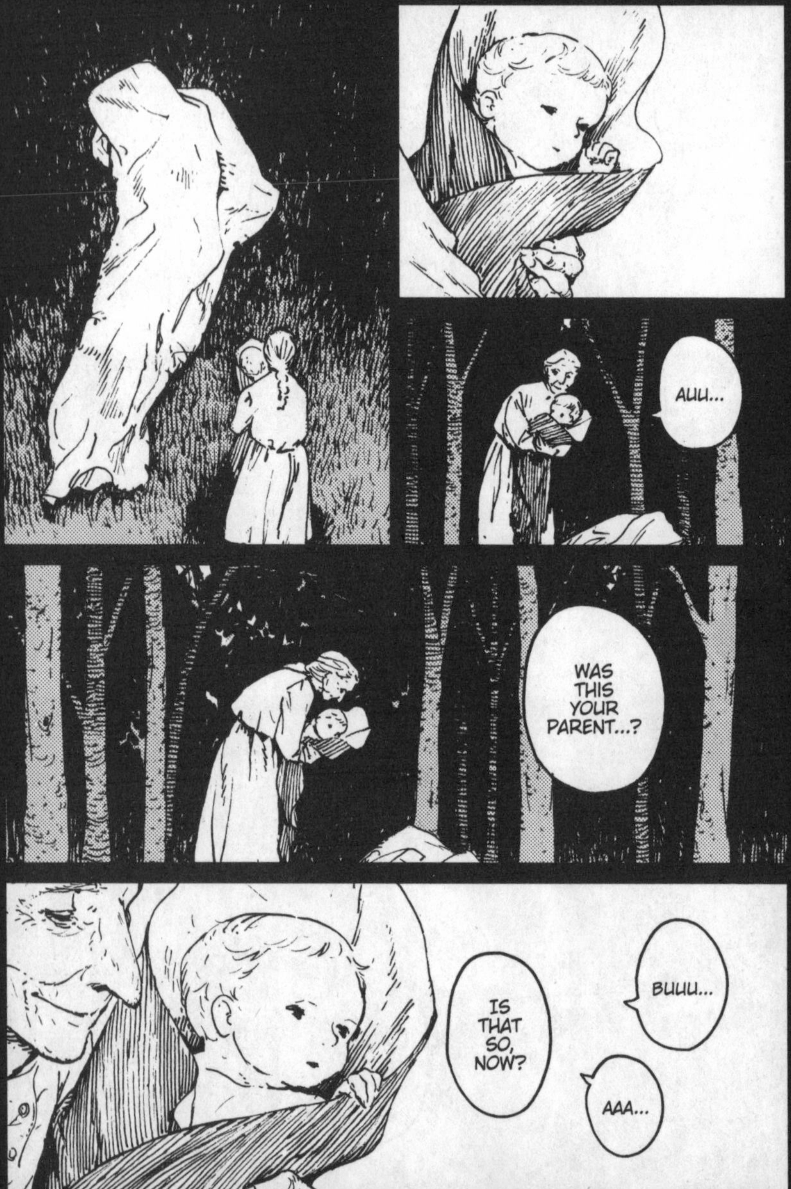
AUU...
WAS THIS YOUR PARENT...?
BUUU...
IS THAT SO, NOW?
AAA...

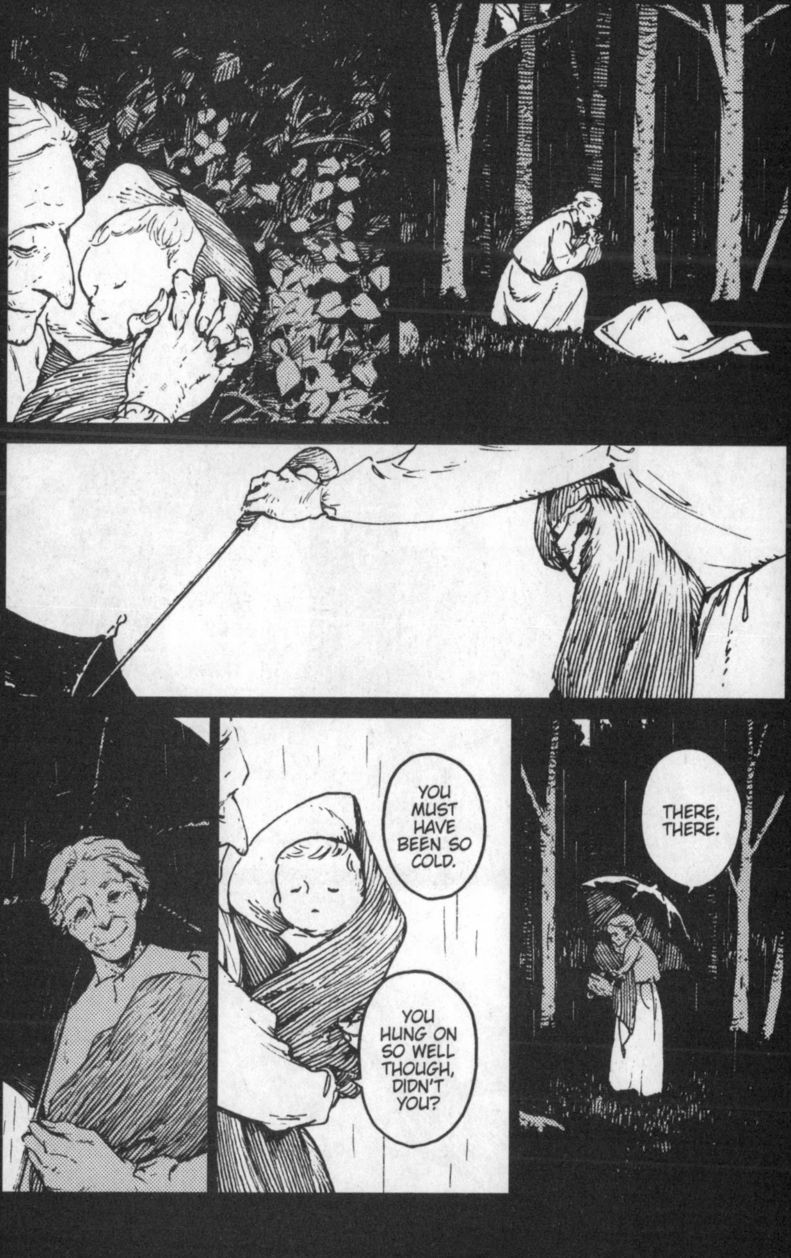
THERE, THERE.
YOU MUST HAVE BEEN SO COLD.
YOU HUNG ON SO WELL THOUGH, DIDN'T YOU?

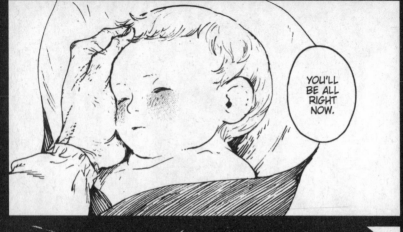

YOU'LL BE ALL RIGHT NOW.

DON'T YOU WORRY ABOUT A THING.

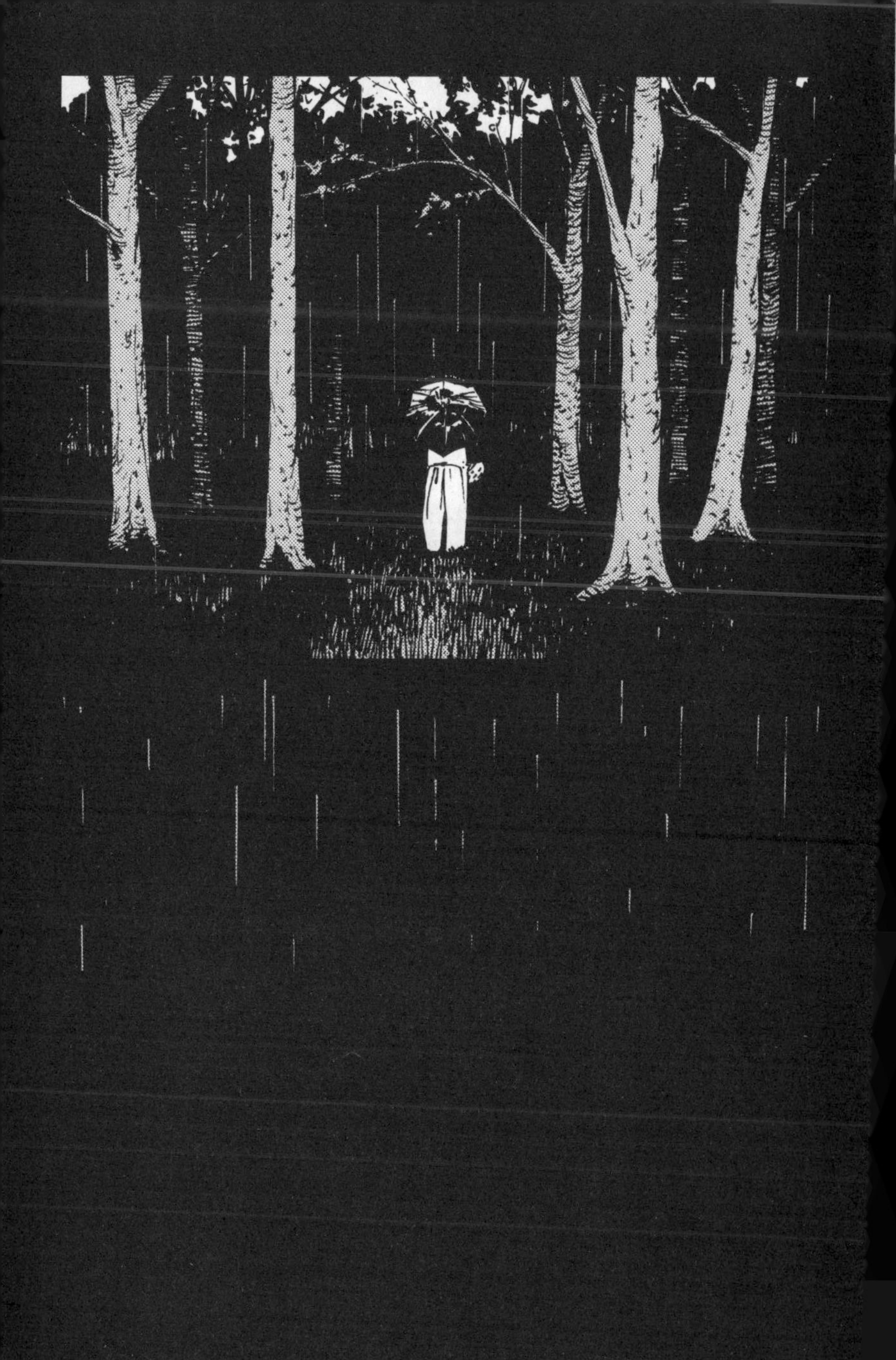

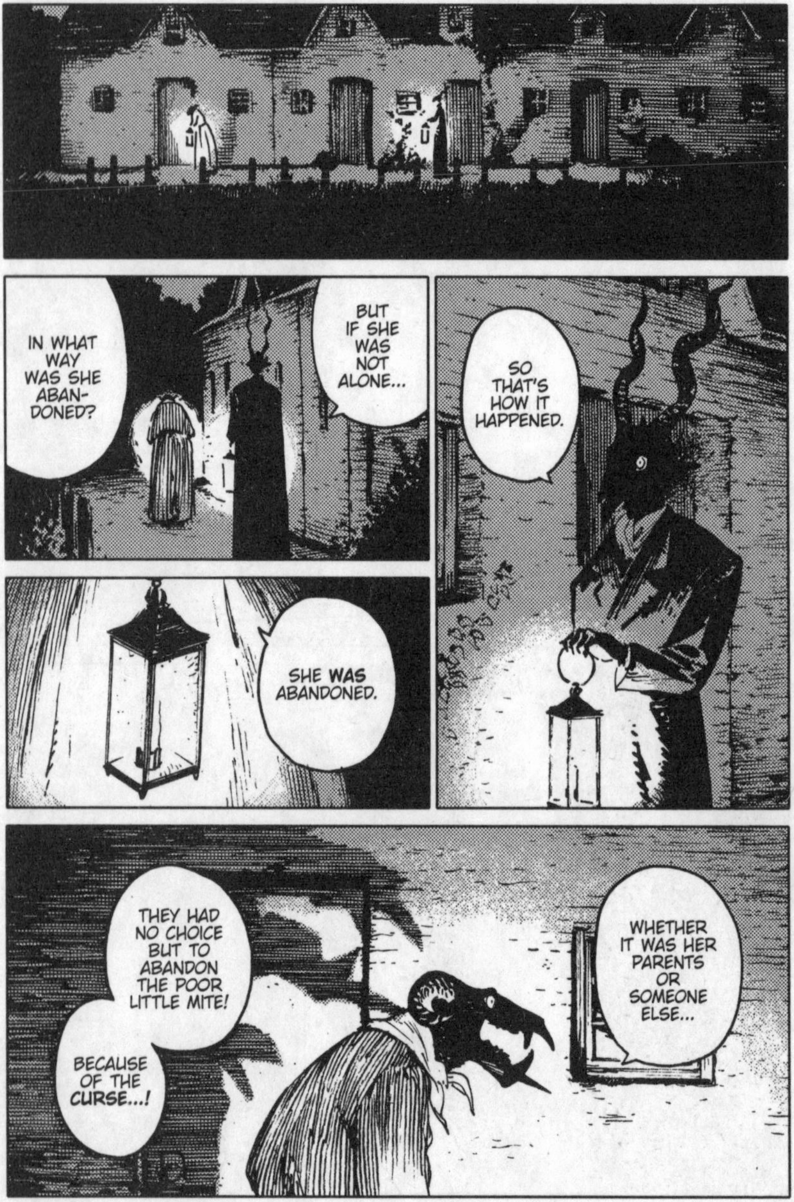
SO THAT'S HOW IT HAPPENED.
BUT IF SHE WAS NOT ALONE...
IN WHAT WAY WAS SHE ABANDONED?
SHE WAS ABANDONED.
WHETHER IT WAS HER PARENTS OR SOMEONE ELSE...
THEY HAD NO CHOICE BUT TO ABANDON THE POOR LITTLE MITE!
BECAUSE OF THE CURSE...!

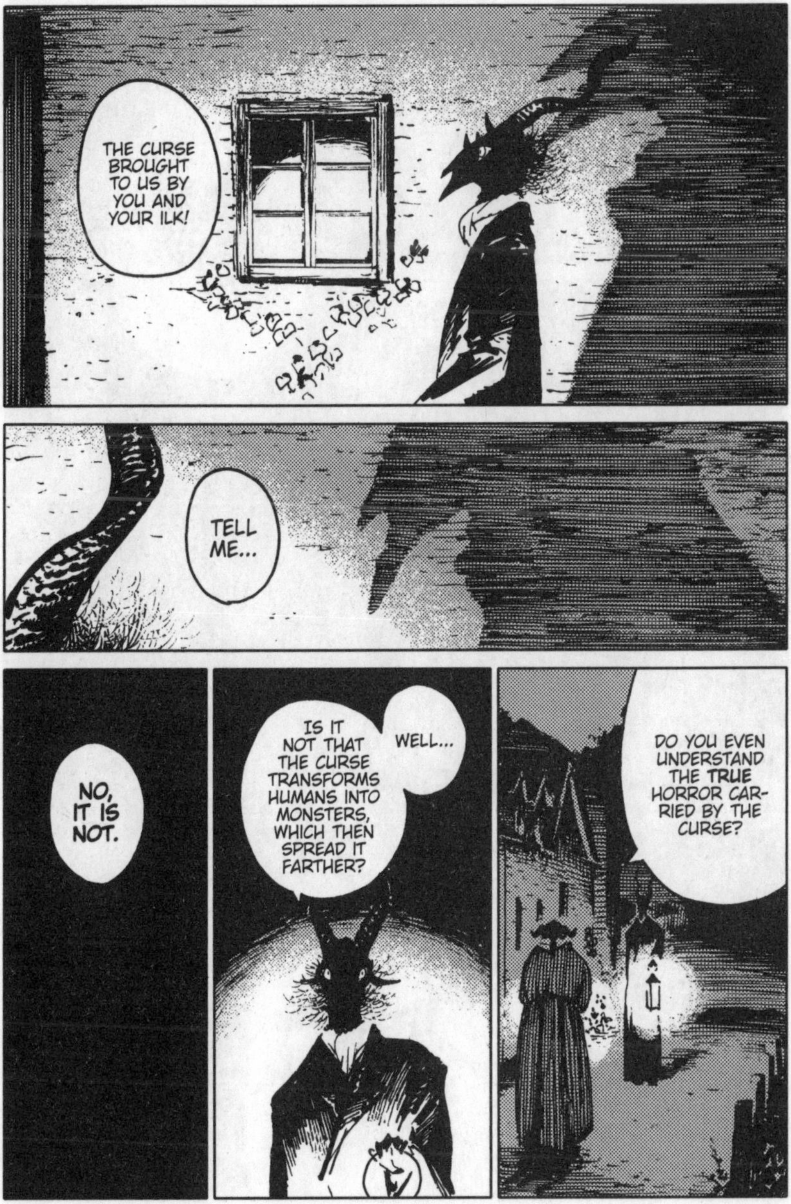
THE CURSE BROUGHT TO US BY YOU AND YOUR ILK!
TELL ME...
DO YOU EVEN UNDERSTAND THE **TRUE** HORROR CARRIED BY THE CURSE?
WELL...
IS IT NOT THAT THE CURSE TRANSFORMS HUMANS INTO MONSTERS, WHICH THEN SPREAD IT FARTHER?
NO, IT IS NOT.

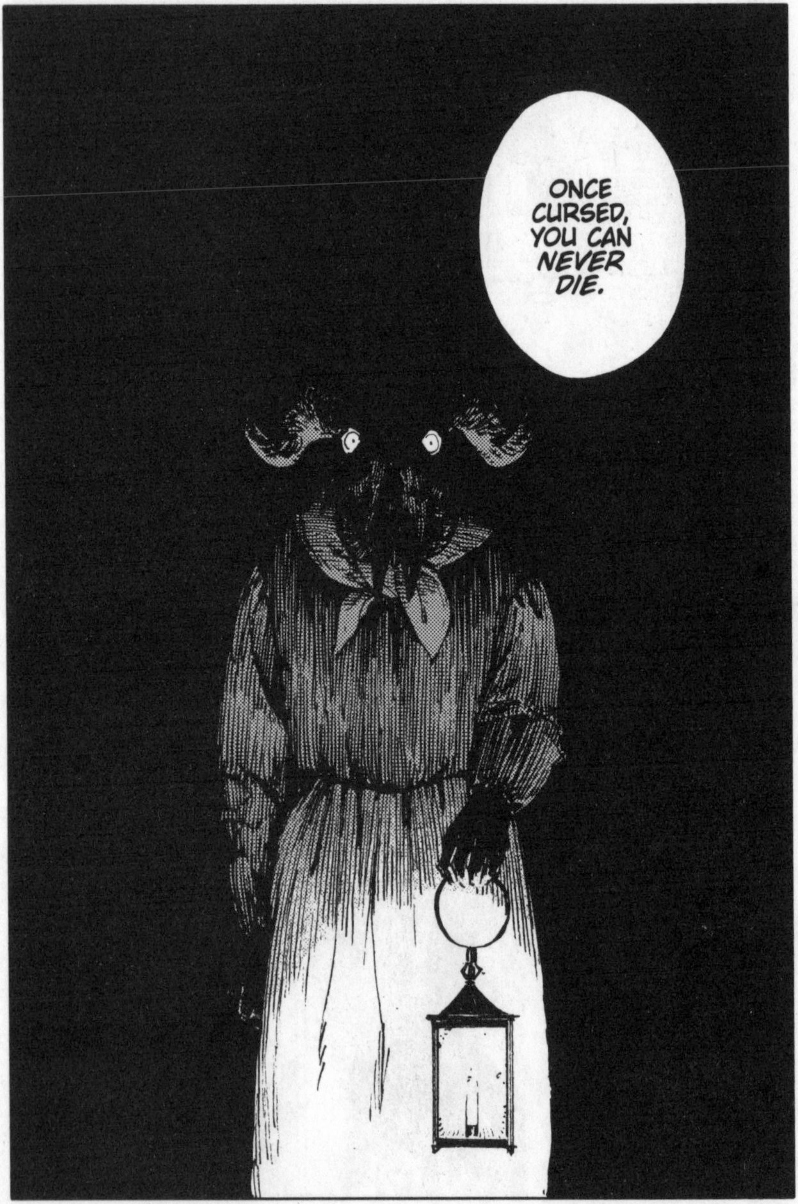
ONCE CURSED, YOU CAN NEVER DIE.

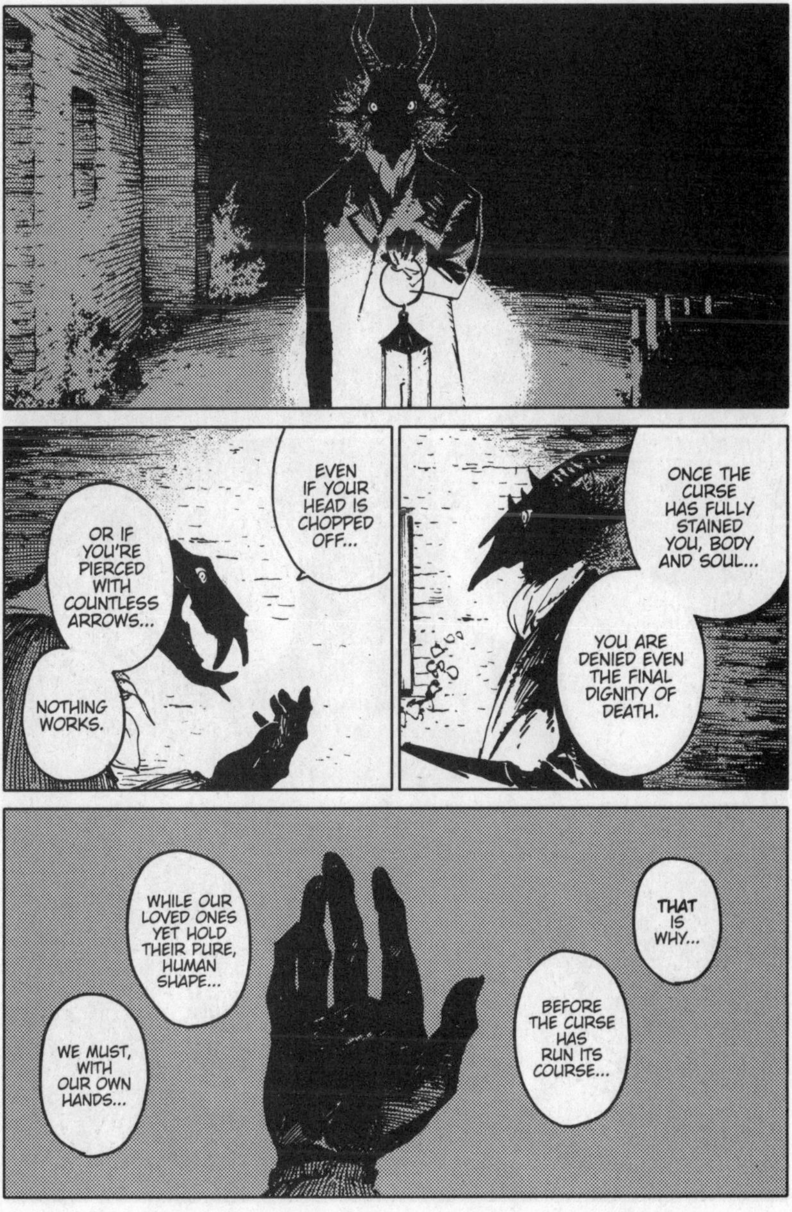
ONCE THE CURSE HAS FULLY STAINED YOU, BODY AND SOUL...
YOU ARE DENIED EVEN THE FINAL DIGNITY OF DEATH.
EVEN IF YOUR HEAD IS CHOPPED OFF...
OR IF YOU'RE PIERCED WITH COUNTLESS ARROWS...
NOTHING WORKS.
THAT IS WHY...
BEFORE THE CURSE HAS RUN ITS COURSE...
WHILE OUR LOVED ONES YET HOLD THEIR PURE, HUMAN SHAPE...
WE MUST, WITH OUR OWN HANDS...

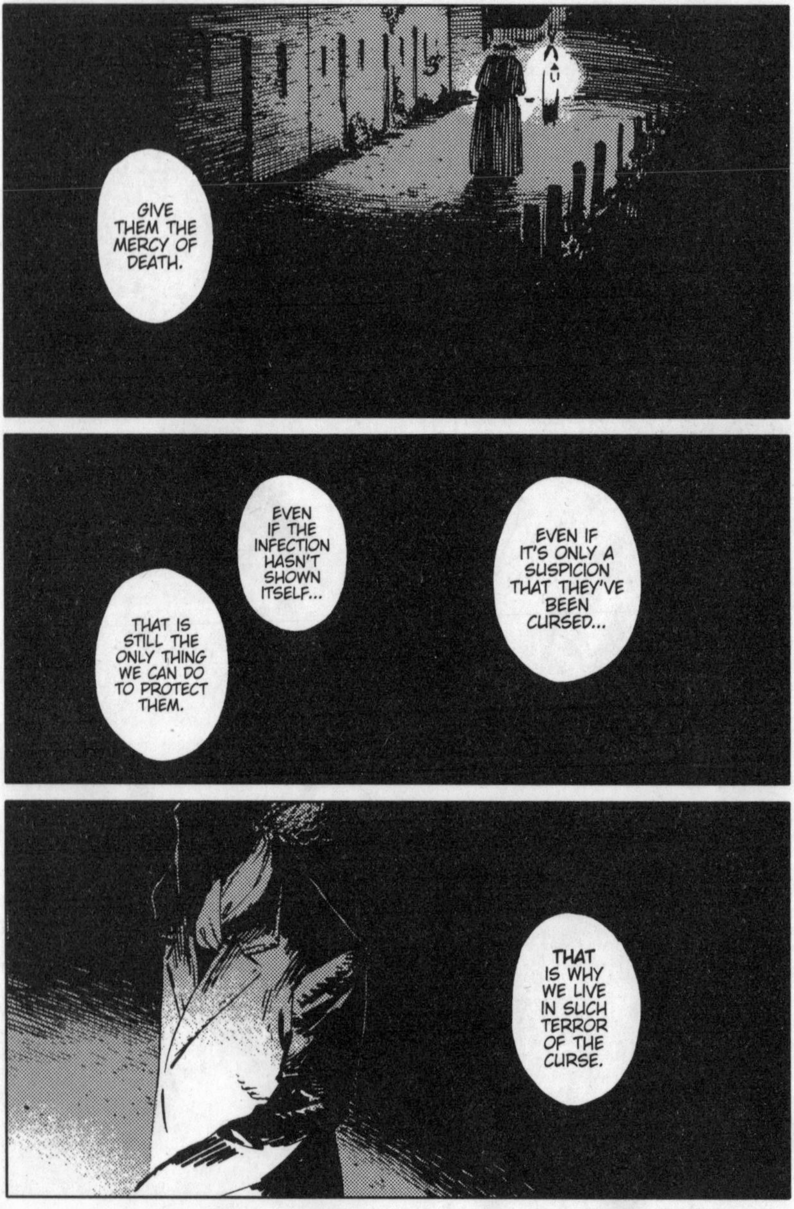
GIVE THEM THE MERCY OF DEATH.
EVEN IF IT'S ONLY A SUSPICION THAT THEY'VE BEEN CURSED...
EVEN IF THE INFECTION HASN'T SHOWN ITSELF...
THAT IS STILL THE ONLY THING WE CAN DO TO PROTECT THEM.
THAT IS WHY WE LIVE IN SUCH TERROR OF THE CURSE.

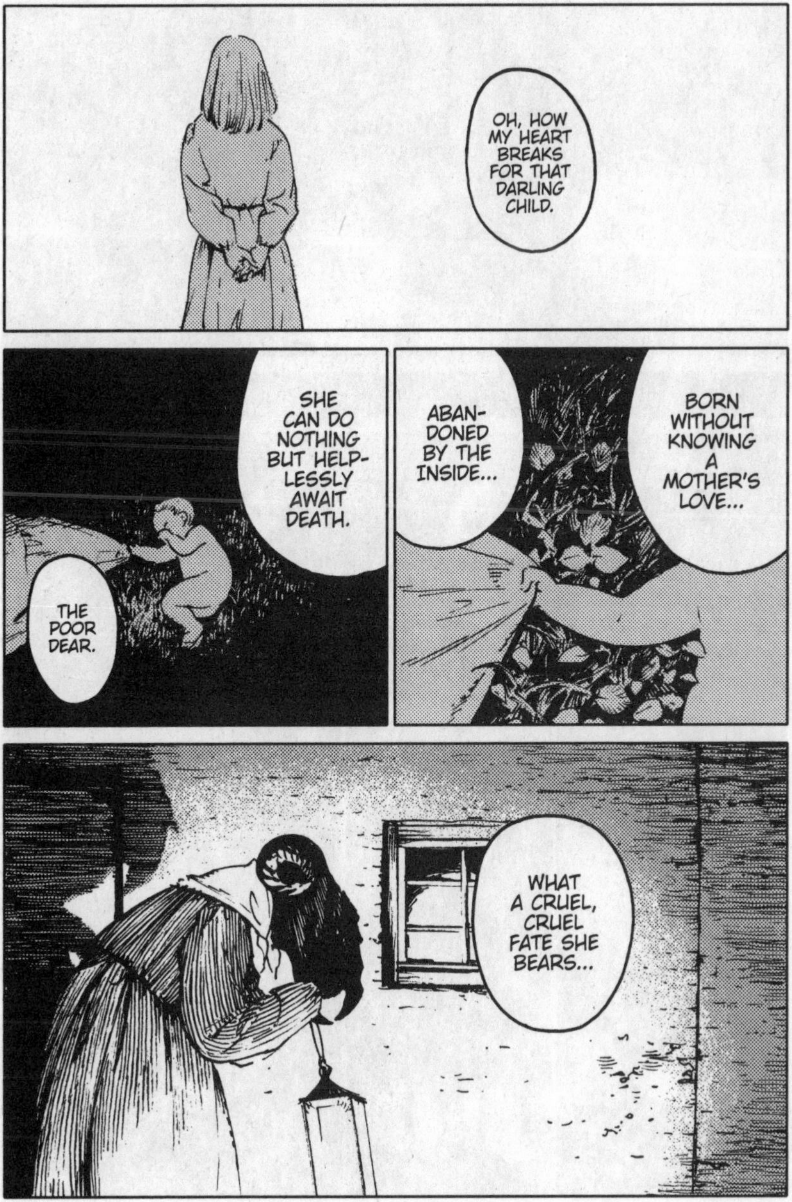
OH, HOW MY HEART BREAKS FOR THAT DARLING CHILD.
BORN WITHOUT KNOWING A MOTHER'S LOVE...
ABAN-DONED BY THE INSIDE...
SHE CAN DO NOTHING BUT HELP-LESSLY AWAIT DEATH.
THE POOR DEAR.
WHAT A CRUEL, CRUEL FATE SHE BEARS...

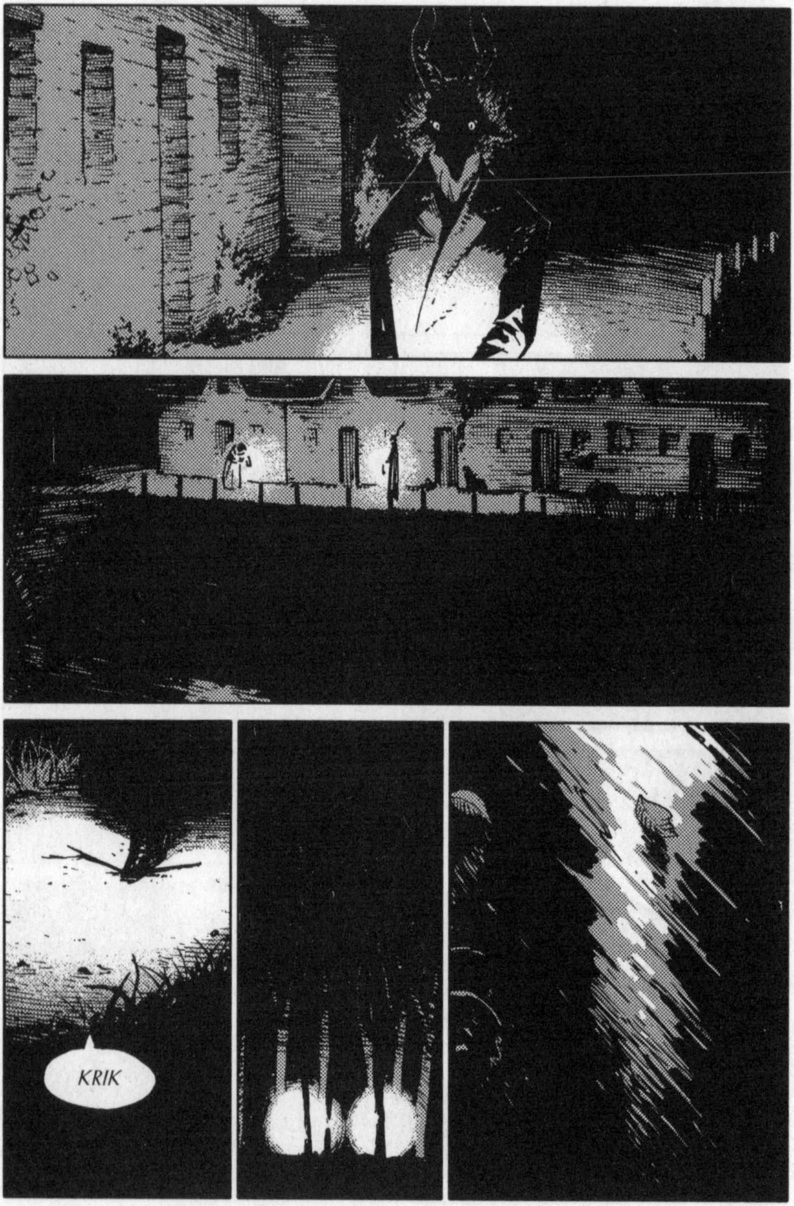
KRIK

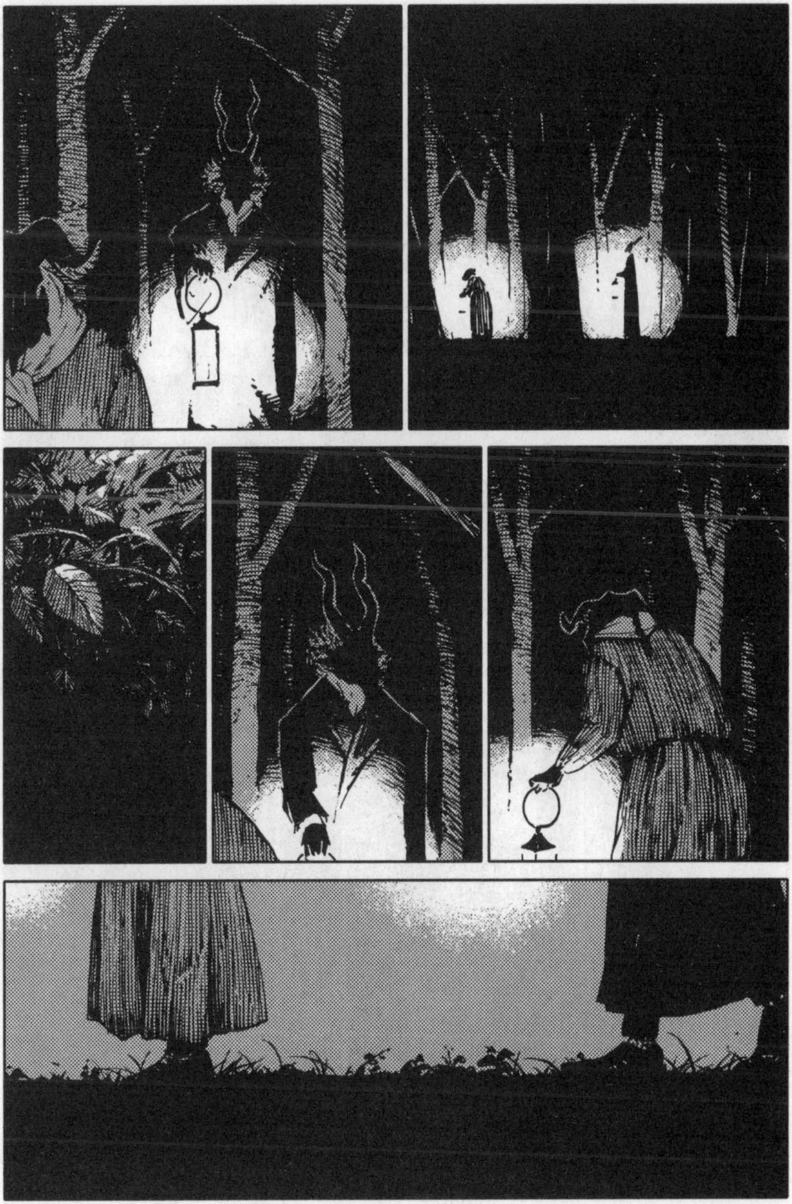

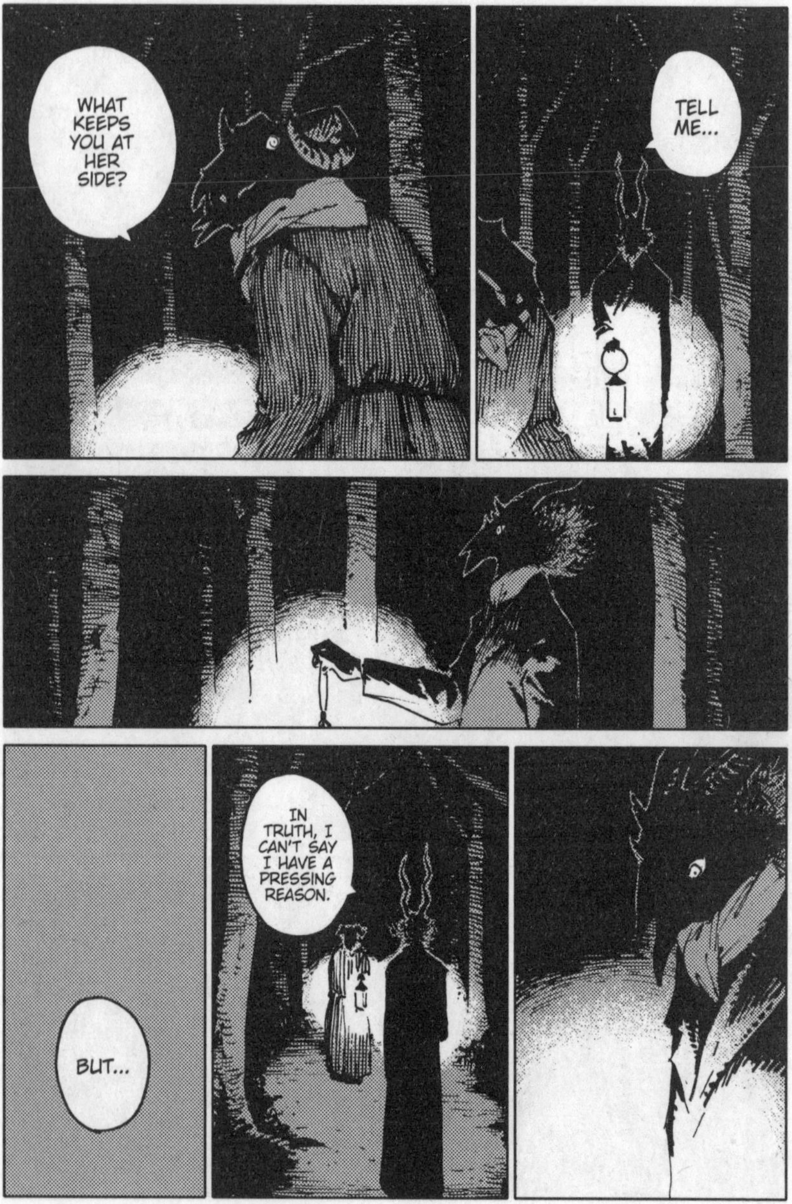
WHAT KEEPS YOU AT HER SIDE?
TELL ME...
IN TRUTH, I CAN'T SAY I HAVE A PRESSING REASON.
BUT...

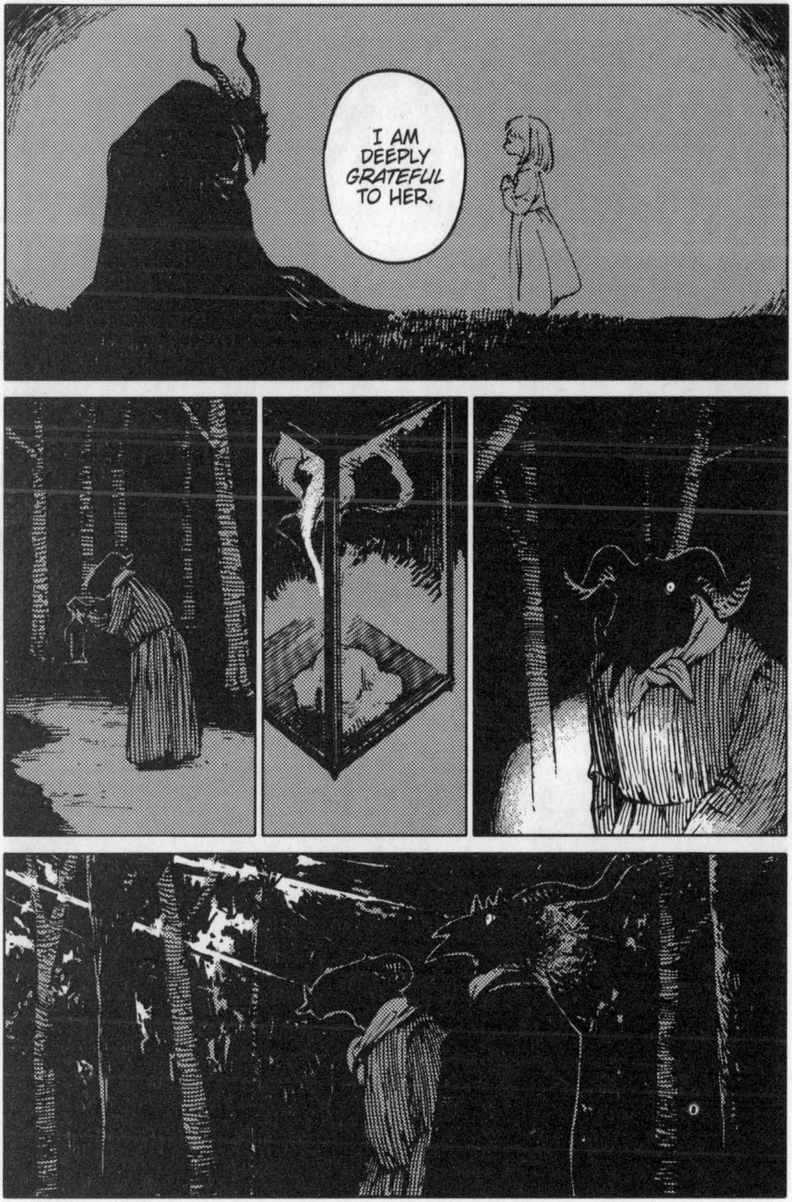
I AM DEEPLY GRATEFUL TO HER.

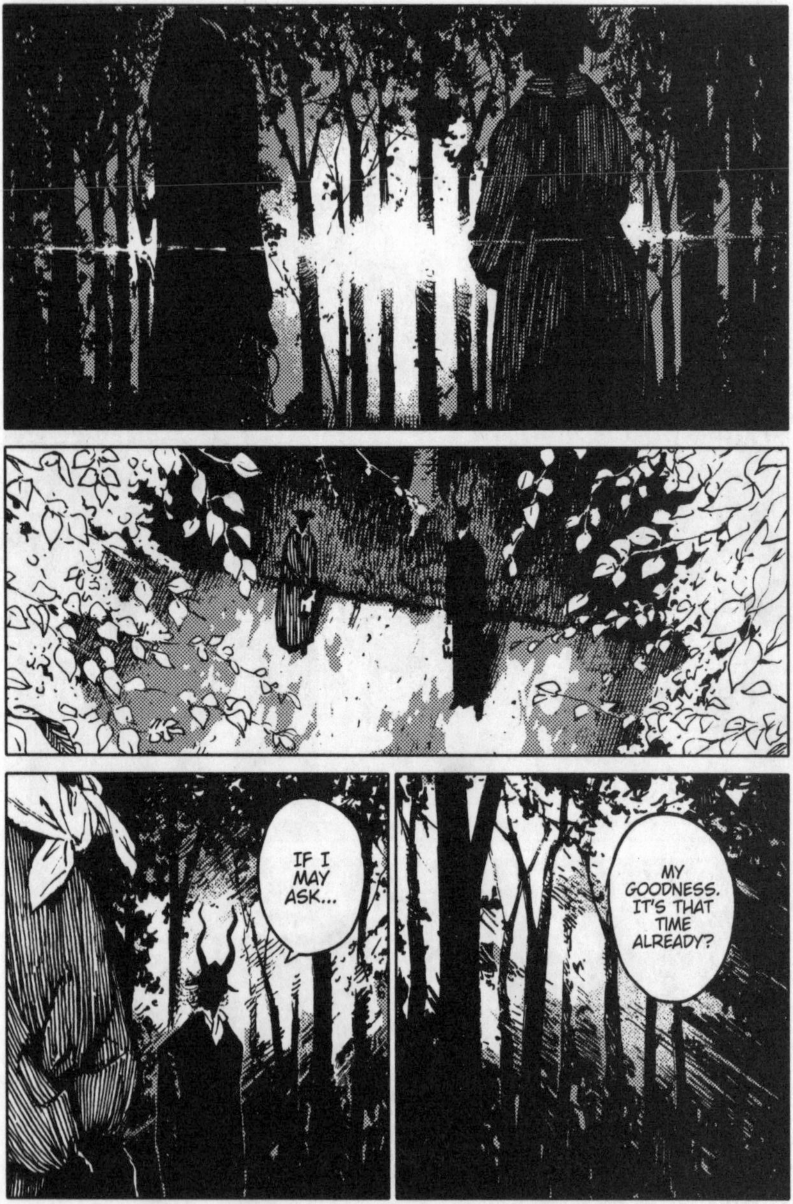
MY GOODNESS. IT'S THAT TIME ALREADY?
IF I MAY ASK...

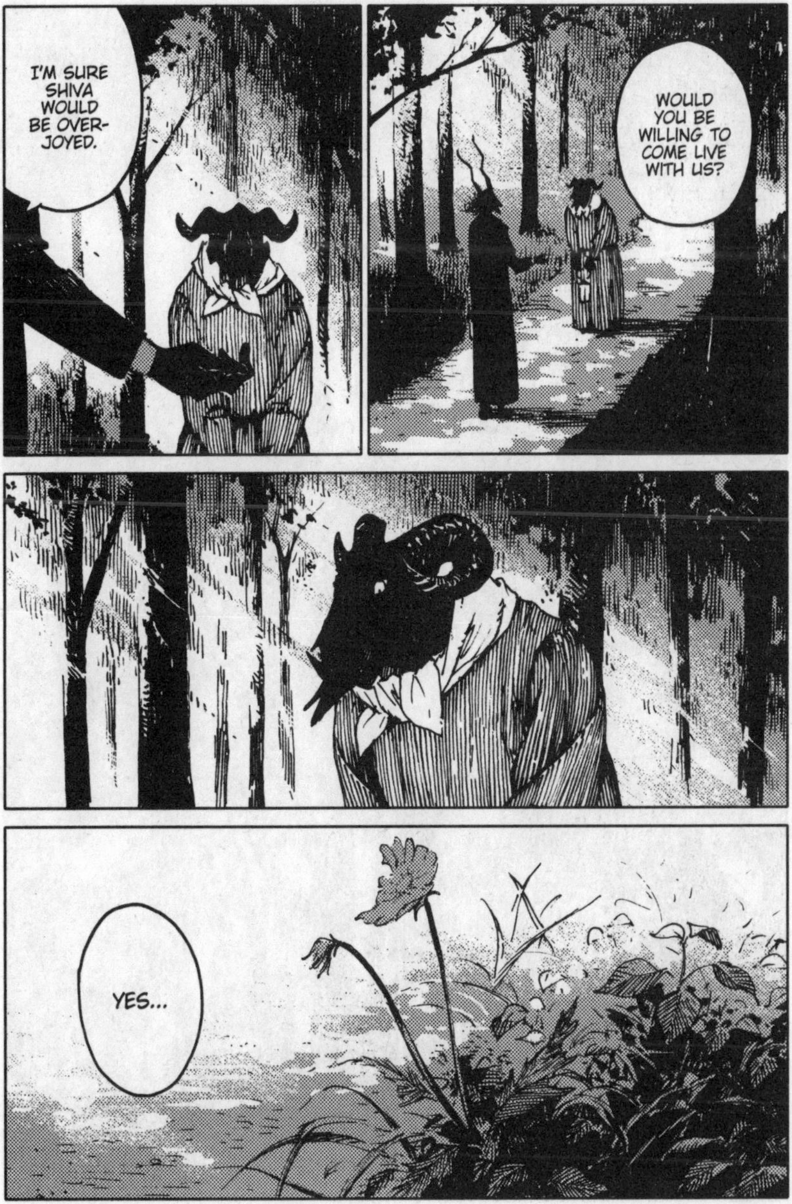
WOULD YOU BE WILLING TO COME LIVE WITH US?
I'M SURE SHIVA WOULD BE OVER-JOYED.
YES...

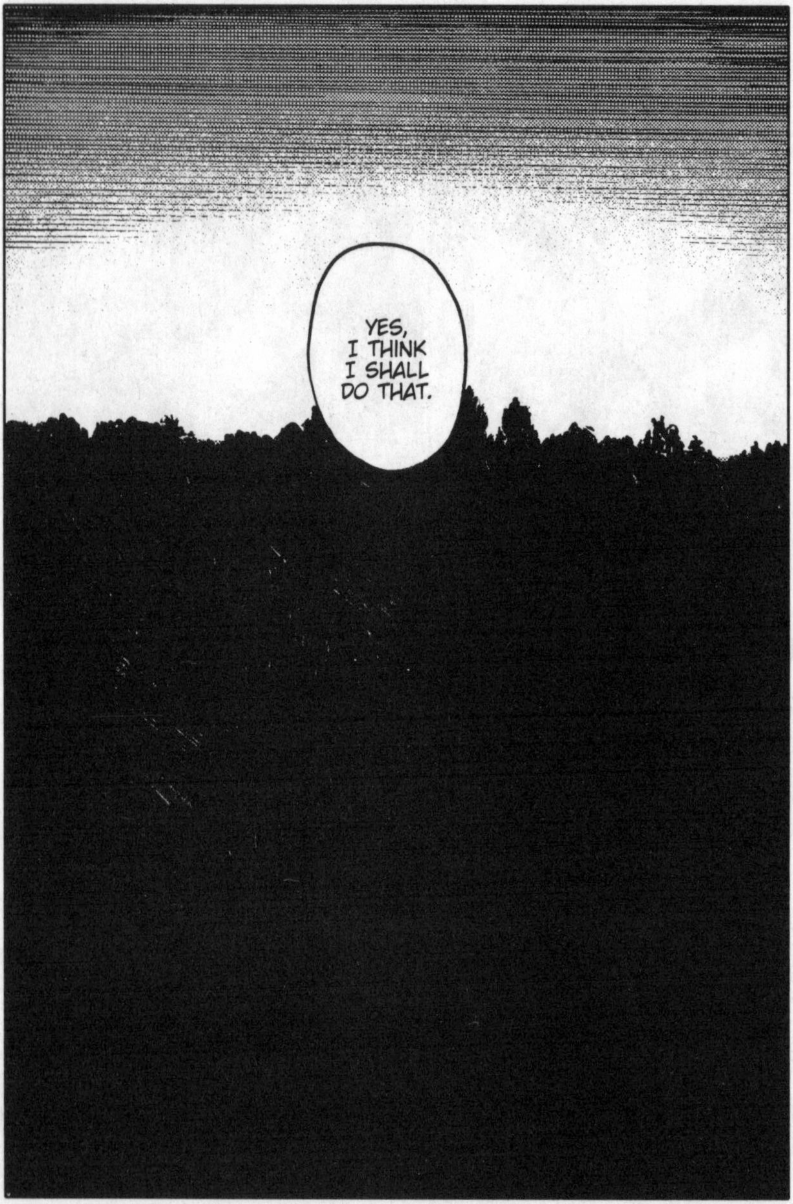
YES, I THINK I SHALL DO THAT.

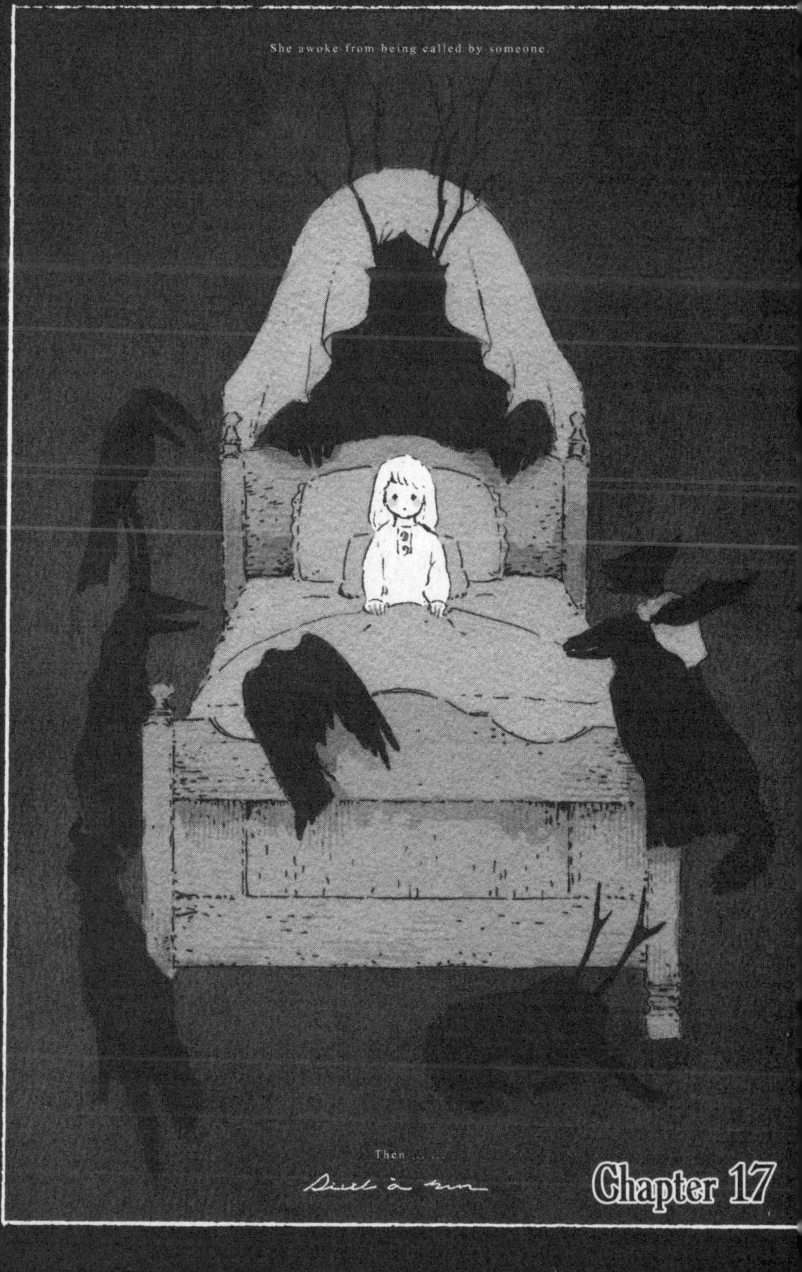
She awoke from being called by someone.
Then ... ...
Chapter 17

She calls for you.

Let's go.

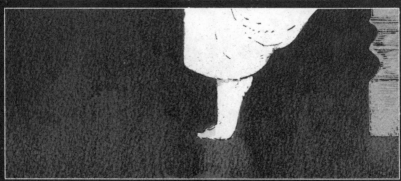

WHO IS IT,
THOUGH?
WHO'S
CALLING?

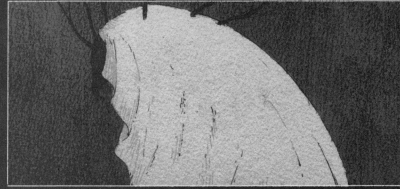

Mother.

Siúil, a Rún
The Girl from the Other Side

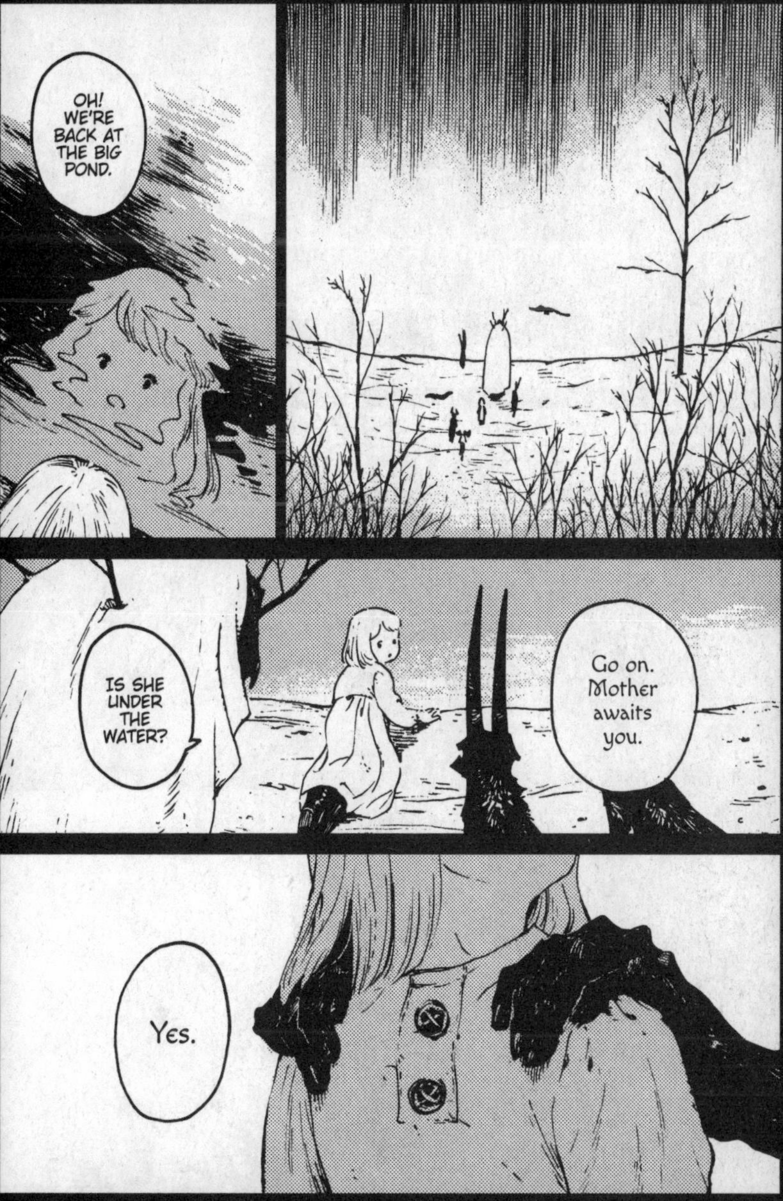
OH! WE'RE BACK AT THE BIG POND.
IS SHE UNDER THE WATER?
Go on. Mother awaits you.
Yes.

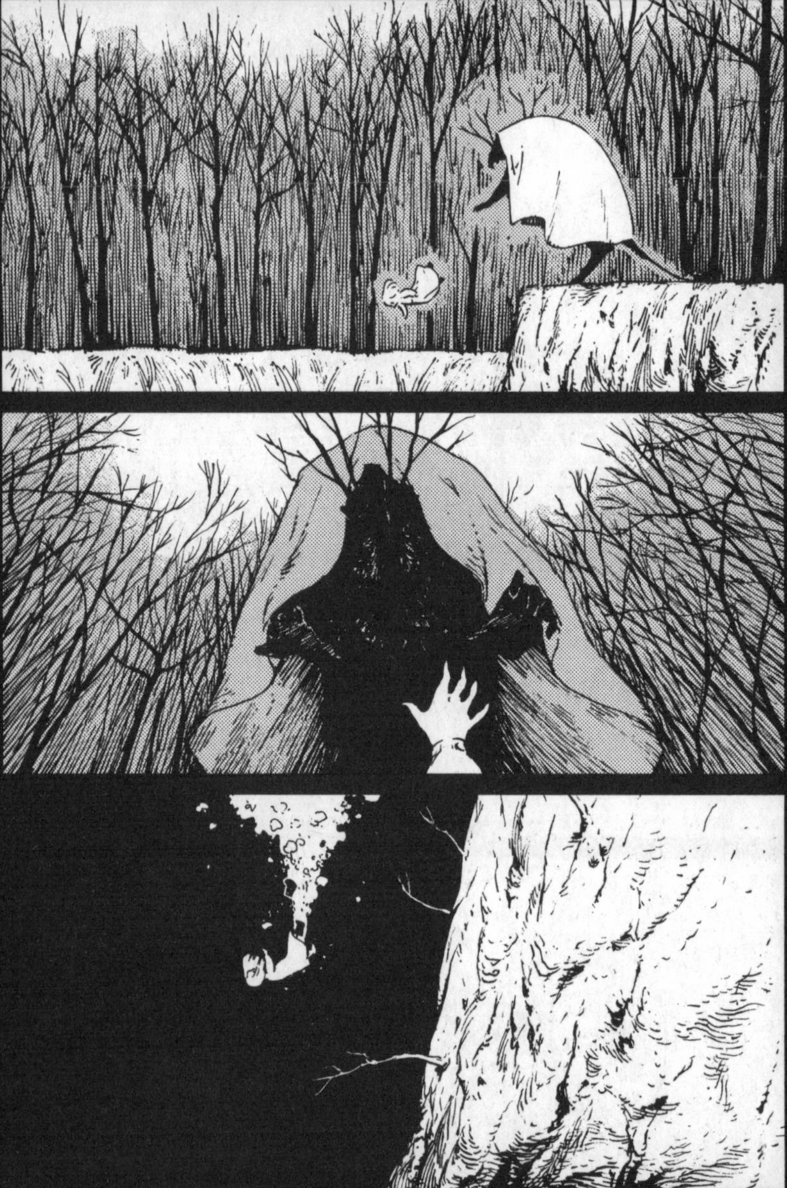

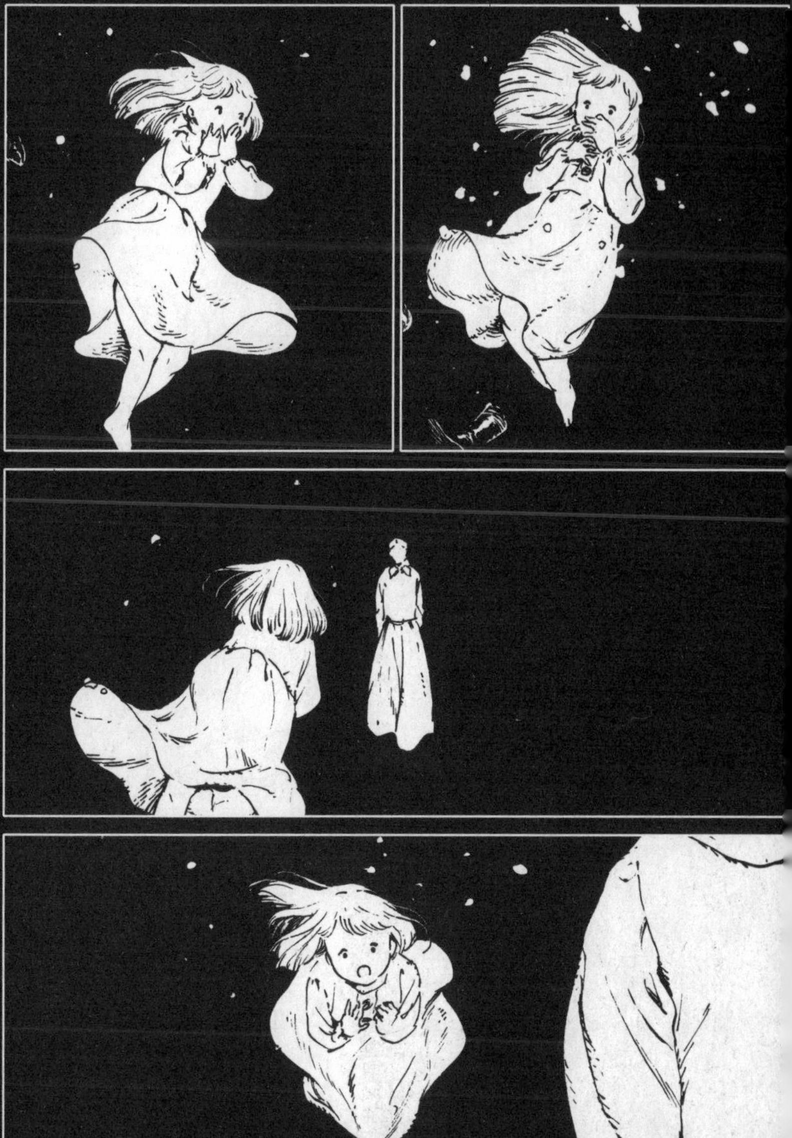

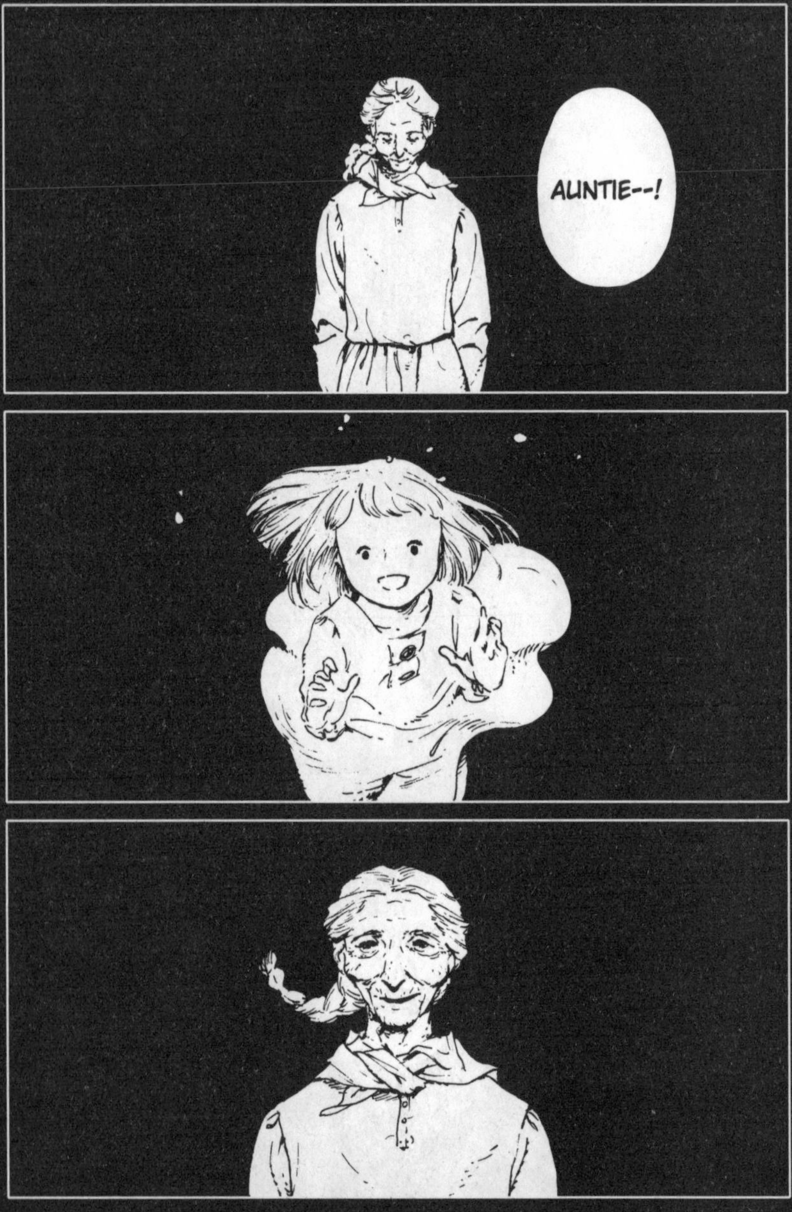
AUNTIE--!

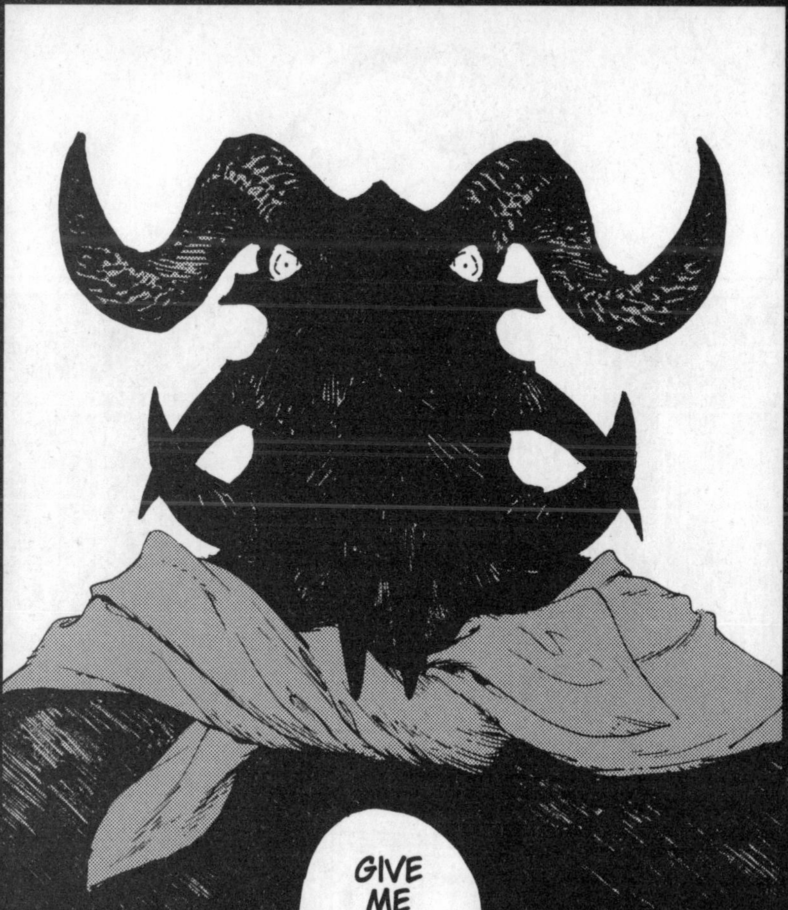
GIVE ME BACK MY SELF.

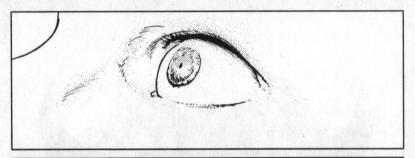

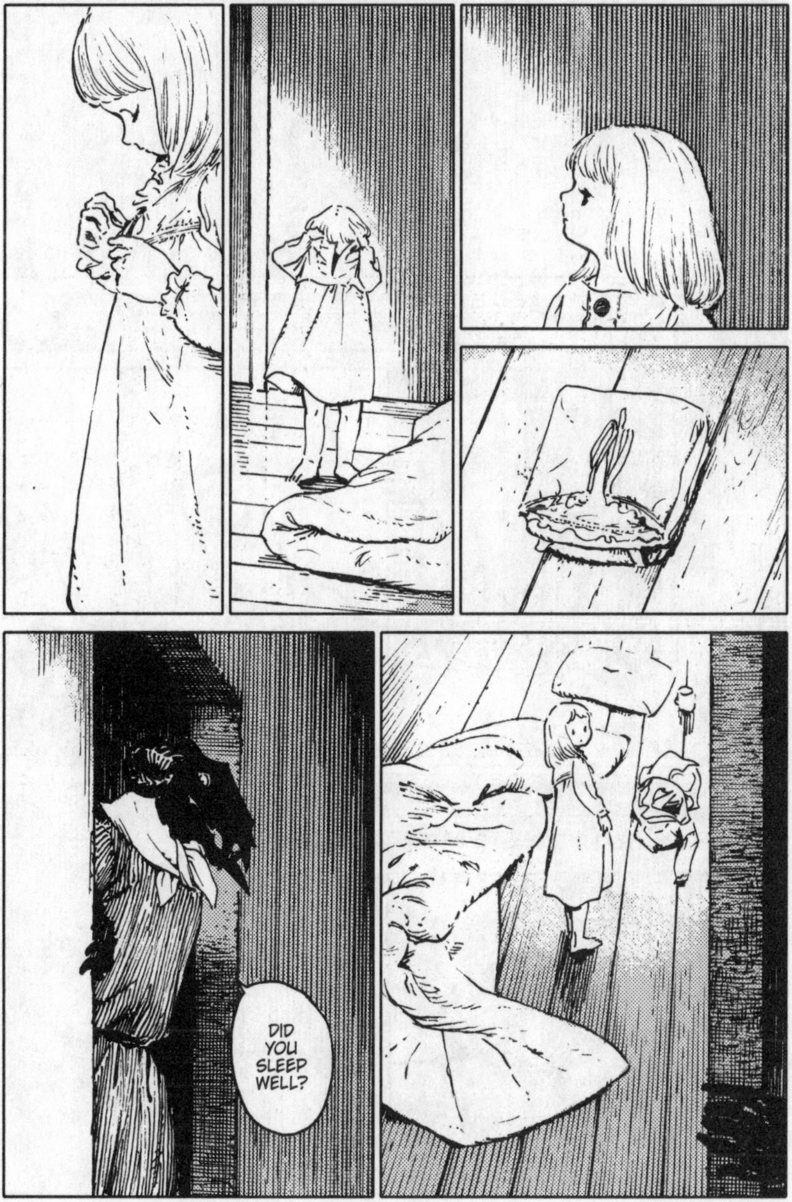
DID YOU SLEEP WELL?

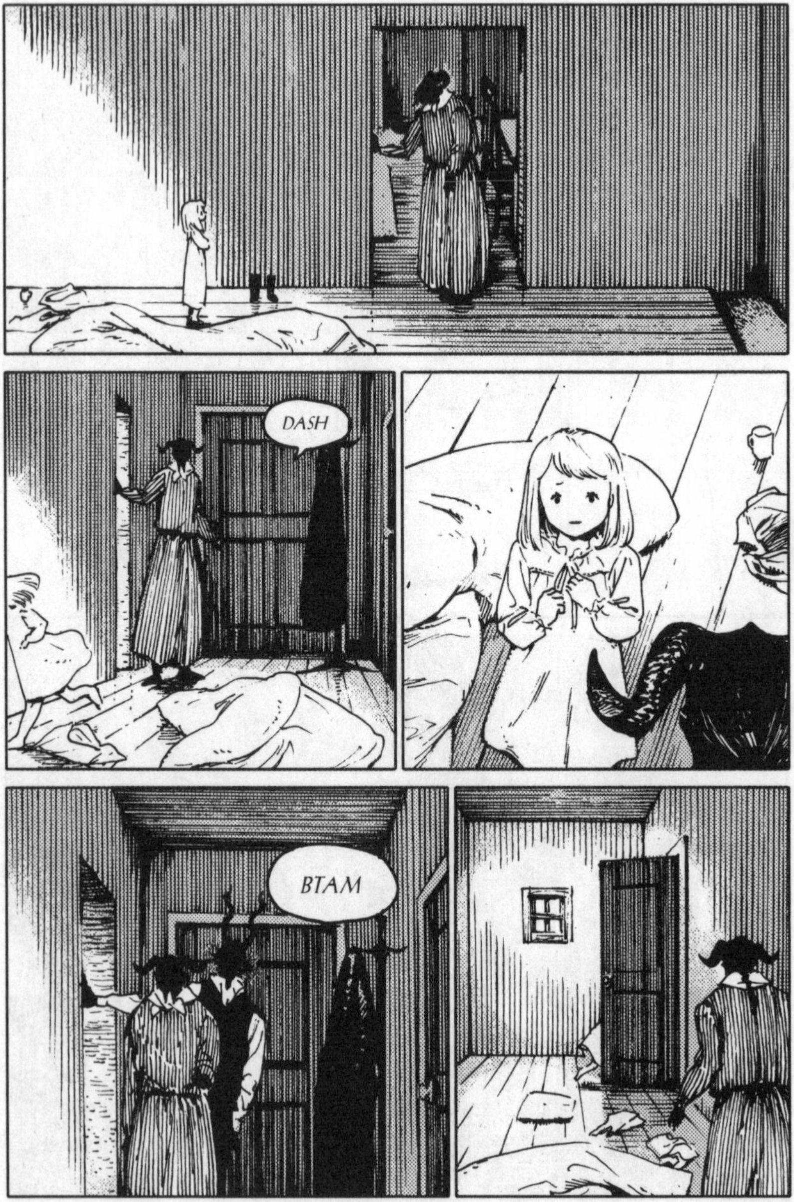
DASH
BTAM

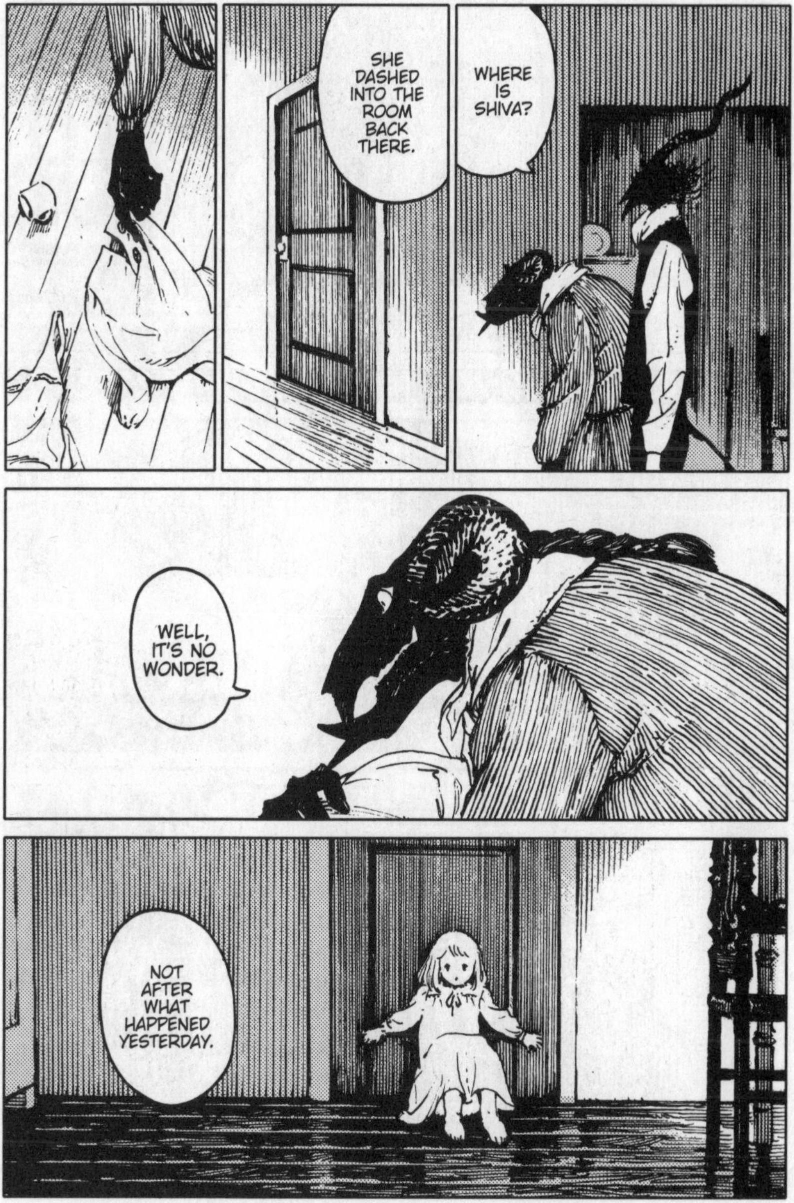

WHERE IS SHIVA?
SHE DASHED INTO THE ROOM BACK THERE.
WELL, IT'S NO WONDER.
NOT AFTER WHAT HAPPENED YESTERDAY.

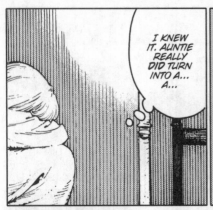

I KNEW IT. AUNTIE REALLY DID TURN INTO A... A...

NOK NOK

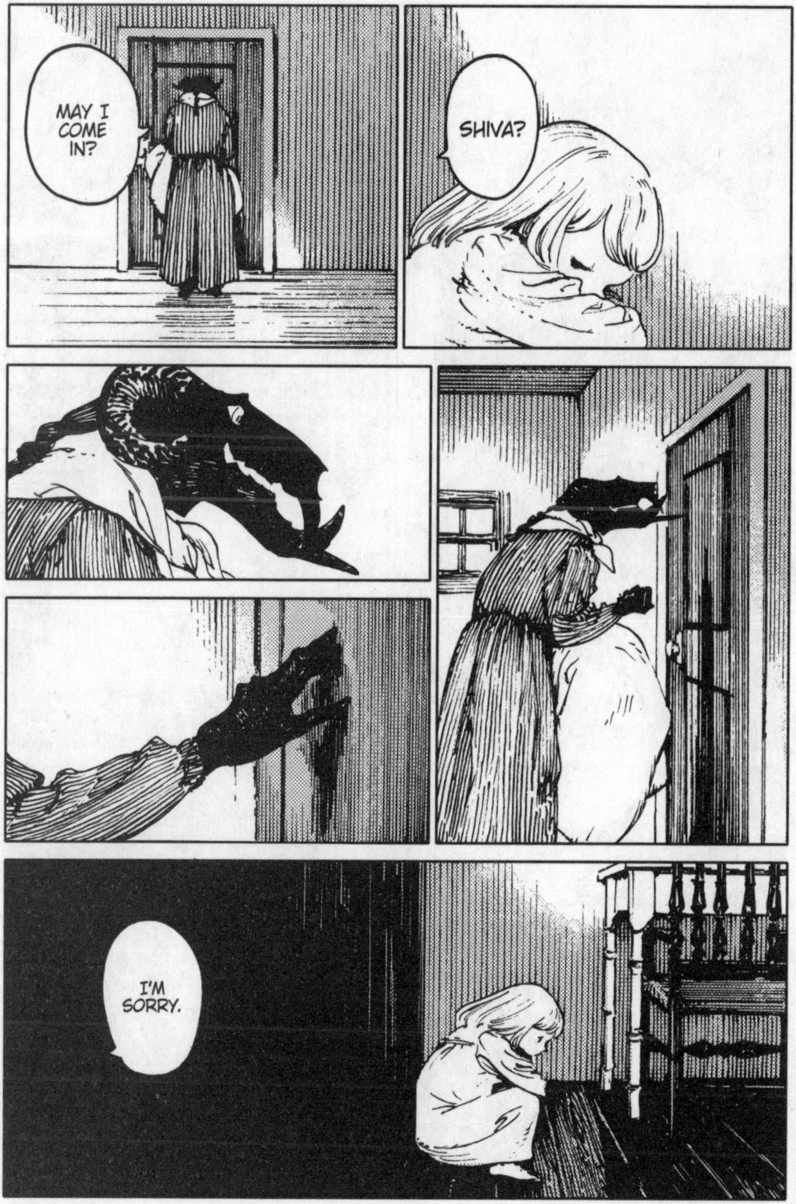
MAY I COME IN?
SHIVA?
I'M SORRY.

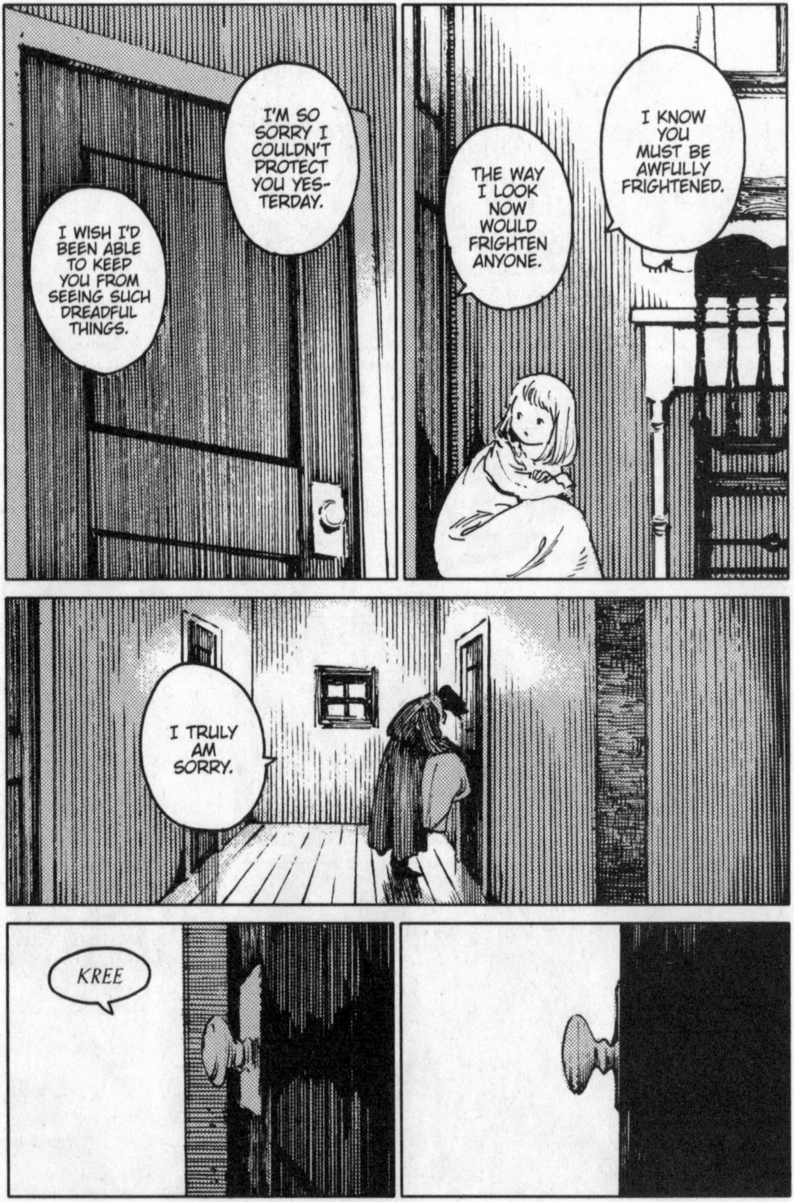
I KNOW YOU MUST BE AWFULLY FRIGHTENED.
THE WAY I LOOK NOW WOULD FRIGHTEN ANYONE.
I'M SO SORRY I COULDN'T PROTECT YOU YES-TERDAY.
I WISH I'D BEEN ABLE TO KEEP YOU FROM SEEING SUCH DREADFUL THINGS.
I TRULY AM SORRY.
KREE

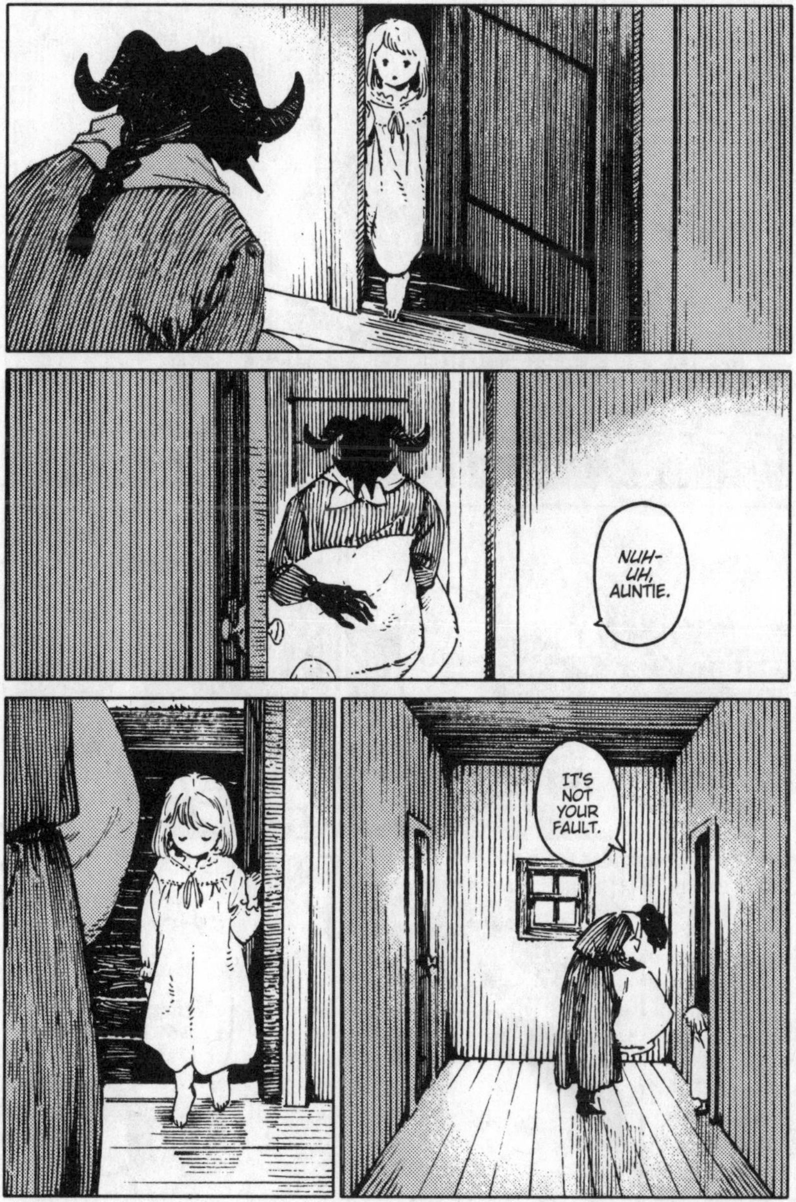
NUH-UH, AUNTIE.
IT'S NOT YOUR FAULT.

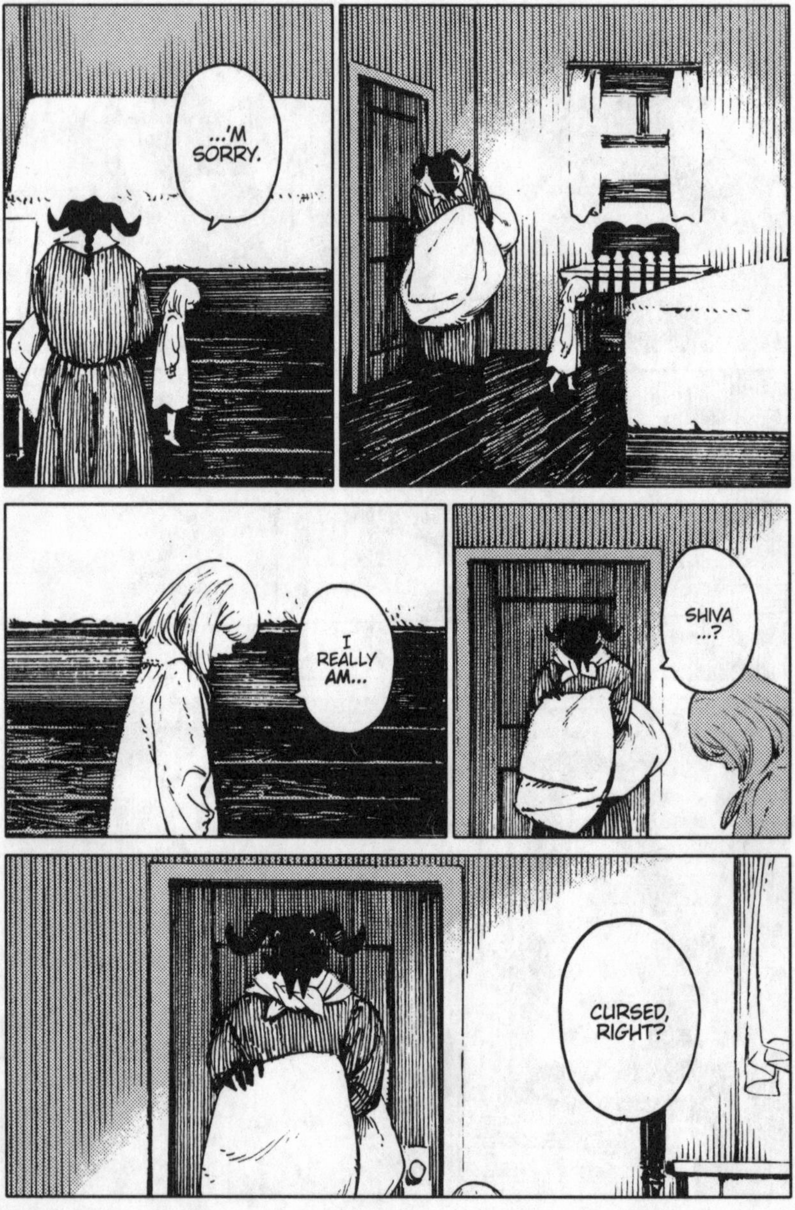
...'M SORRY.
I REALLY AM...
SHIVA ...?
CURSED, RIGHT?

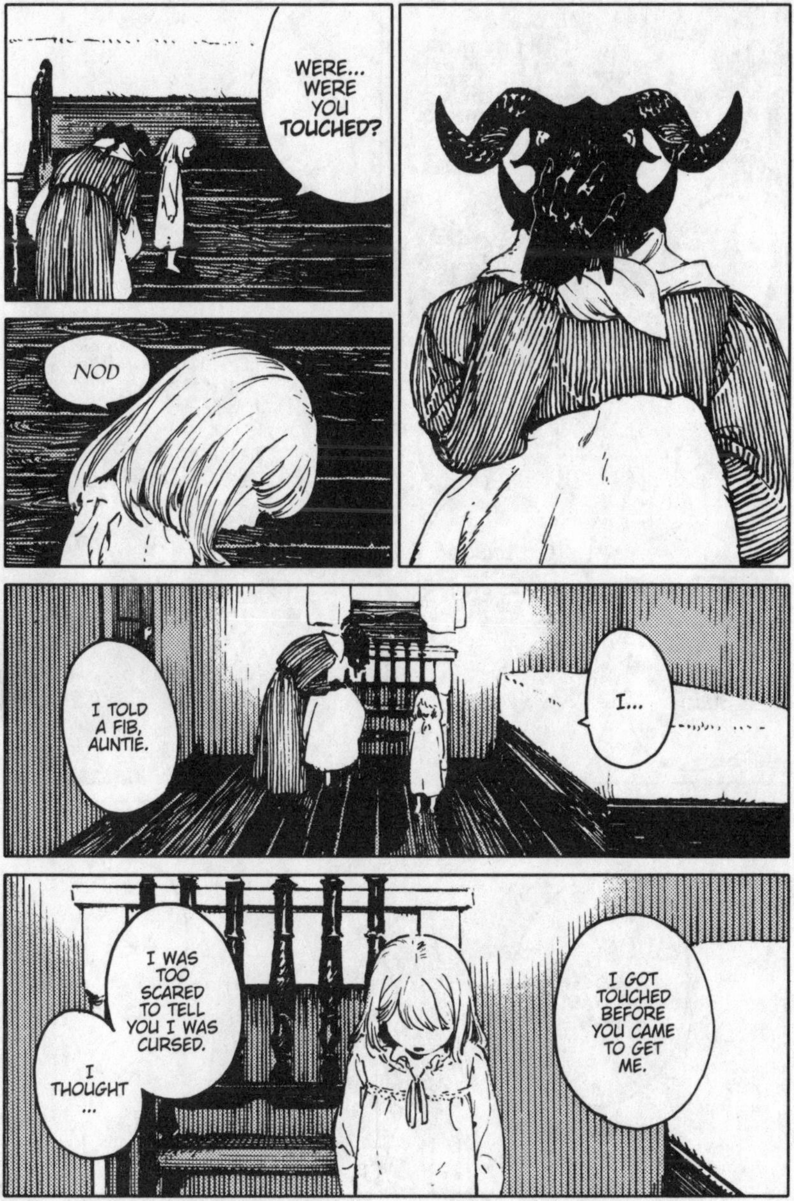
WERE... WERE YOU TOUCHED?
NOD
I...
I TOLD A FIB, AUNTIE.
I GOT TOUCHED BEFORE YOU CAME TO GET ME.
I WAS TOO SCARED TO TELL YOU I WAS CURSED.
I THOUGHT ...

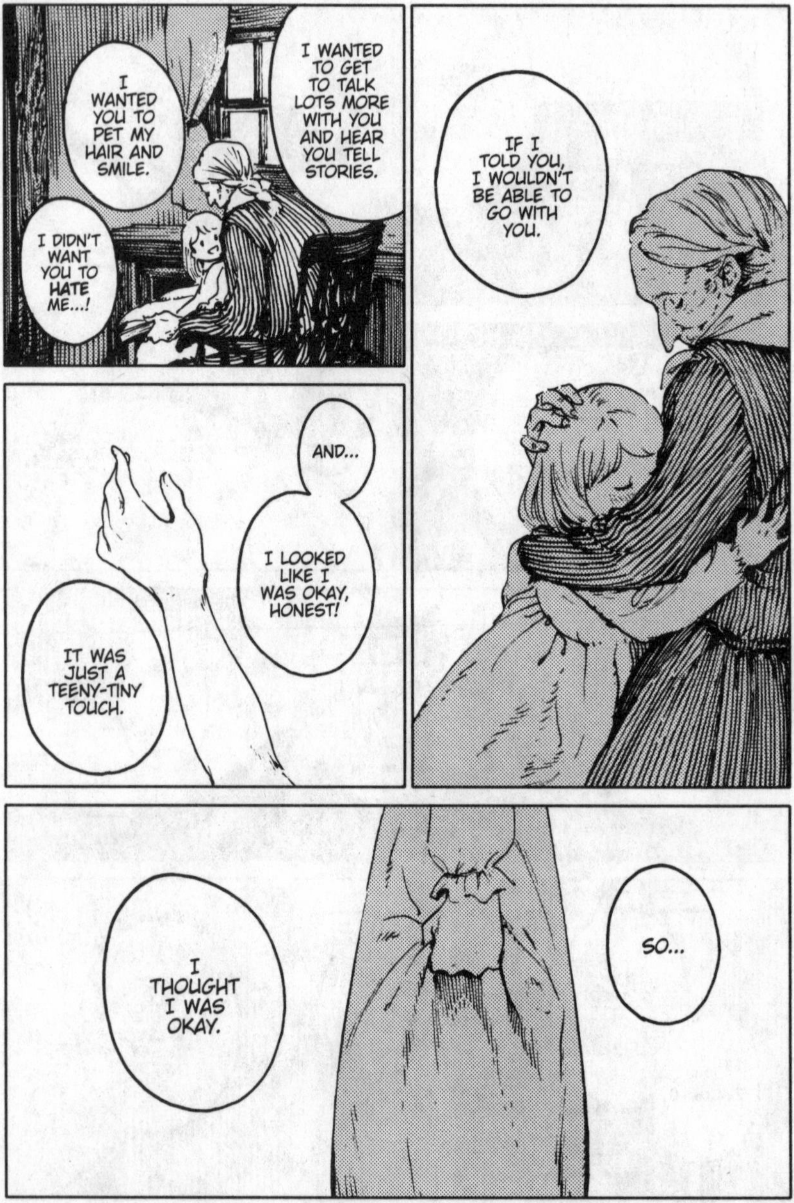
IF I TOLD YOU, I WOULDN'T BE ABLE TO GO WITH YOU.
I WANTED TO GET TO TALK LOTS MORE WITH YOU AND HEAR YOU TELL STORIES.
I WANTED YOU TO PET MY HAIR AND SMILE.
I DIDN'T WANT YOU TO HATE ME...!
AND...
I LOOKED LIKE I WAS OKAY, HONEST!
IT WAS JUST A TEENY-TINY TOUCH.
SO...
I THOUGHT I WAS OKAY.

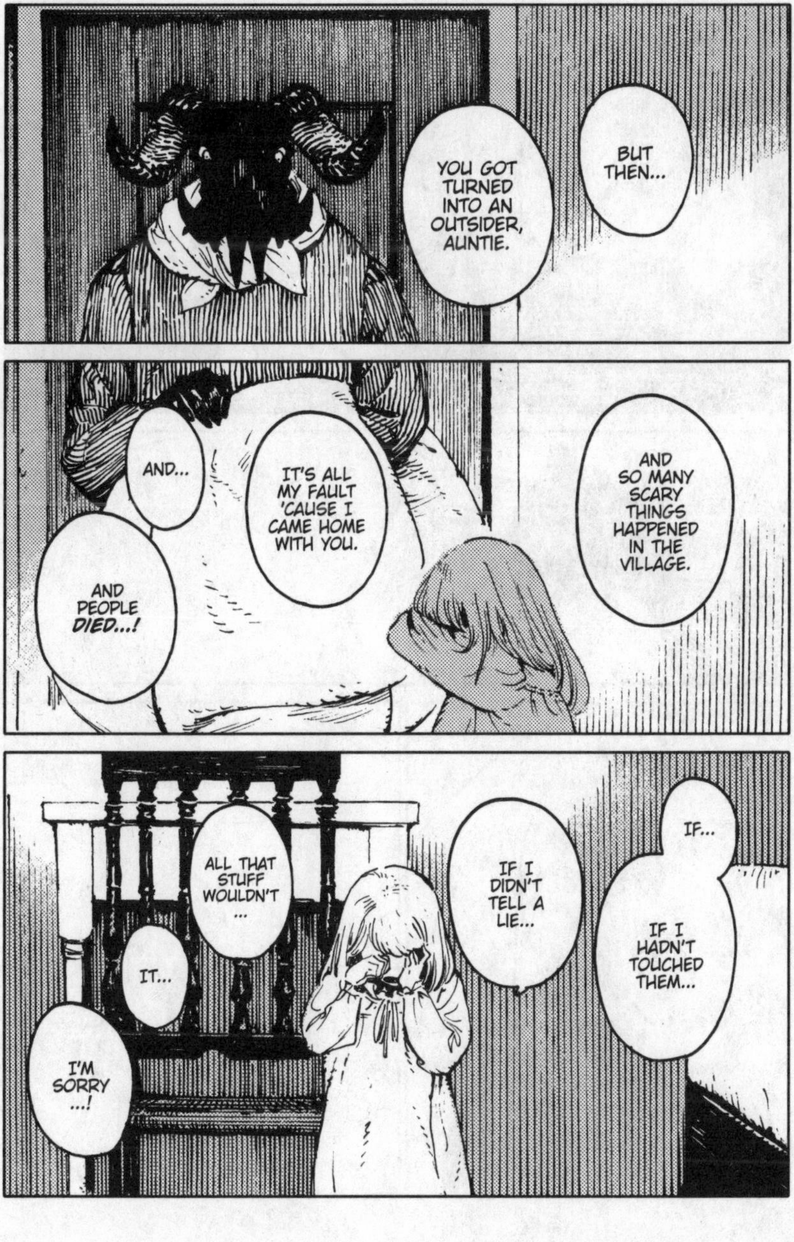
BUT THEN...
YOU GOT TURNED INTO AN OUTSIDER, AUNTIE.
AND SO MANY SCARY THINGS HAPPENED IN THE VILLAGE.
IT'S ALL MY FAULT 'CAUSE I CAME HOME WITH YOU.
AND...
AND PEOPLE *DIED*...!
IF...
IF I HADN'T TOUCHED THEM...
IF I DIDN'T TELL A LIE...
ALL THAT STUFF WOULDN'T ...
IT...
I'M SORRY ...!

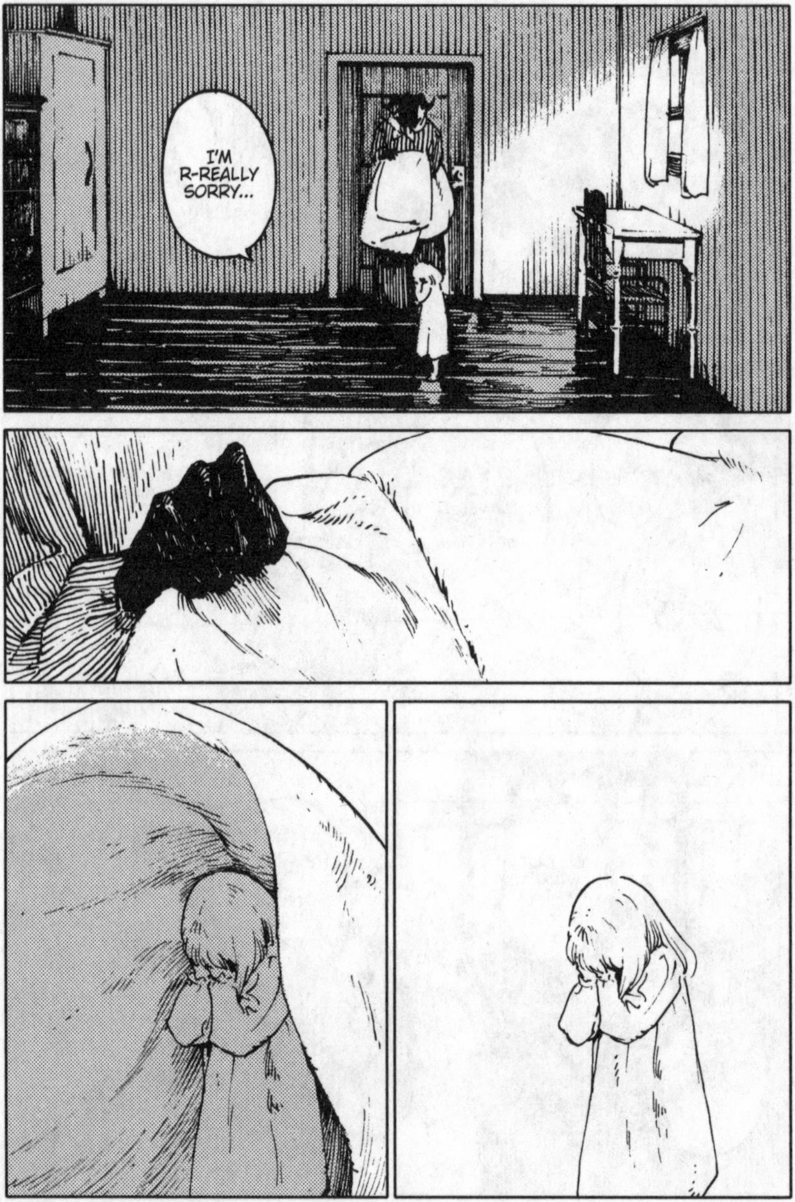
I'M R-REALLY SORRY...

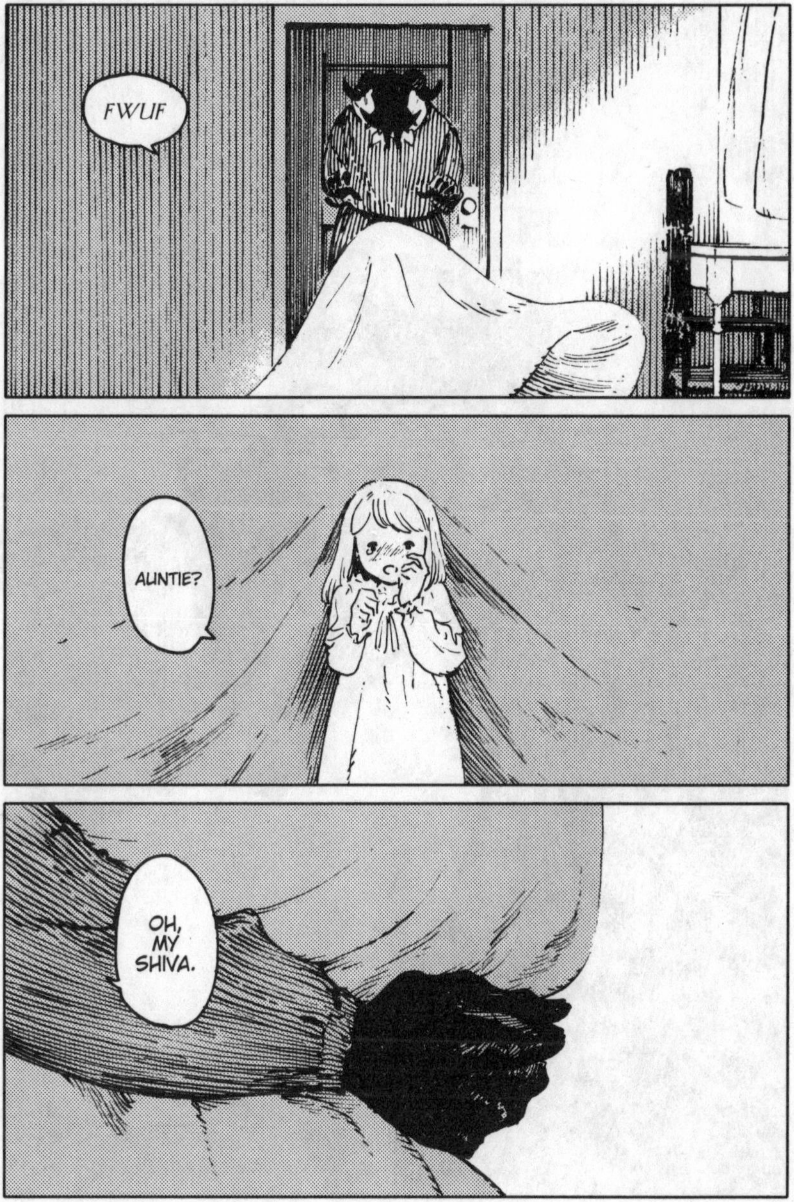
FWUF
AUNTIE?
OH, MY SHIVA.

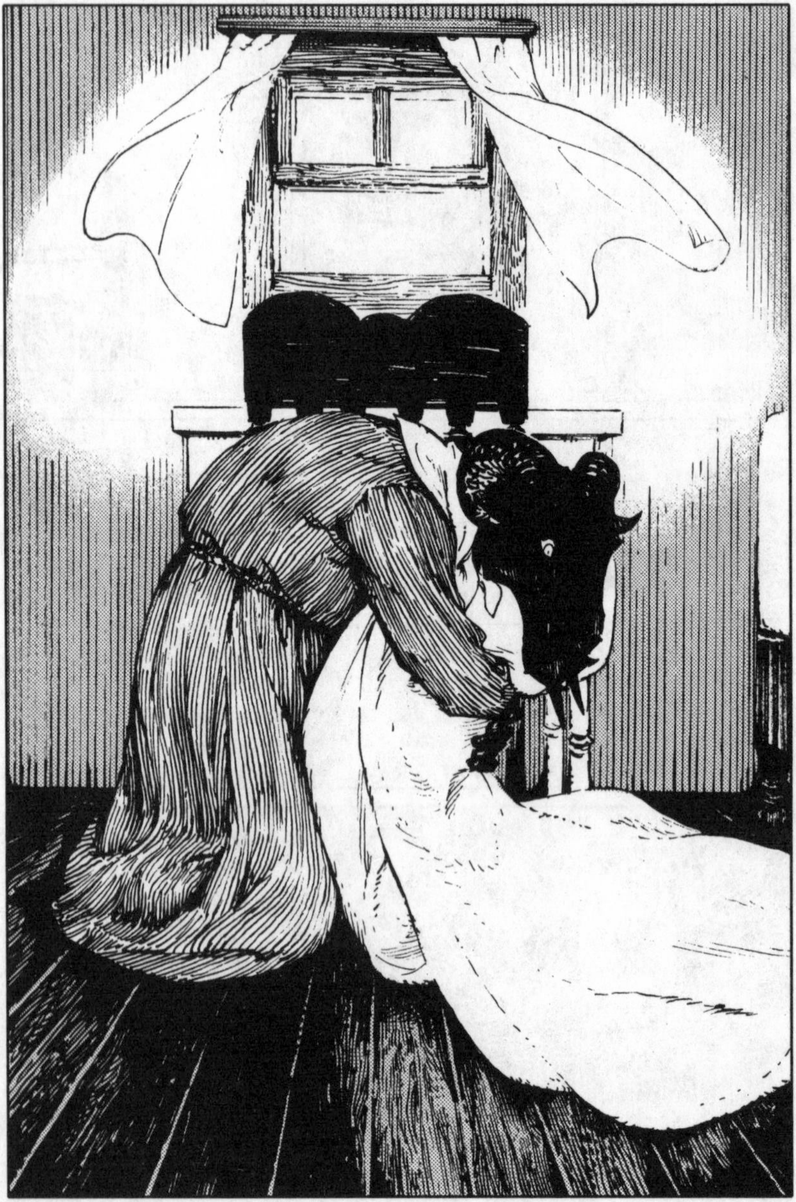

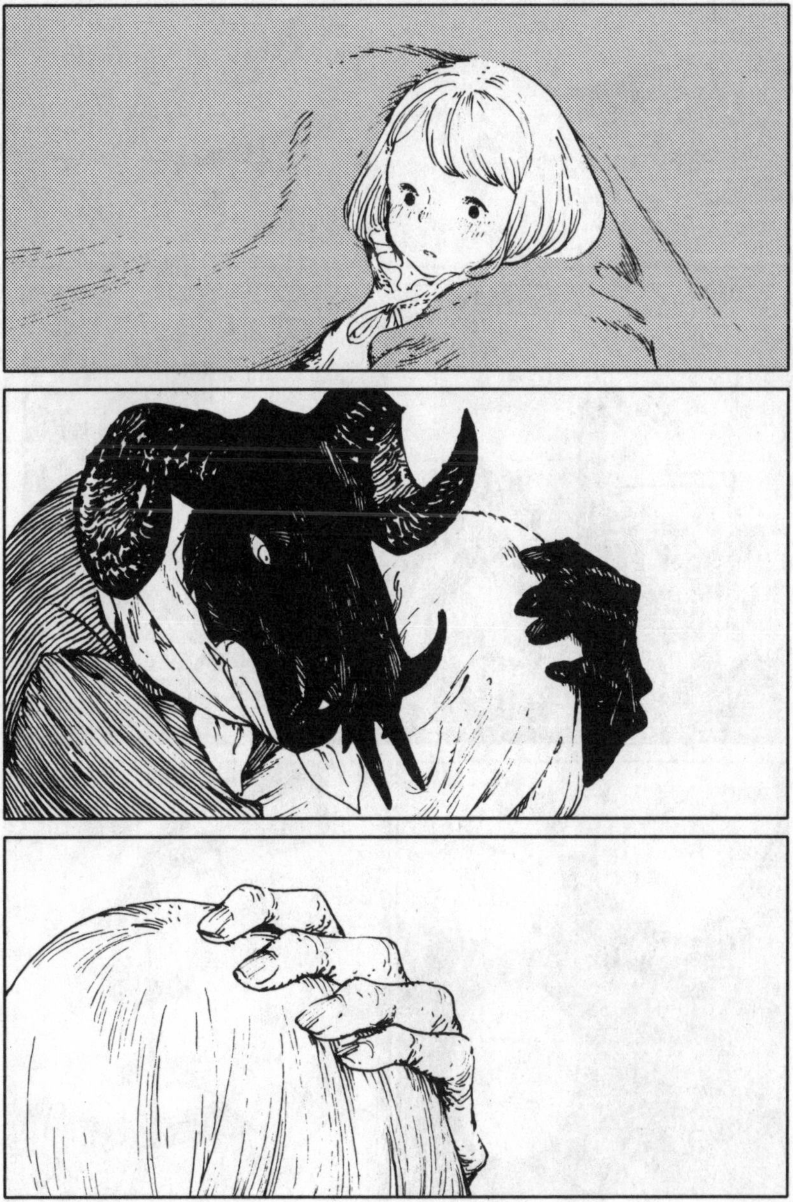

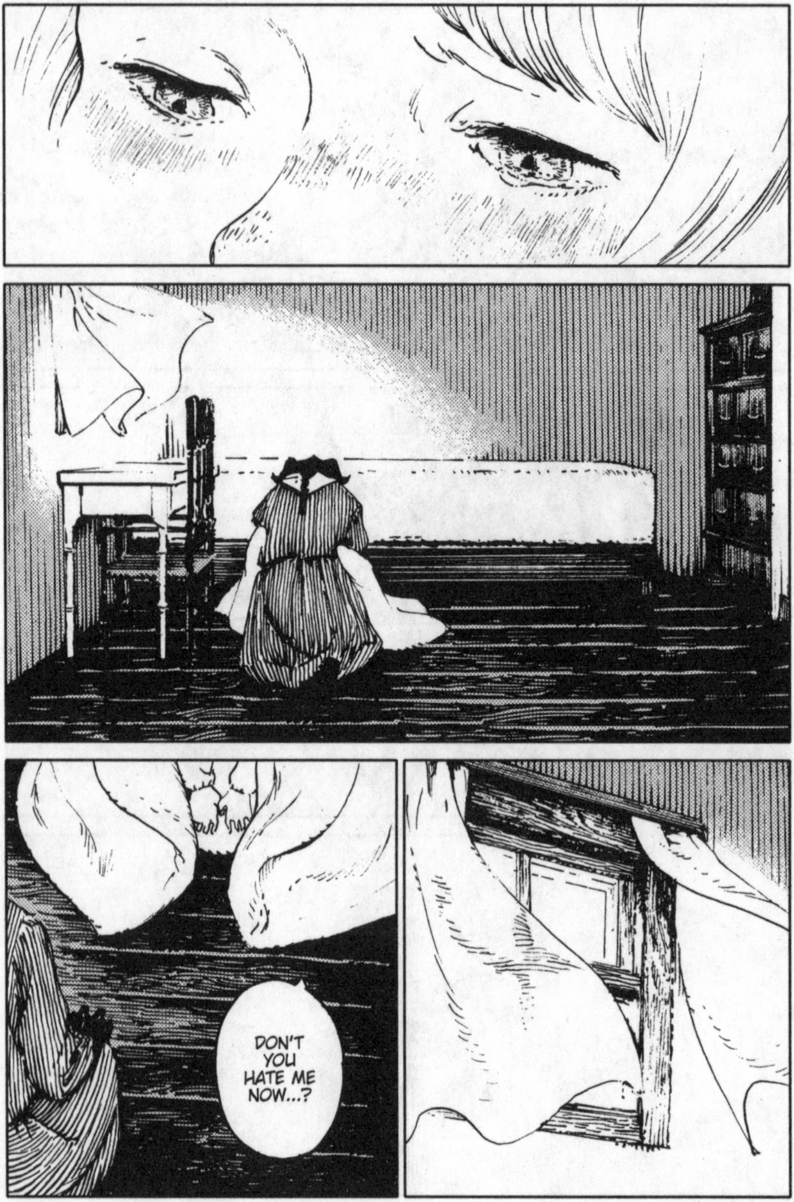
DON'T YOU HATE ME NOW...?

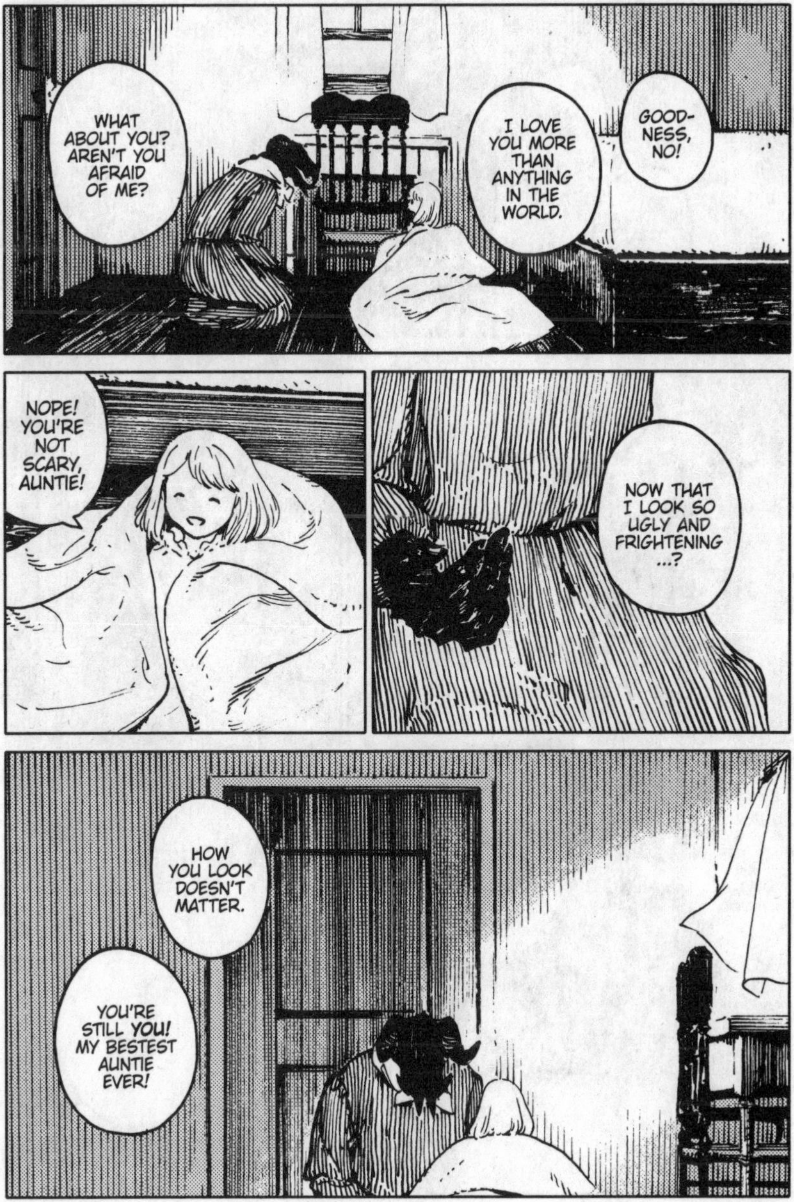
GOOD-NESS, NO!
I LOVE YOU MORE THAN ANYTHING IN THE WORLD.
WHAT ABOUT YOU? AREN'T YOU AFRAID OF ME?
NOW THAT I LOOK SO UGLY AND FRIGHTENING ...?
NOPE! YOU'RE NOT SCARY, AUNTIE!
HOW YOU LOOK DOESN'T MATTER.
YOU'RE STILL YOU! MY BESTEST AUNTIE EVER!

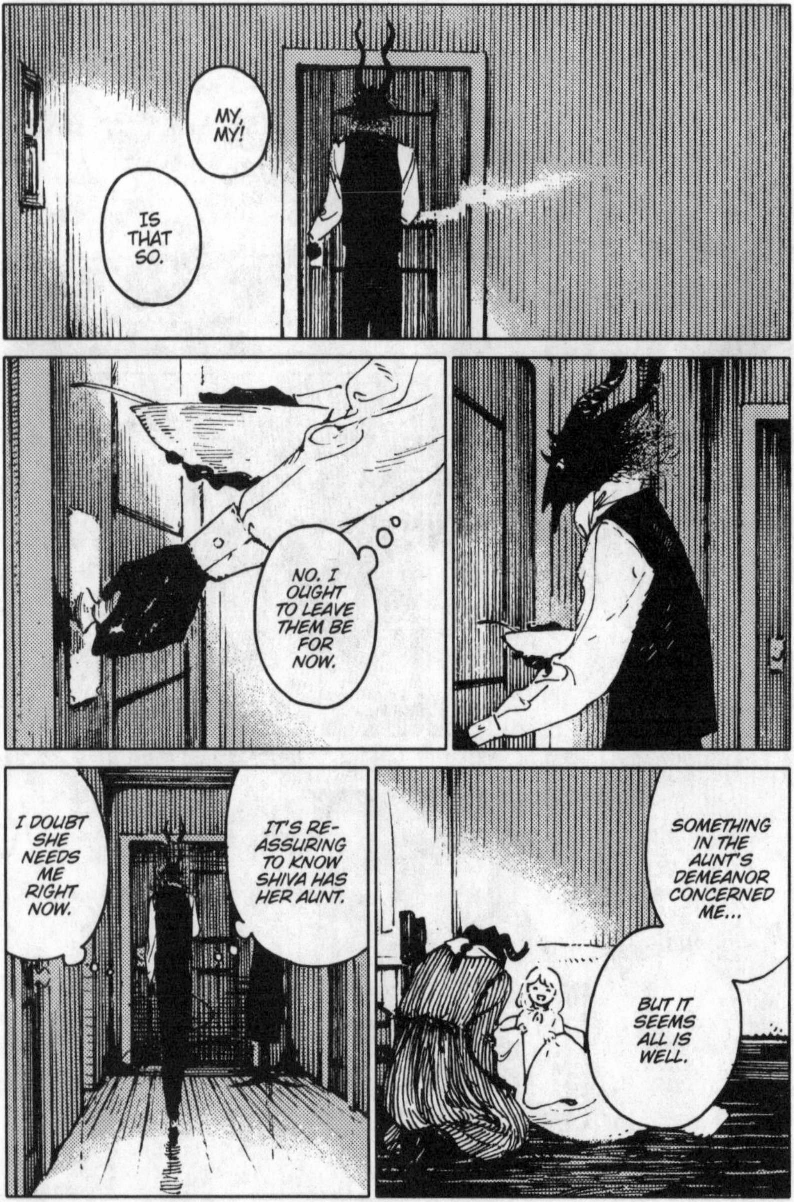

MY, MY!
IS THAT SO.
NO. I OUGHT TO LEAVE THEM BE FOR NOW.
IT'S RE-ASSURING TO KNOW SHIVA HAS HER AUNT.
I DOUBT SHE NEEDS ME RIGHT NOW.
SOMETHING IN THE AUNT'S DEMEANOR CONCERNED ME...
BUT IT SEEMS ALL IS WELL.

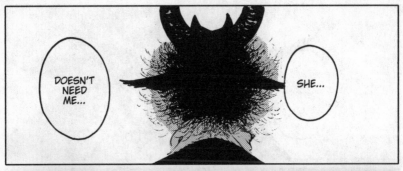

DOESN'T NEED ME...

SHE...

KRASH

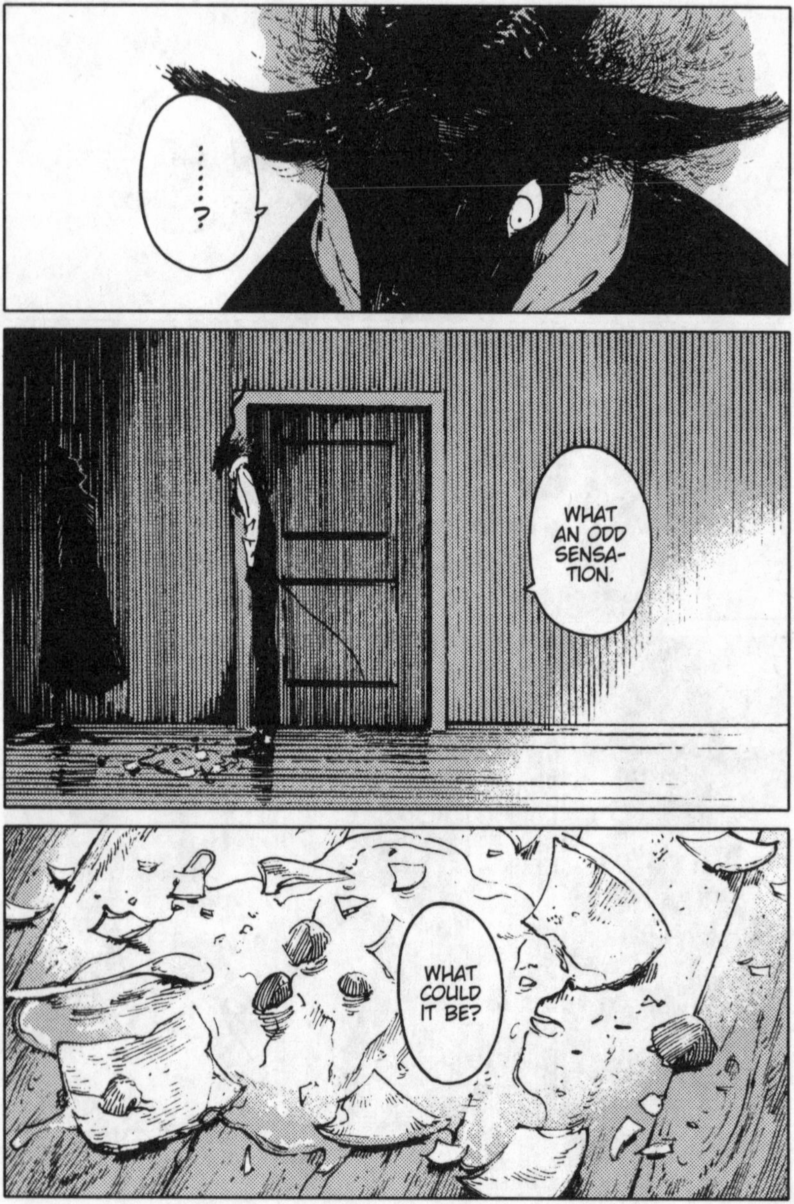
……?
WHAT AN ODD SENSATION.
WHAT COULD IT BE?

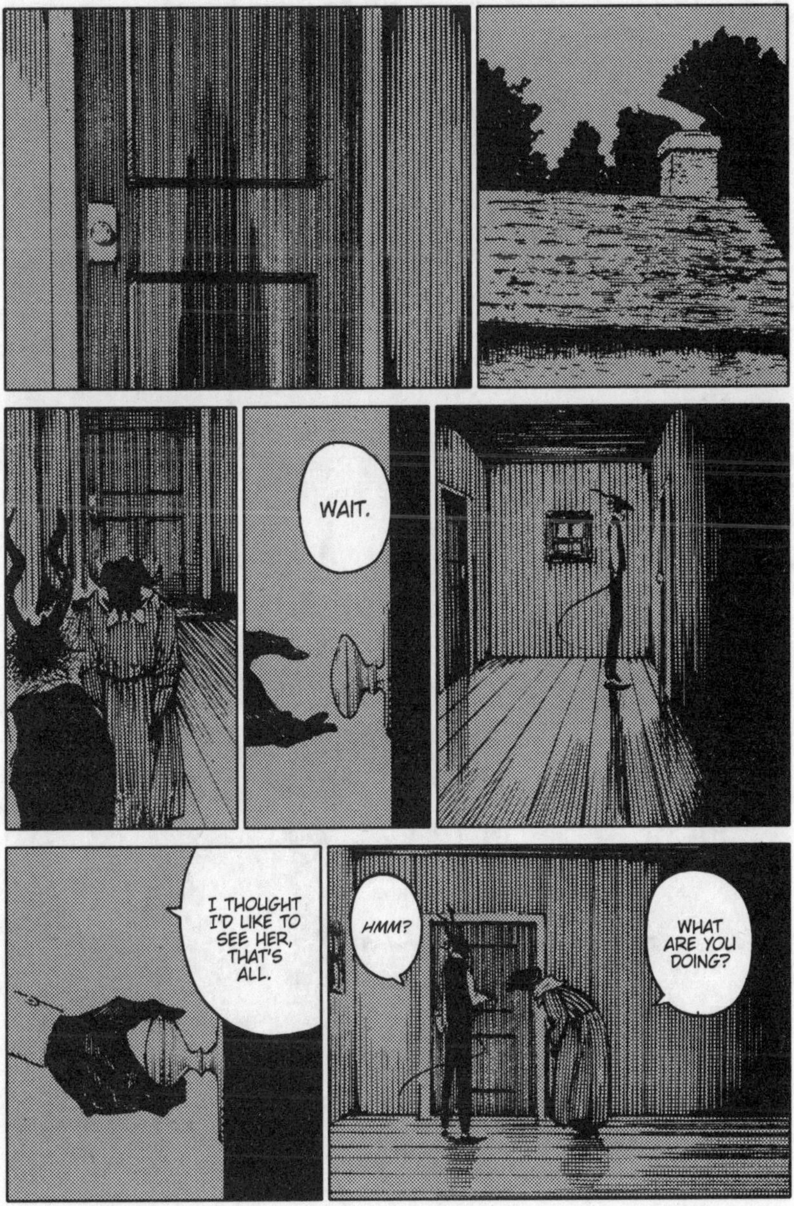
WAIT.
WHAT ARE YOU DOING?
HMM?
I THOUGHT I'D LIKE TO SEE HER, THAT'S ALL.

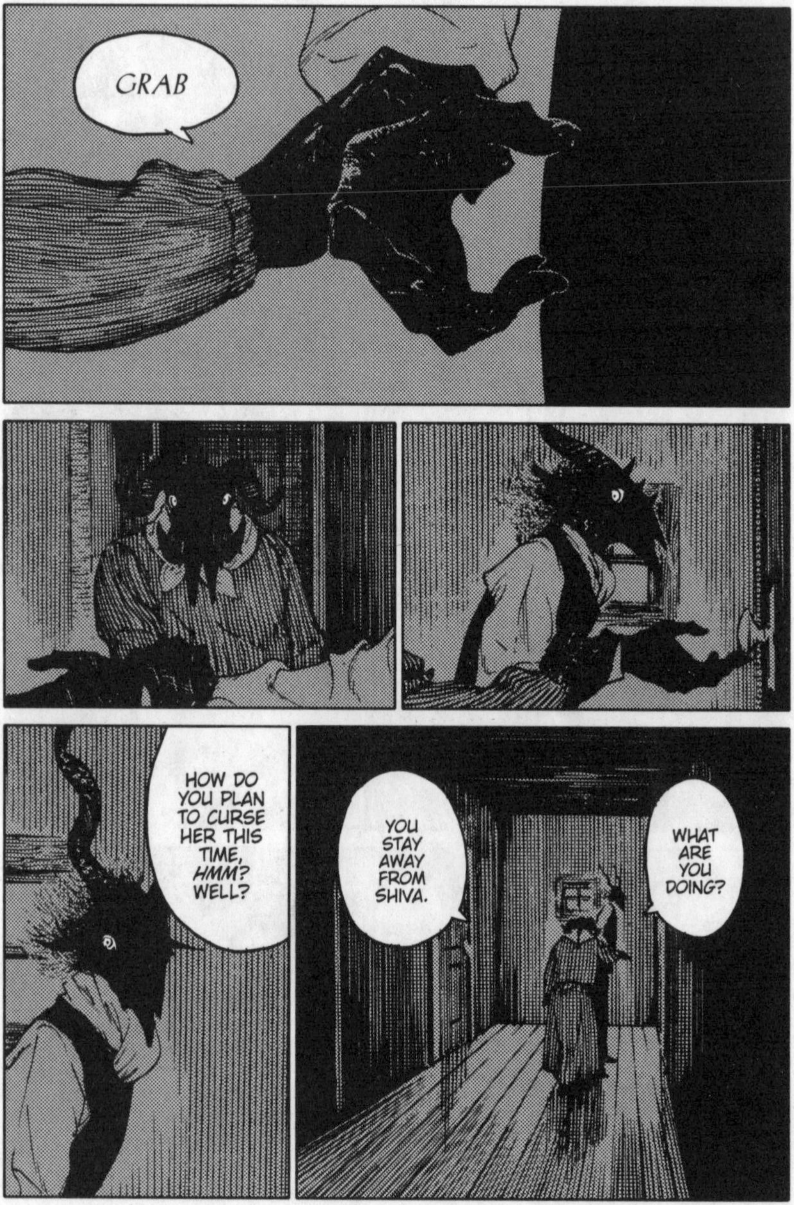
GRAB
HOW DO YOU PLAN TO CURSE HER THIS TIME, *HMM*? WELL?
YOU STAY AWAY FROM SHIVA.
WHAT ARE YOU DOING?

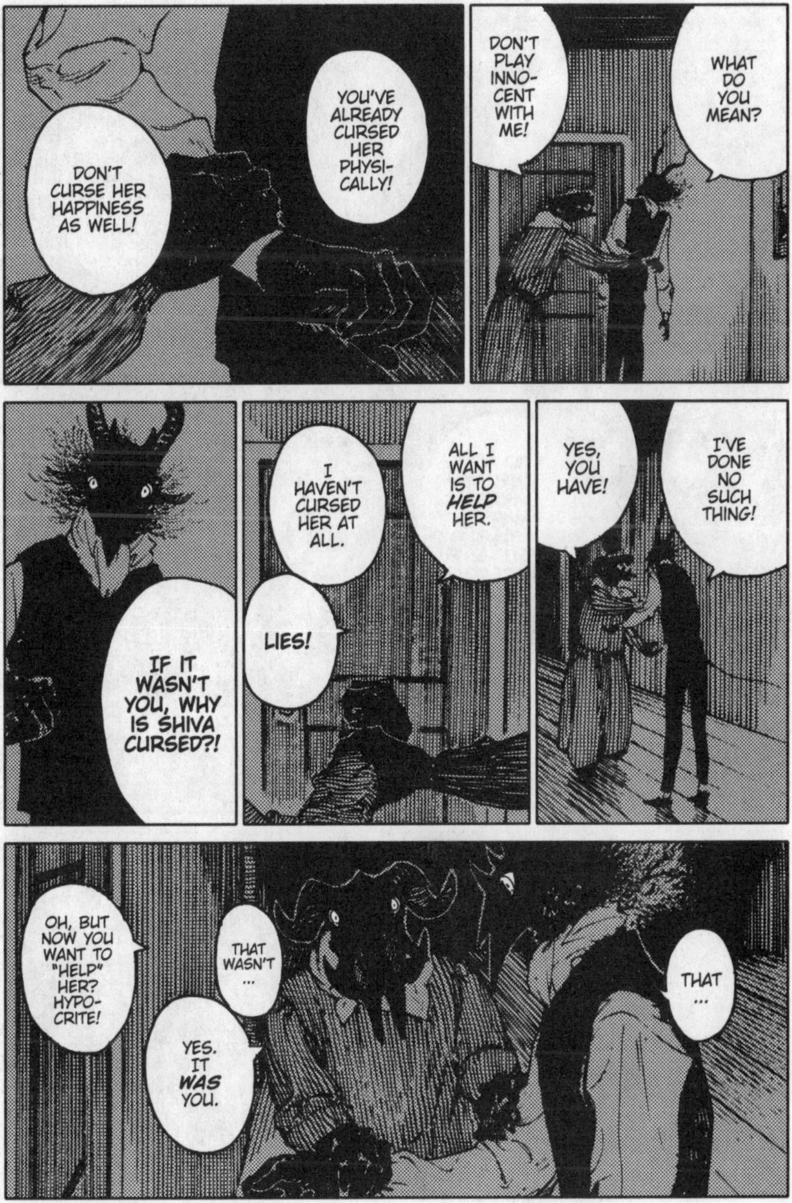
WHAT DO YOU MEAN?
DON'T PLAY INNO-CENT WITH ME!
YOU'VE ALREADY CURSED HER PHYSI-CALLY!
DON'T CURSE HER HAPPINESS AS WELL!
I'VE DONE NO SUCH THING!
YES, YOU HAVE!
ALL I WANT IS TO *HELP* HER.
I HAVEN'T CURSED HER AT ALL.
LIES!
IF IT WASN'T YOU, WHY IS SHIVA CURSED?!
THAT ...
THAT WASN'T ...
YES. IT *WAS* YOU.
OH, BUT NOW YOU WANT TO "HELP" HER? HYPO-CRITE!

IF IT WEREN'T FOR YOU, SHIVA NEVER WOULD HAVE BEEN CURSED TO BEGIN WITH.
SHE WOULDN'T HAVE HAD TO ENDURE SUCH TERRORS.
THIS IS YOUR FAULT!
DO NOT INFLICT MORE MISERY THAN YOU HAVE ALREADY.

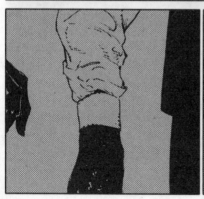

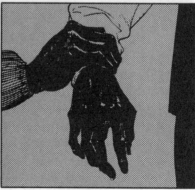

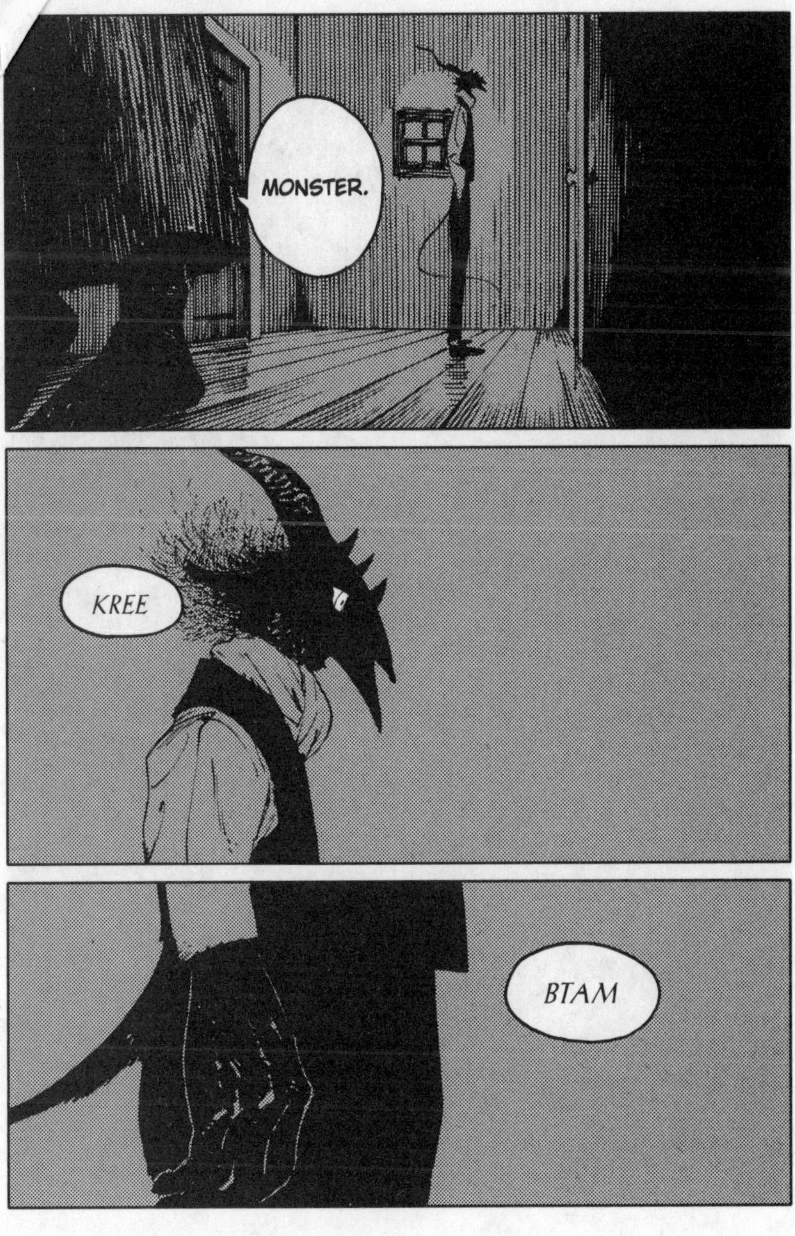
MONSTER.
KREE
BTAM

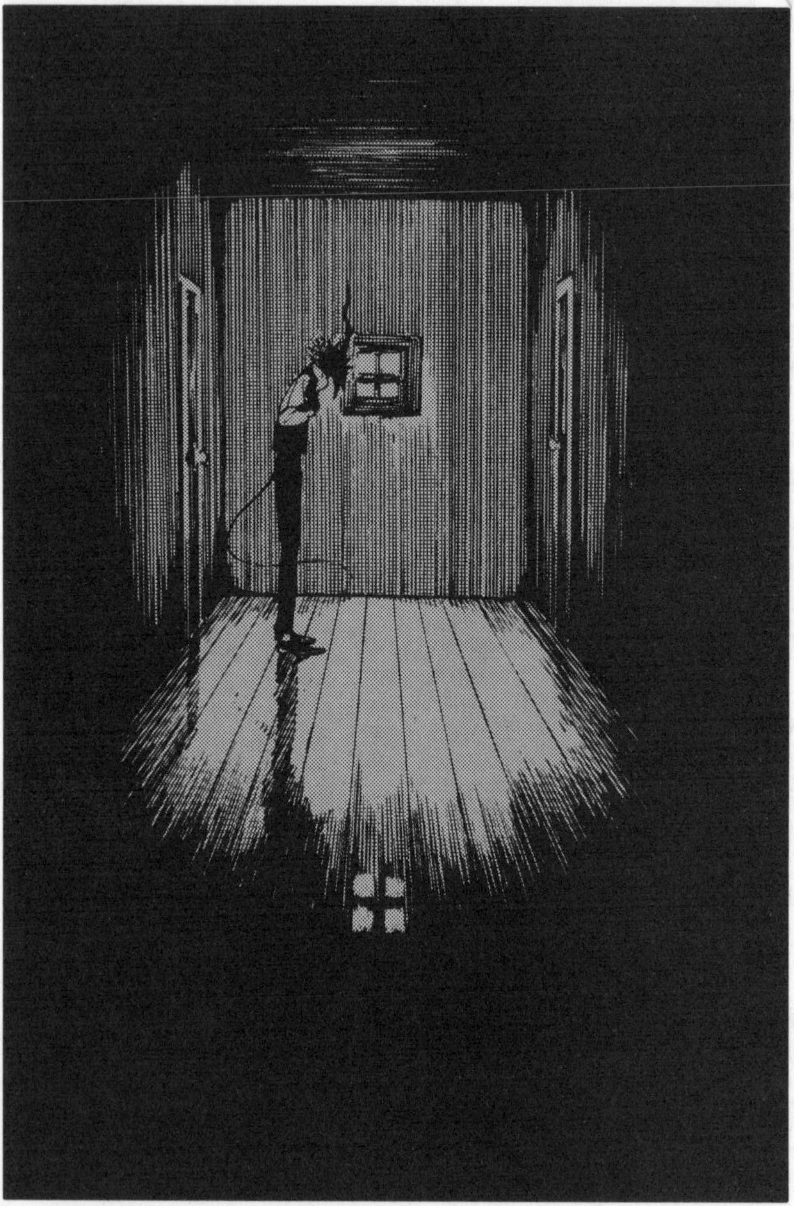

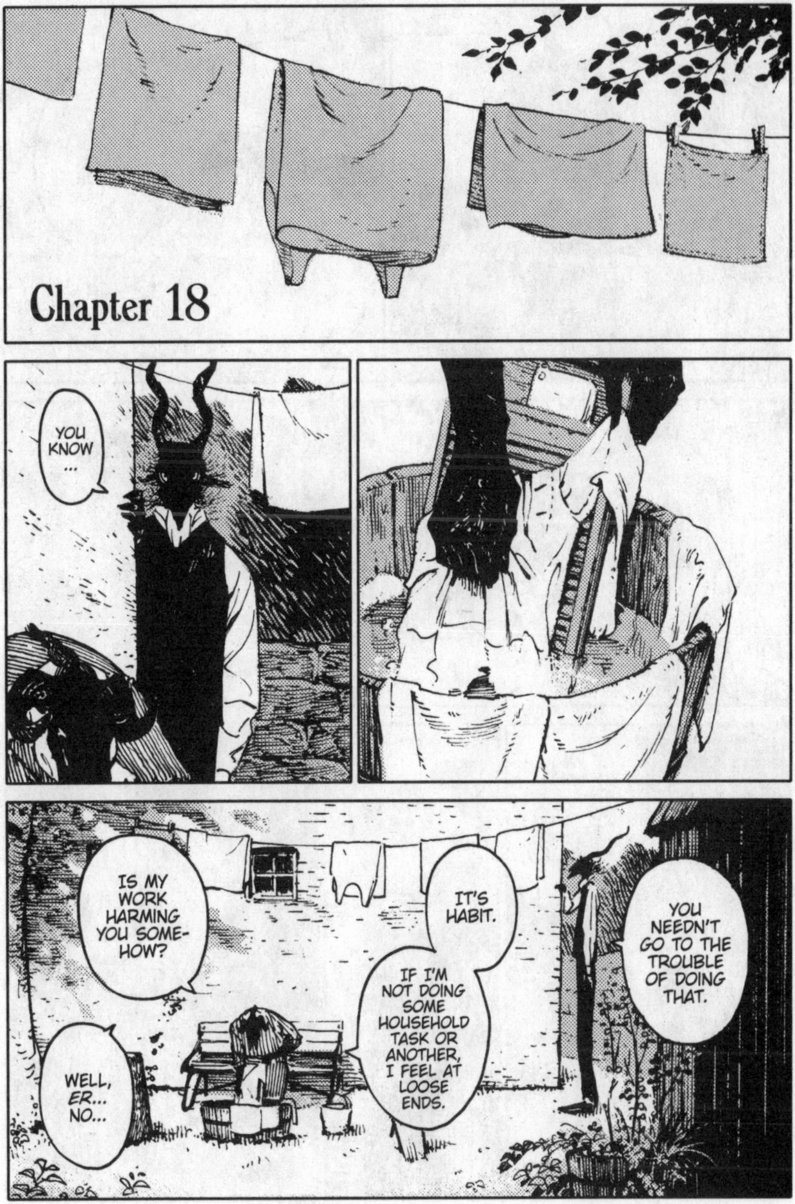
Chapter 18
YOU KNOW ...
YOU NEEDN'T GO TO THE TROUBLE OF DOING THAT.
IT'S HABIT.
IF I'M NOT DOING SOME HOUSEHOLD TASK OR ANOTHER, I FEEL AT LOOSE ENDS.
IS MY WORK HARMING YOU SOMEHOW?
WELL, ER... NO...

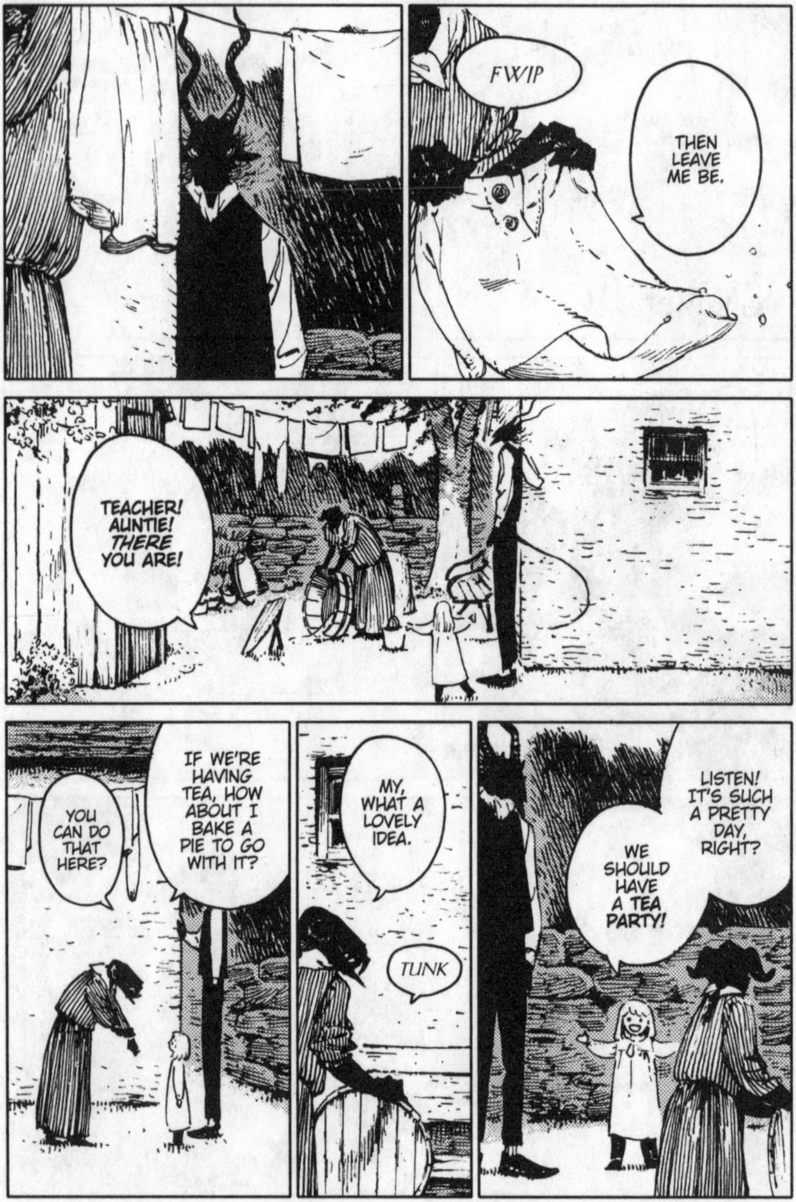
FWIP
THEN LEAVE ME BE.
TEACHER! AUNTIE! *THERE* YOU ARE!
YOU CAN DO THAT HERE?
IF WE'RE HAVING TEA, HOW ABOUT I BAKE A PIE TO GO WITH IT?
MY, WHAT A LOVELY IDEA.
TUNK
LISTEN! IT'S SUCH A PRETTY DAY, RIGHT?
WE SHOULD HAVE A TEA PARTY!

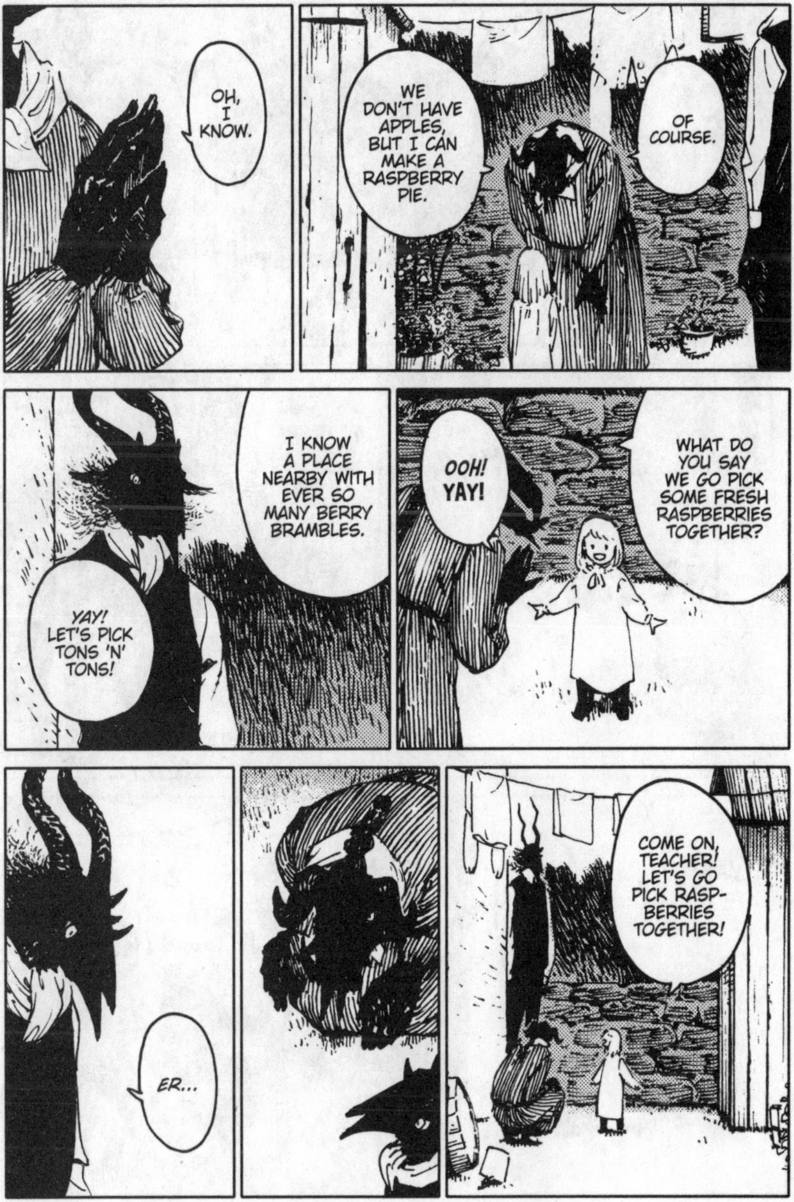
OF COURSE.
WE DON'T HAVE APPLES, BUT I CAN MAKE A RASPBERRY PIE.
OH, I KNOW.
WHAT DO YOU SAY WE GO PICK SOME FRESH RASPBERRIES TOGETHER?
OOH! YAY!
I KNOW A PLACE NEARBY WITH EVER SO MANY BERRY BRAMBLES.
YAY! LET'S PICK TONS 'N' TONS!
COME ON, TEACHER! LET'S GO PICK RASP-BERRIES TOGETHER!
ER...

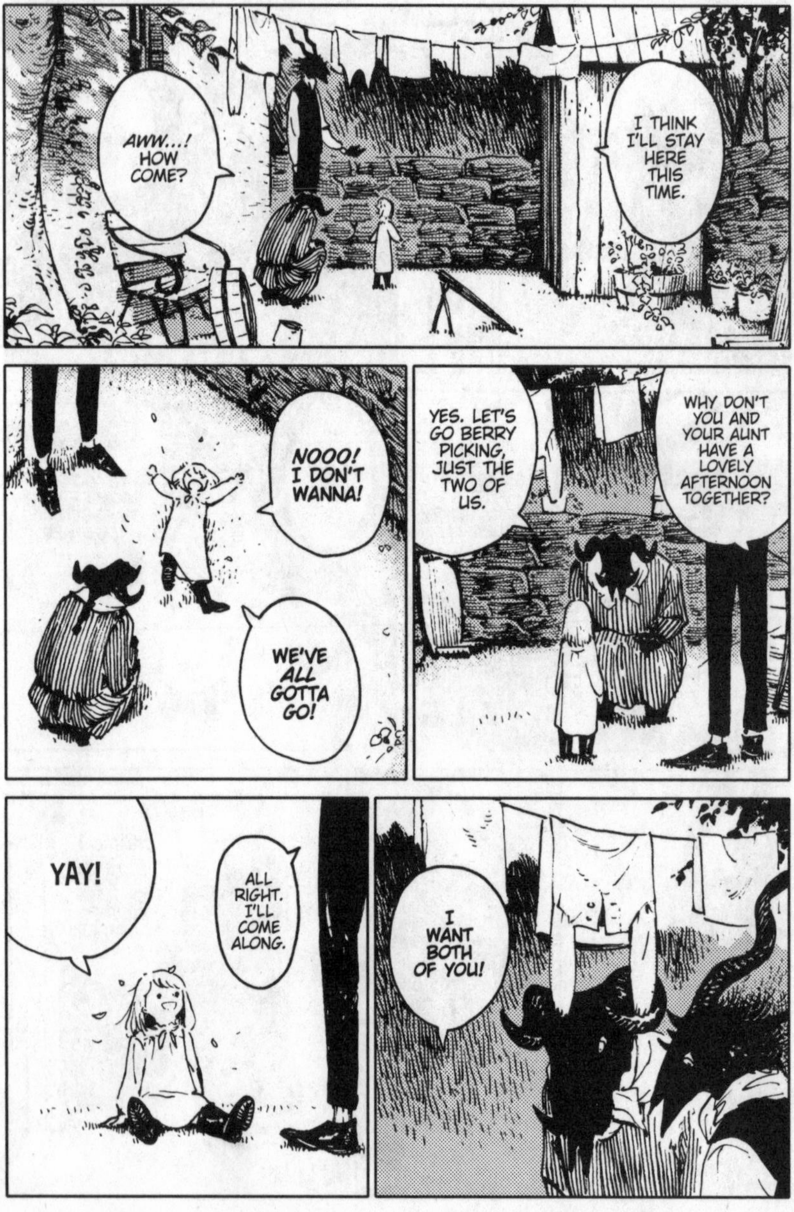
I THINK I'LL STAY HERE THIS TIME.
AWW...! HOW COME?
WHY DON'T YOU AND YOUR AUNT HAVE A LOVELY AFTERNOON TOGETHER?
YES. LET'S GO BERRY PICKING, JUST THE TWO OF US.
NOOO! I DON'T WANNA!
WE'VE *ALL* GOTTA GO!
I WANT BOTH OF YOU!
ALL RIGHT. I'LL COME ALONG.
YAY!

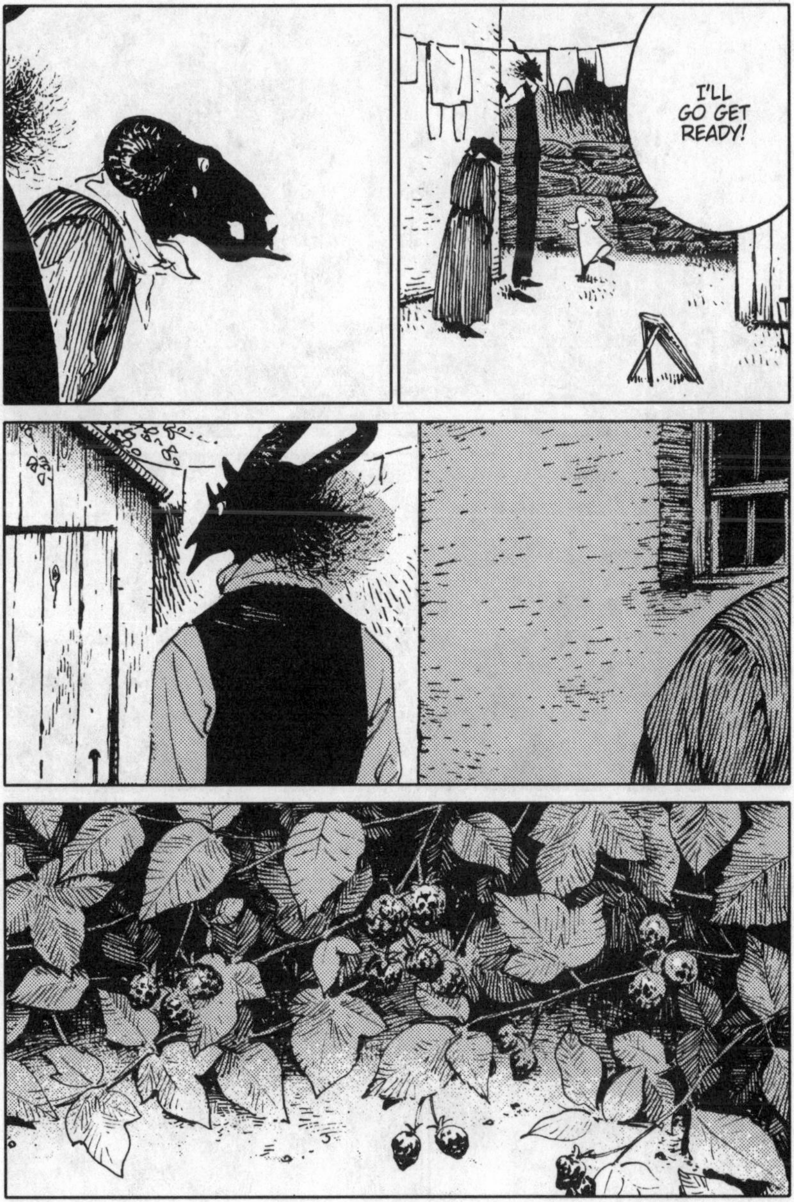
I'LL GO GET READY!

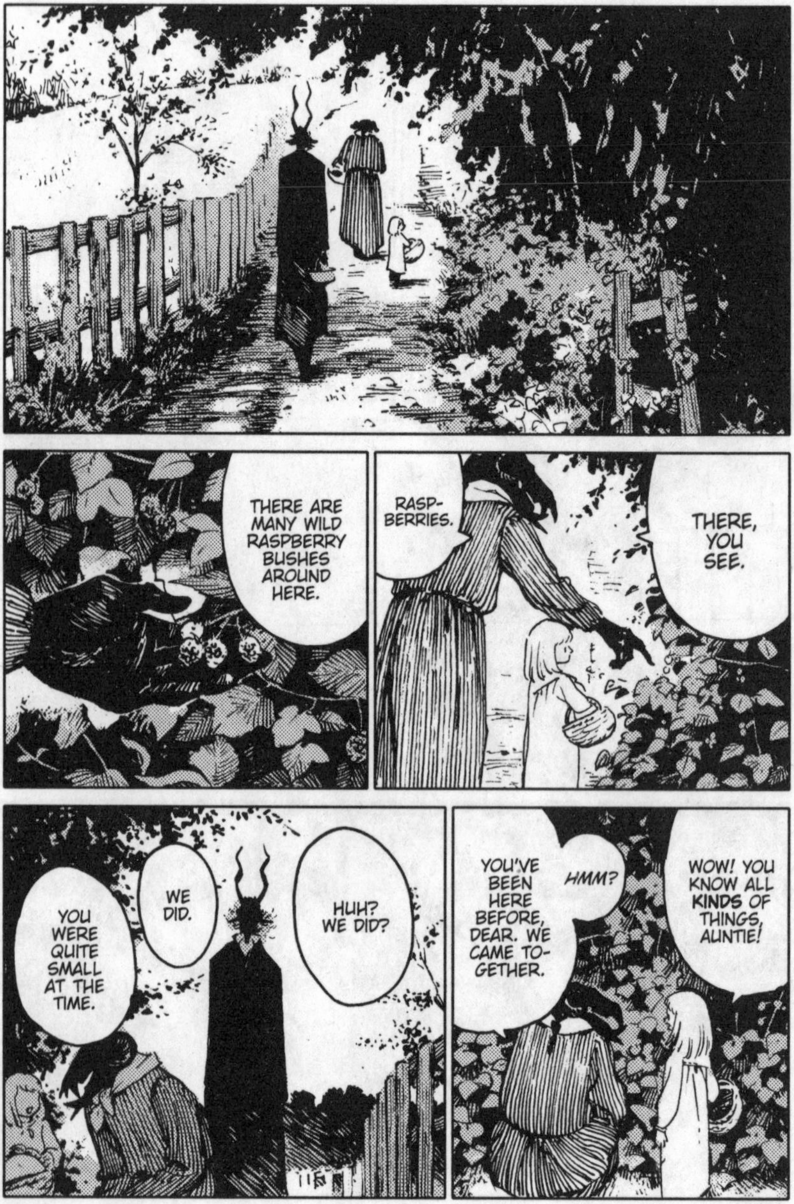
THERE, YOU SEE.
RASP-BERRIES.
THERE ARE MANY WILD RASPBERRY BUSHES AROUND HERE.
WOW! YOU KNOW ALL **KINDS** OF THINGS, AUNTIE!
HMM?
YOU'VE BEEN HERE BEFORE, DEAR. WE CAME TO-GETHER.
HUH? WE DID?
WE DID.
YOU WERE QUITE SMALL AT THE TIME.

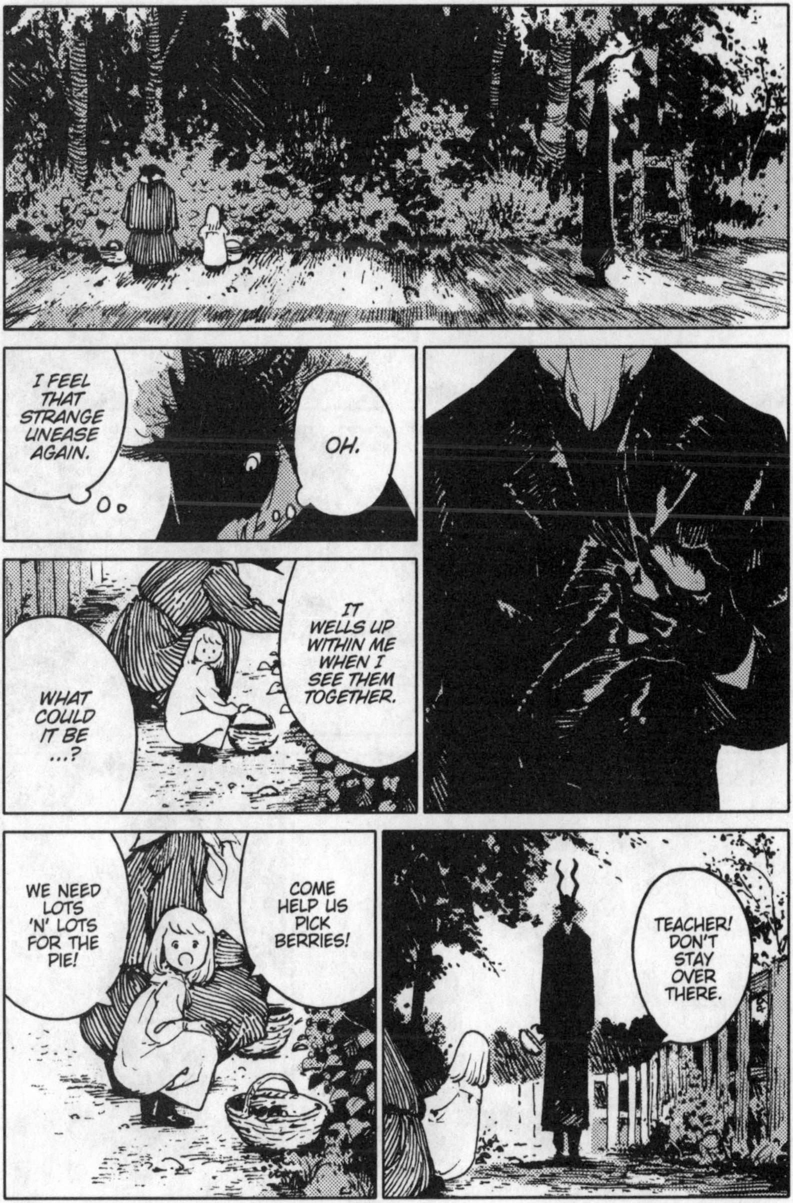
OH.
I FEEL THAT STRANGE UNEASE AGAIN.
IT WELLS UP WITHIN ME WHEN I SEE THEM TOGETHER.
WHAT COULD IT BE ...?
TEACHER! DON'T STAY OVER THERE.
COME HELP US PICK BERRIES!
WE NEED LOTS 'N' LOTS FOR THE PIE!

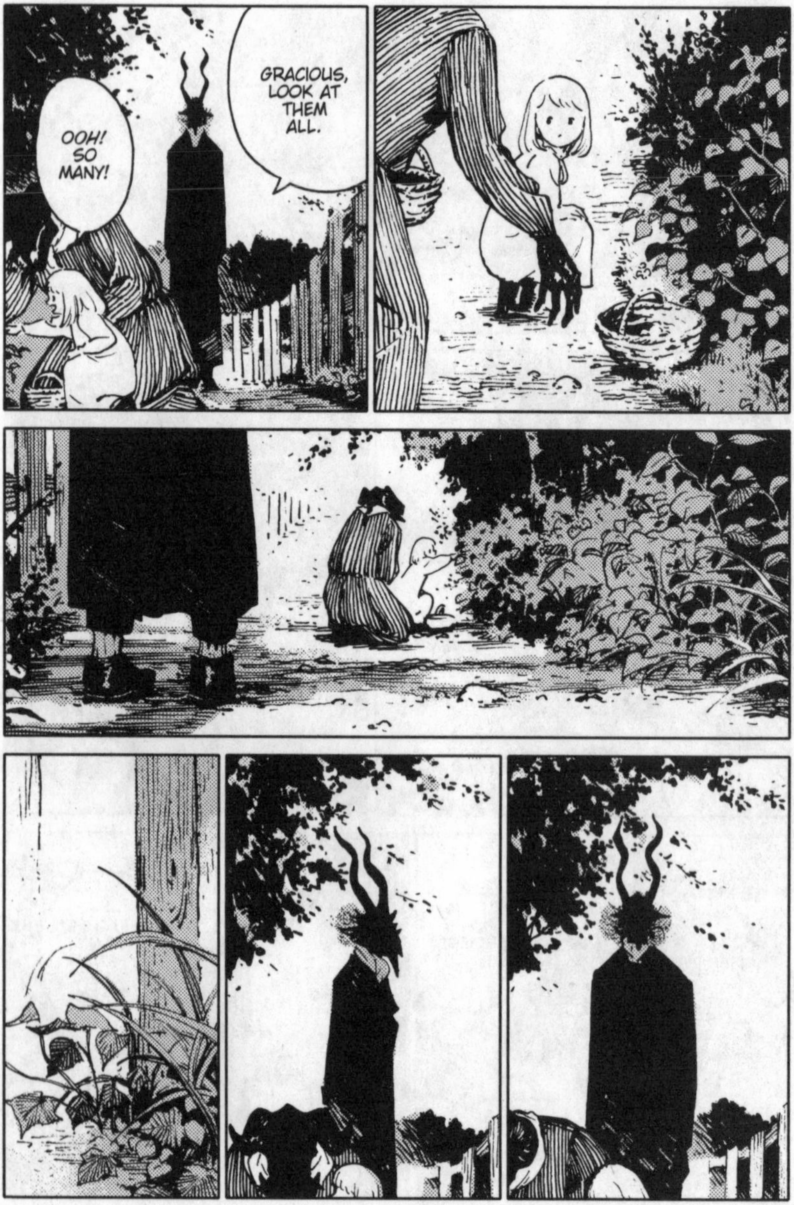
OOH! SO MANY!
GRACIOUS, LOOK AT THEM ALL.

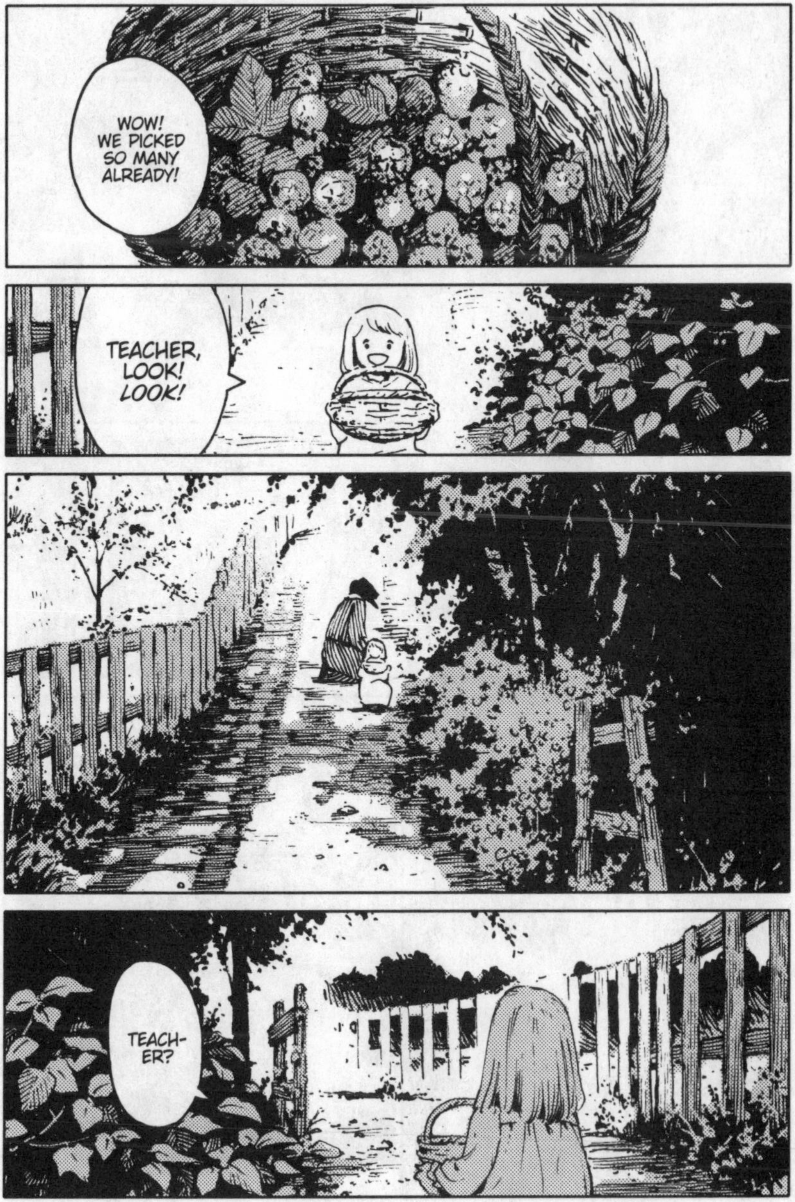
WOW! WE PICKED SO MANY ALREADY!
TEACHER, LOOK! LOOK!
TEACHER?

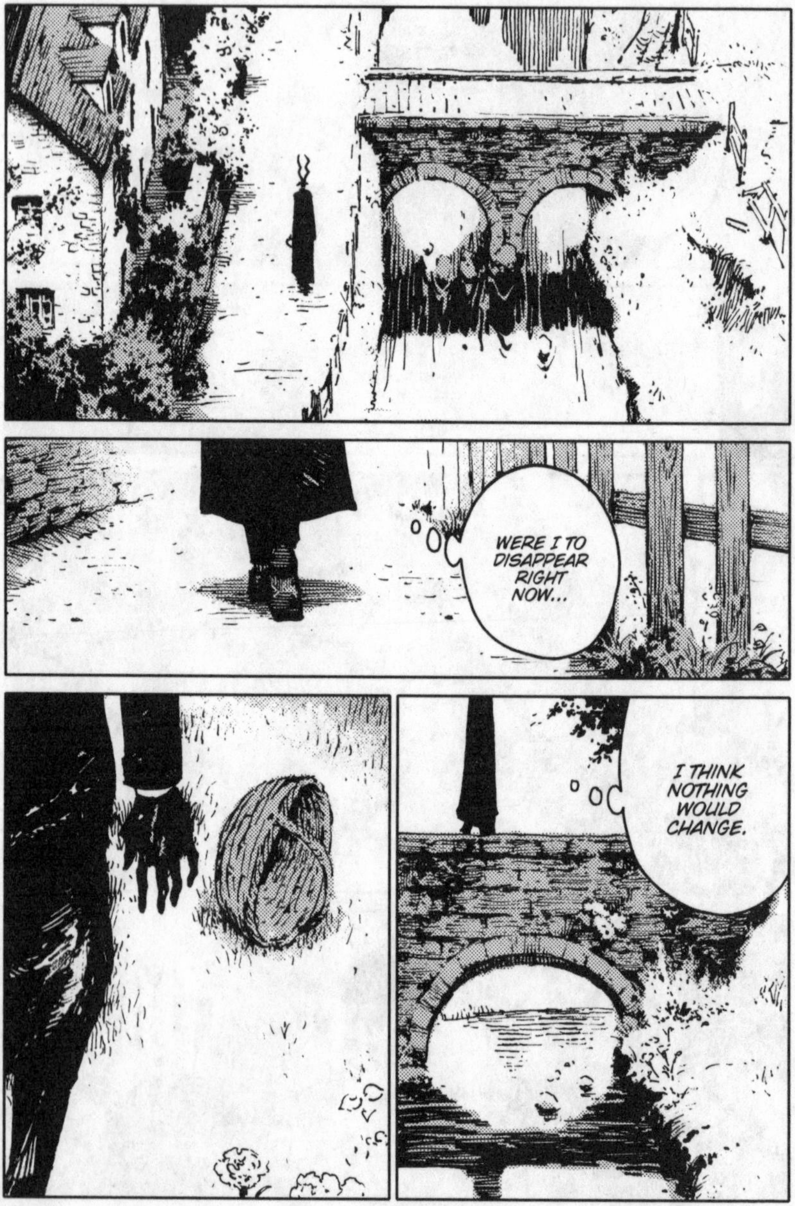
WERE I TO DISAPPEAR RIGHT NOW...
I THINK NOTHING WOULD CHANGE.

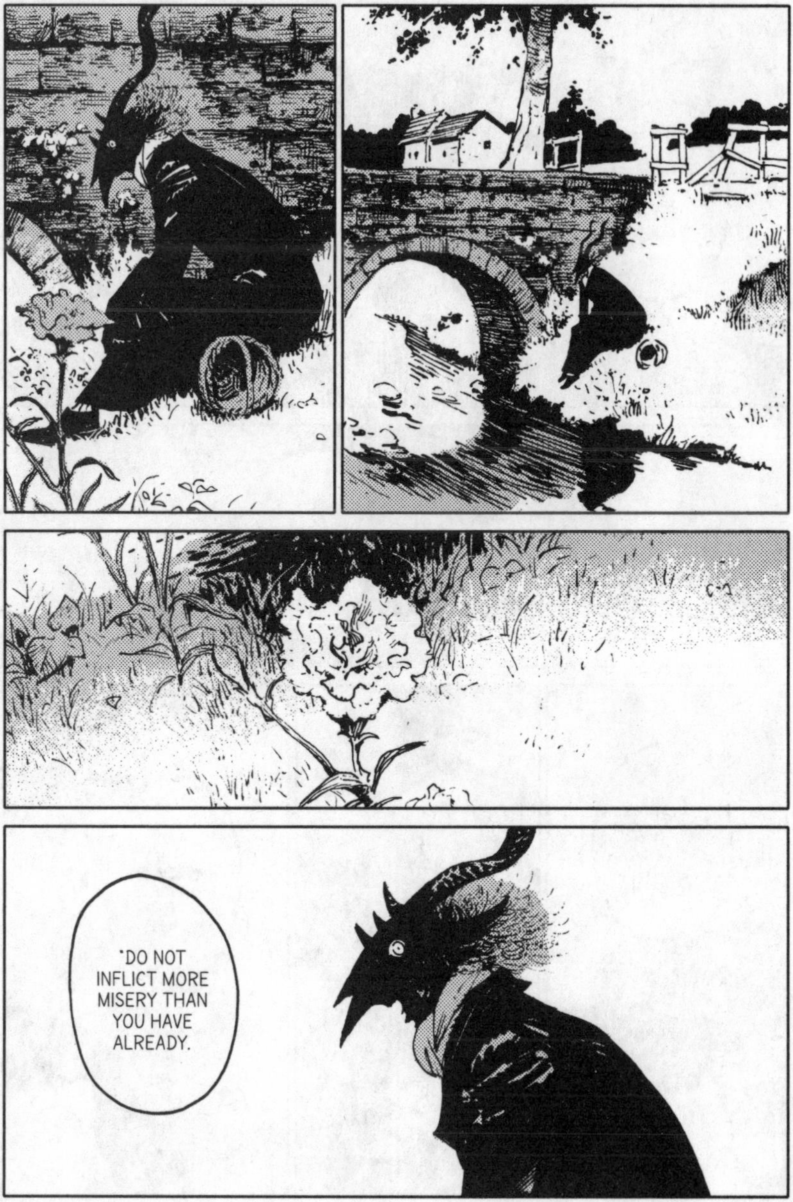
"DO NOT INFLICT MORE MISERY THAN YOU HAVE ALREADY.

"IF IT WEREN'T FOR YOU, SHIVA NEVER WOULD HAVE BEEN CURSED TO BEGIN WITH.
"SHE WOULDN'T HAVE HAD TO ENDURE SUCH TERRORS.
"THIS IS YOUR FAULT!
"MONSTER."
HAVE...
HAVE I BEEN WRONG THIS ENTIRE TIME?
ALL THE THINGS I DID...
THAT I THOUGHT WOULD HELP AND PROTECT HER...
CAN I BE...
TRULY SURE THAT THEY WERE THE RIGHT THINGS TO DO?

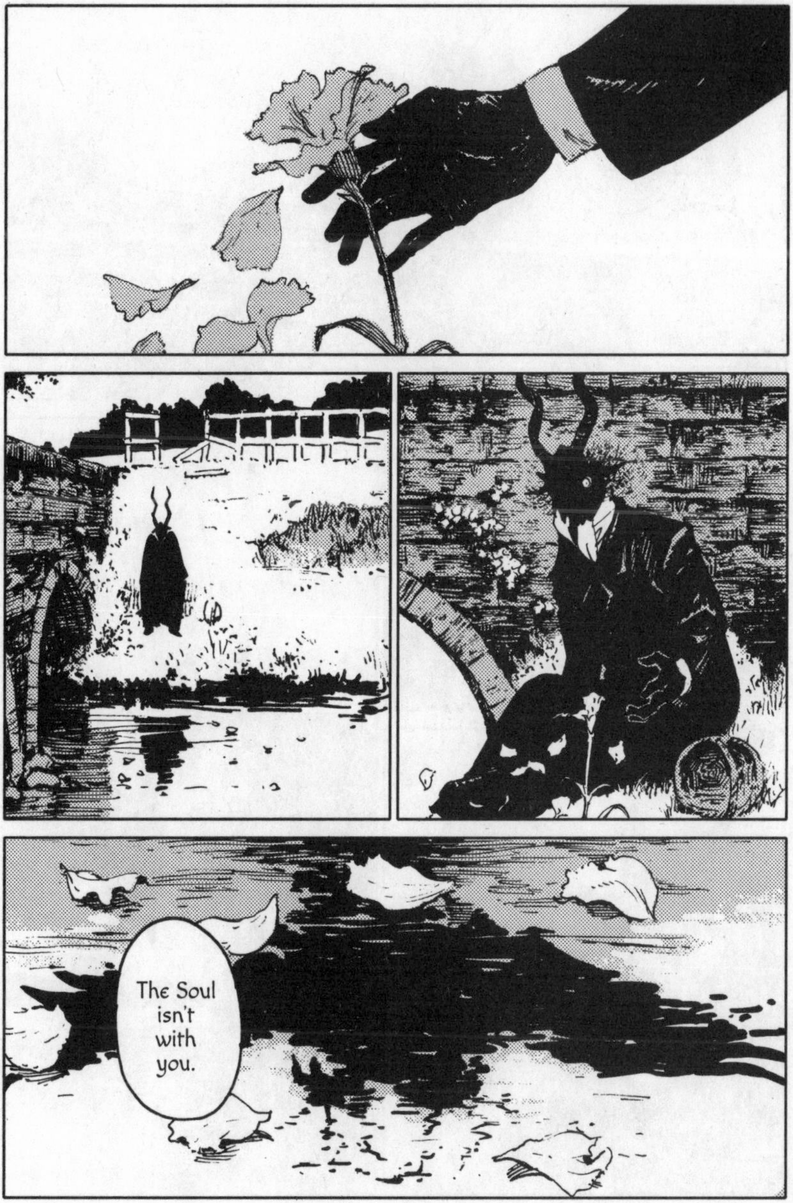
The Soul isn't with you.

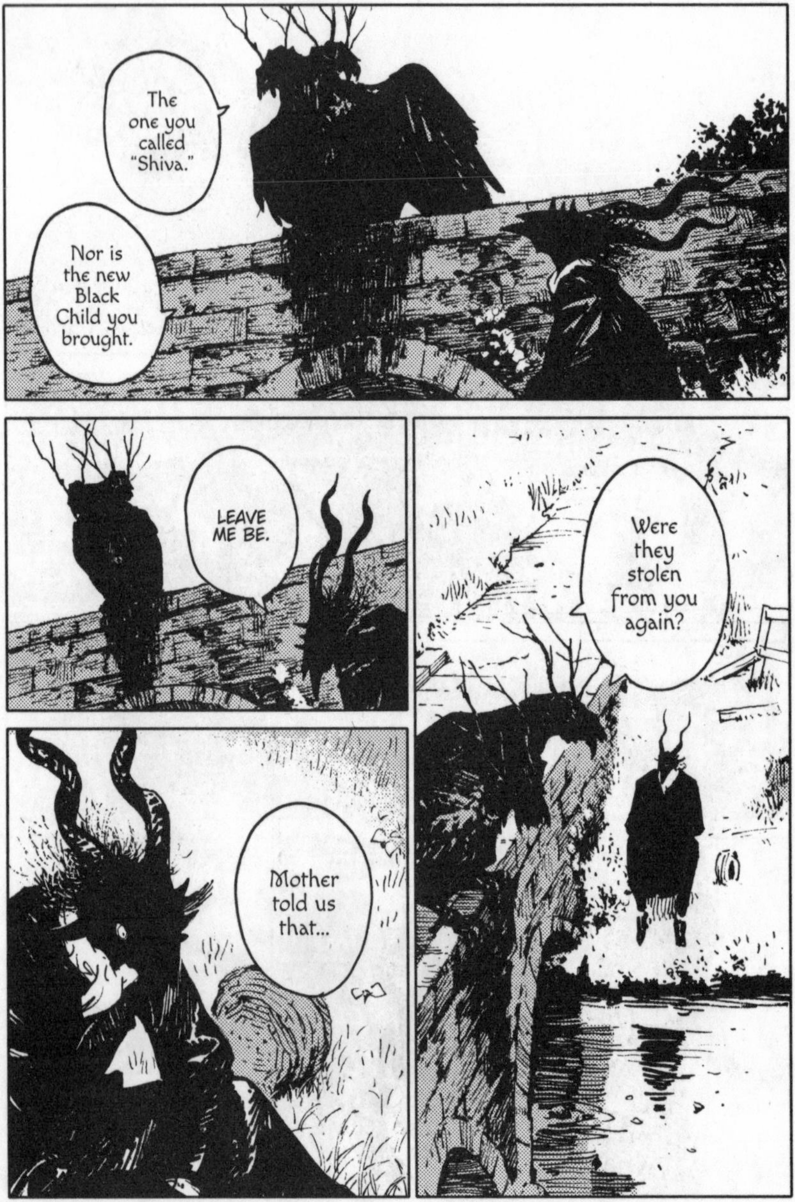
The one you called "Shiva."
Nor is the new Black Child you brought.
LEAVE ME BE.
Were they stolen from you again?
Mother told us that...

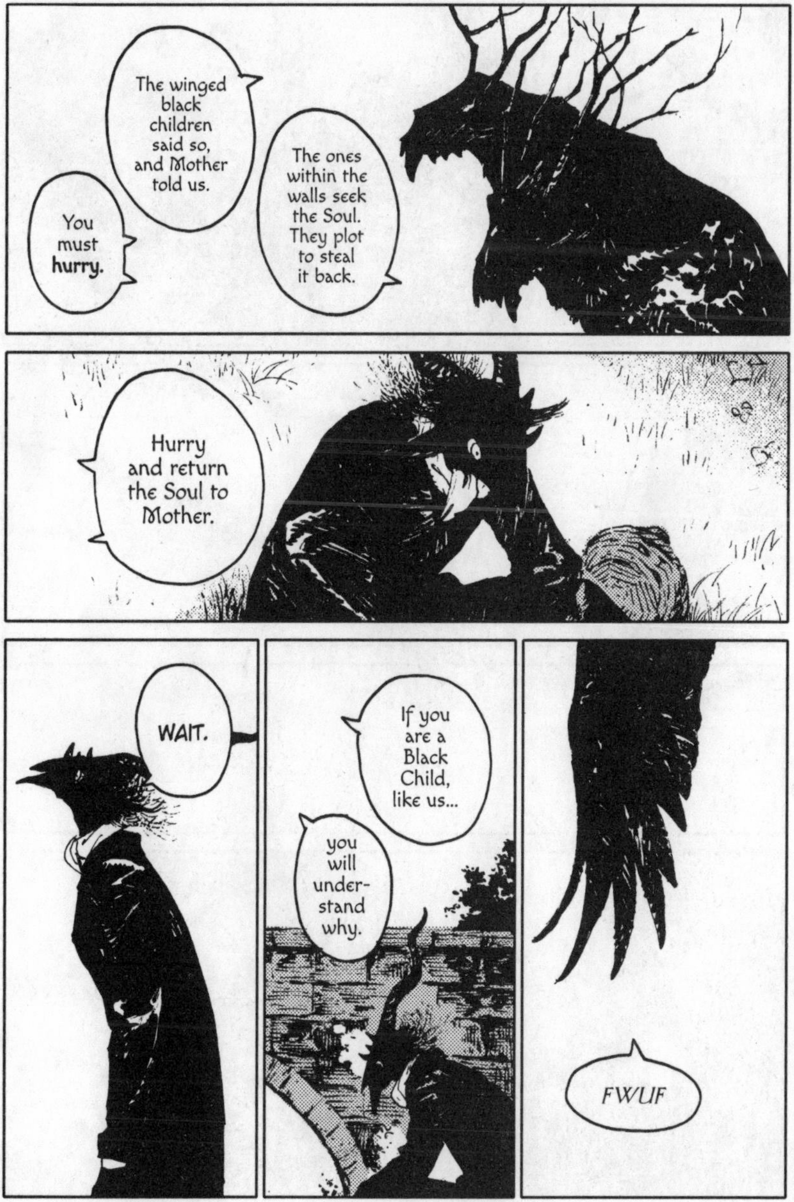
The winged black children said so, and Mother told us.
You must **hurry.**
The ones within the walls seek the Soul. They plot to steal it back.
Hurry and return the Soul to Mother.
WAIT.
If you are a Black Child, like us...
you will under-stand why.
FWUF

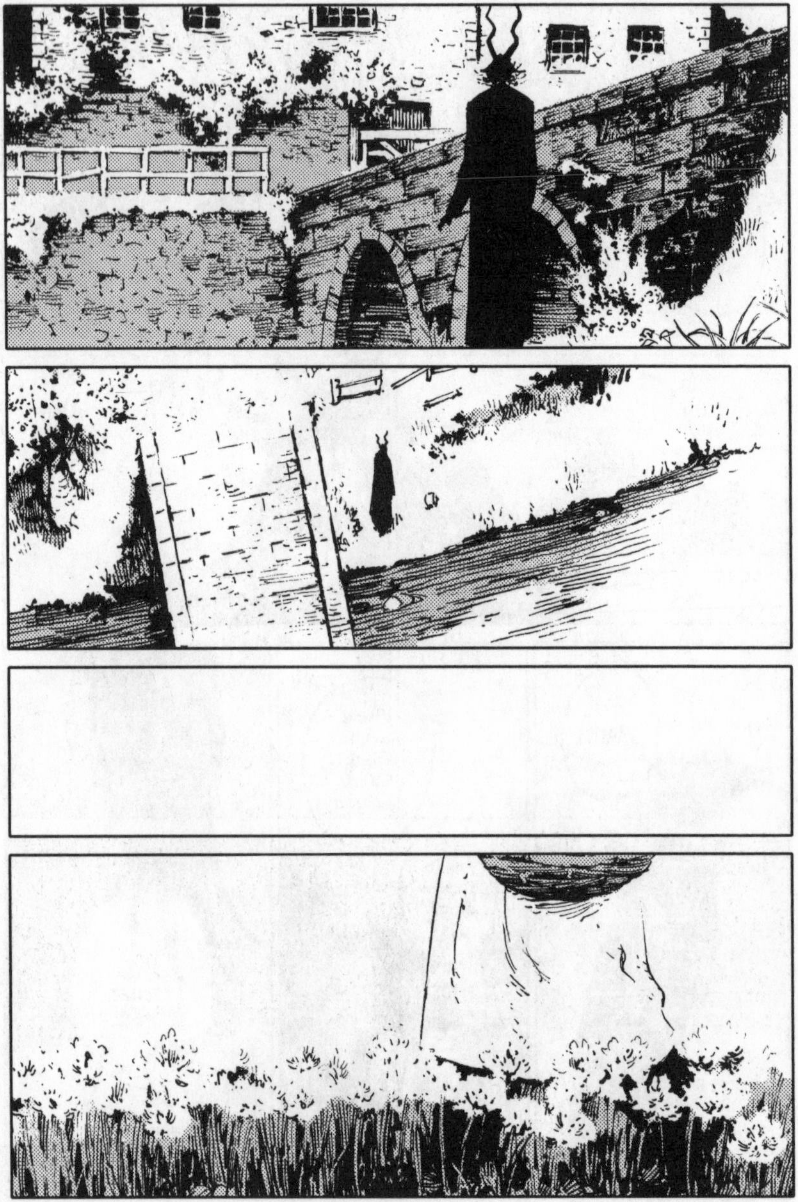

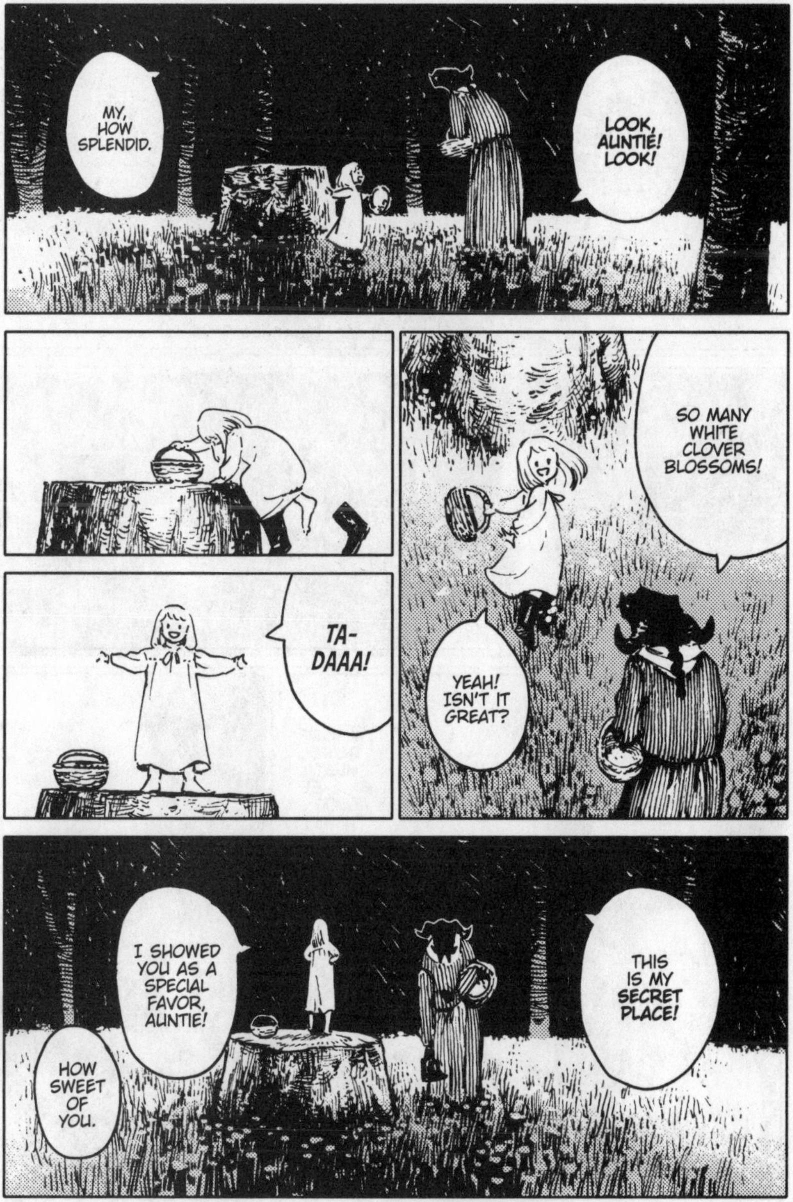
LOOK, AUNTIE! LOOK!
MY, HOW SPLENDID.
SO MANY WHITE CLOVER BLOSSOMS!
YEAH! ISN'T IT GREAT?
TA-DAAA!
THIS IS MY SECRET PLACE!
I SHOWED YOU AS A SPECIAL FAVOR, AUNTIE!
HOW SWEET OF YOU.

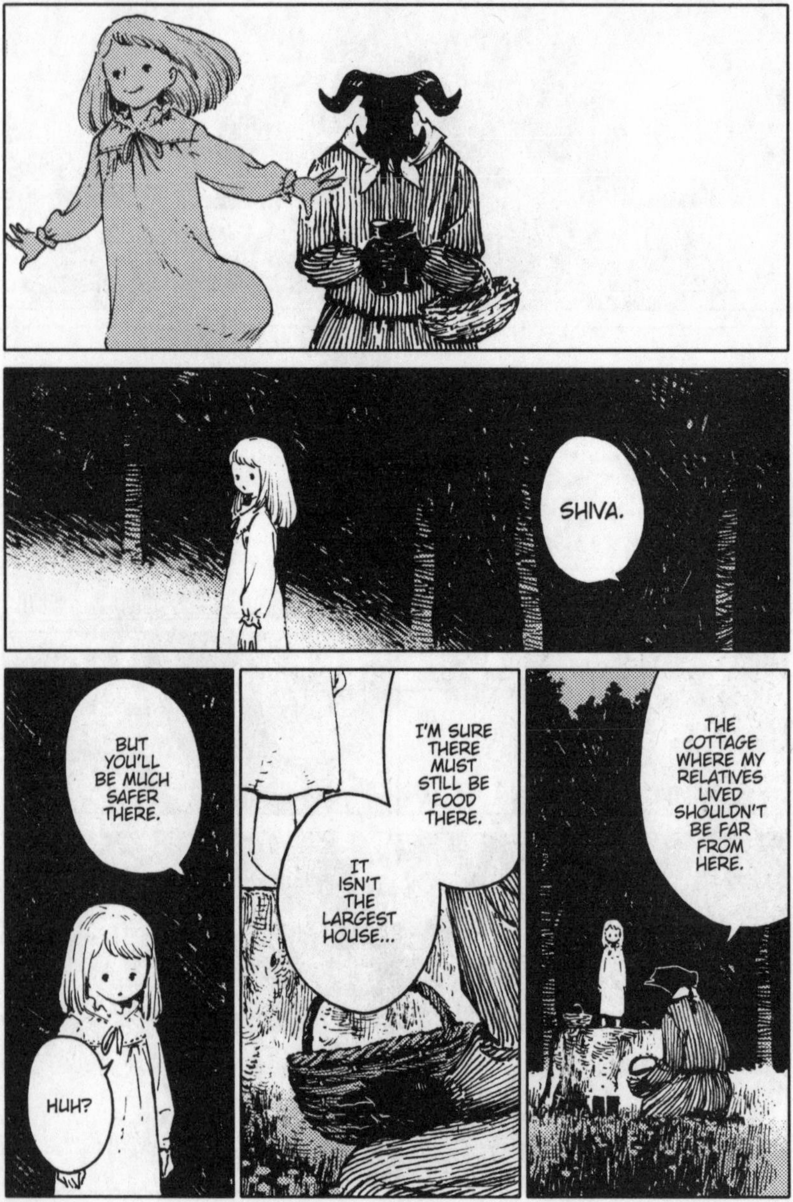
SHIVA.
THE COTTAGE WHERE MY RELATIVES LIVED SHOULDN'T BE FAR FROM HERE.
I'M SURE THERE MUST STILL BE FOOD THERE.
IT ISN'T THE LARGEST HOUSE...
BUT YOU'LL BE MUCH SAFER THERE.
HUH?

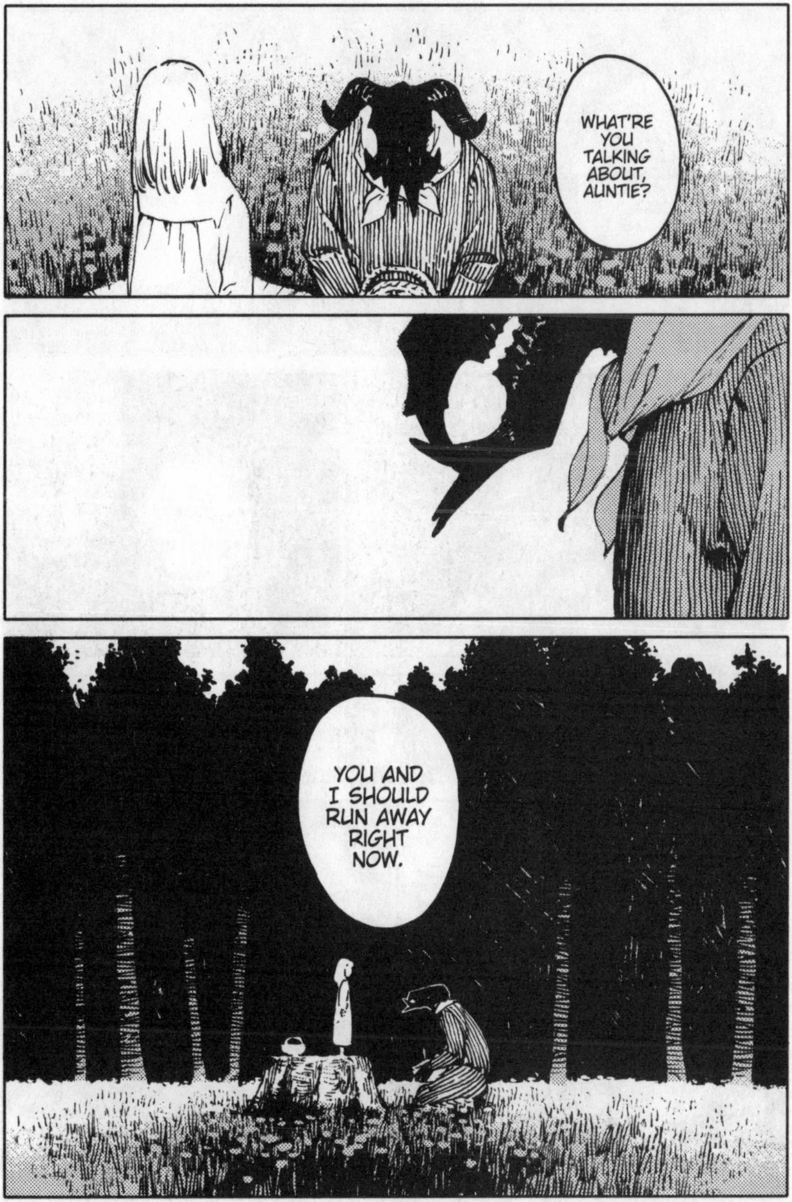
WHAT'RE YOU TALKING ABOUT, AUNTIE?
YOU AND I SHOULD RUN AWAY RIGHT NOW.

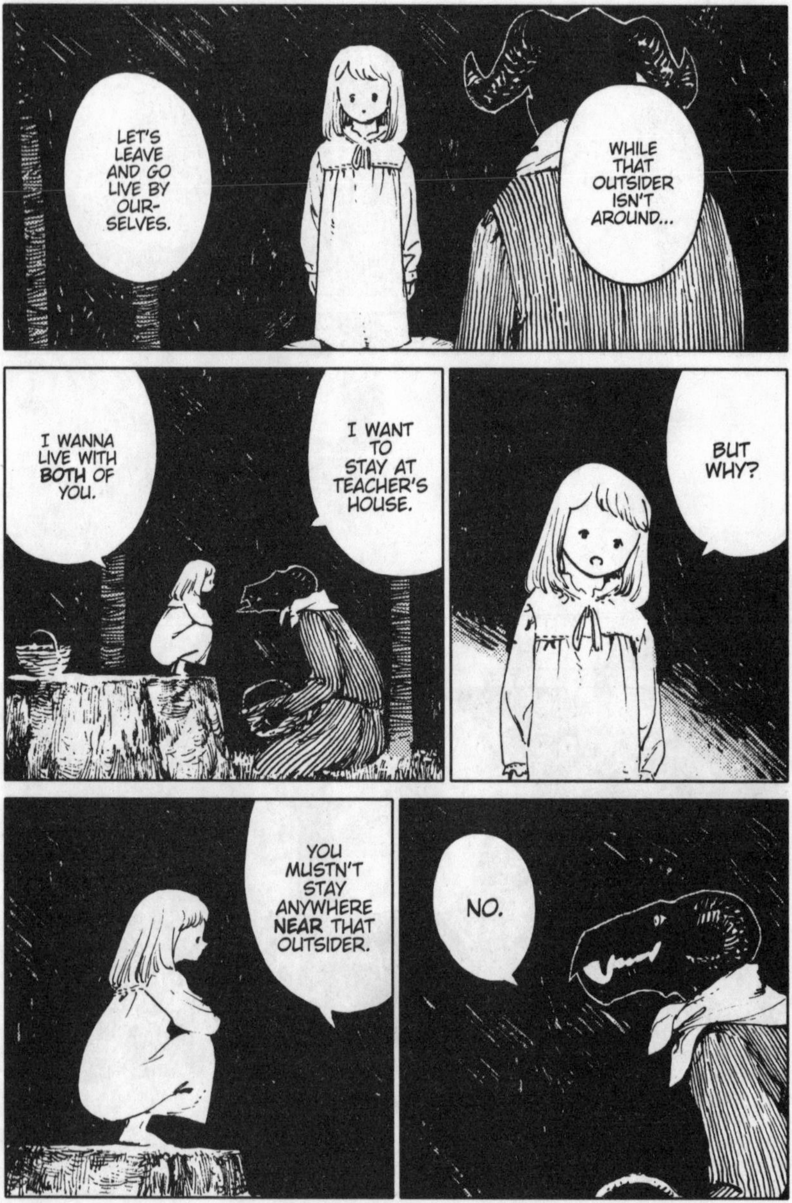
WHILE THAT OUTSIDER ISN'T AROUND...
LET'S LEAVE AND GO LIVE BY OUR-SELVES.
I WANT TO STAY AT TEACHER'S HOUSE.
I WANNA LIVE WITH BOTH OF YOU.
BUT WHY?
NO.
YOU MUSTN'T STAY ANYWHERE NEAR THAT OUTSIDER.

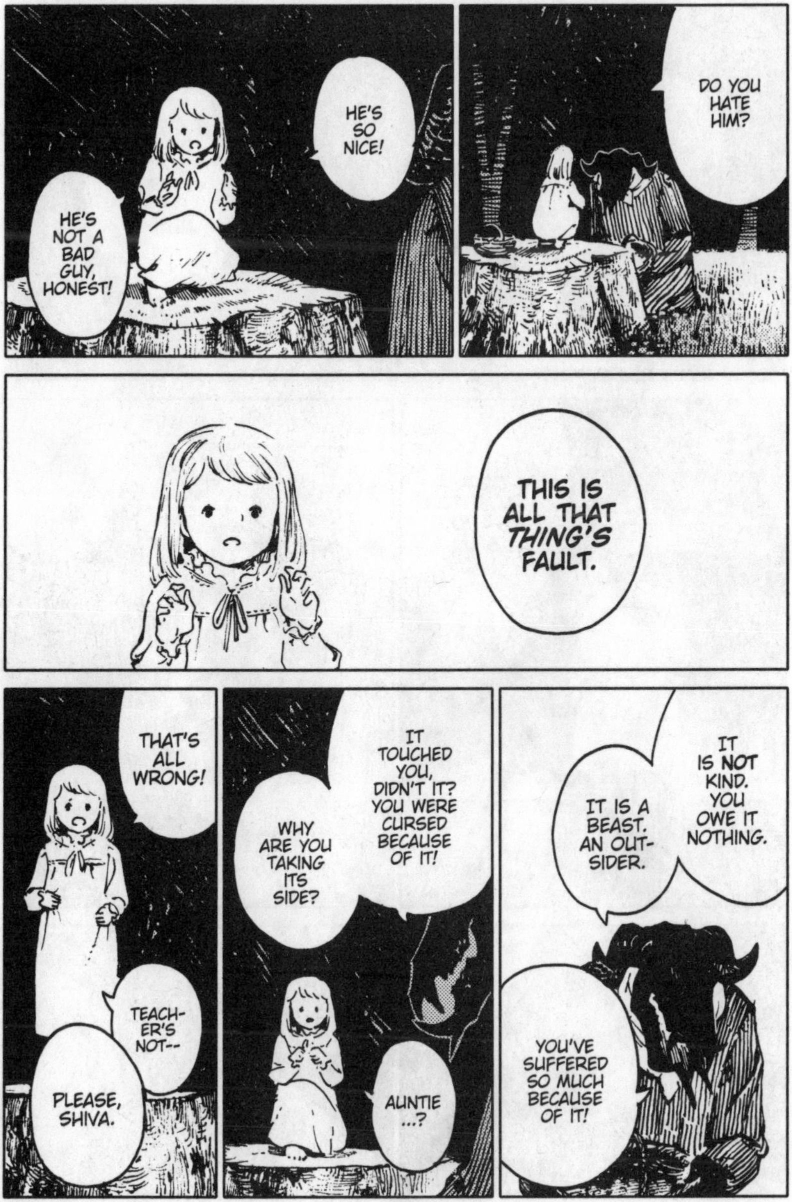
DO YOU HATE HIM?
HE'S SO NICE!
HE'S NOT A BAD GUY, HONEST!
THIS IS ALL THAT *THING'S* FAULT.
IT IS NOT KIND. YOU OWE IT NOTHING.
IT IS A BEAST. AN OUT-SIDER.
YOU'VE SUFFERED SO MUCH BECAUSE OF IT!
IT TOUCHED YOU, DIDN'T IT? YOU WERE CURSED BECAUSE OF IT!
WHY ARE YOU TAKING ITS SIDE?
AUNTIE ...?
THAT'S ALL WRONG!
TEACH-ER'S NOT--
PLEASE, SHIVA.

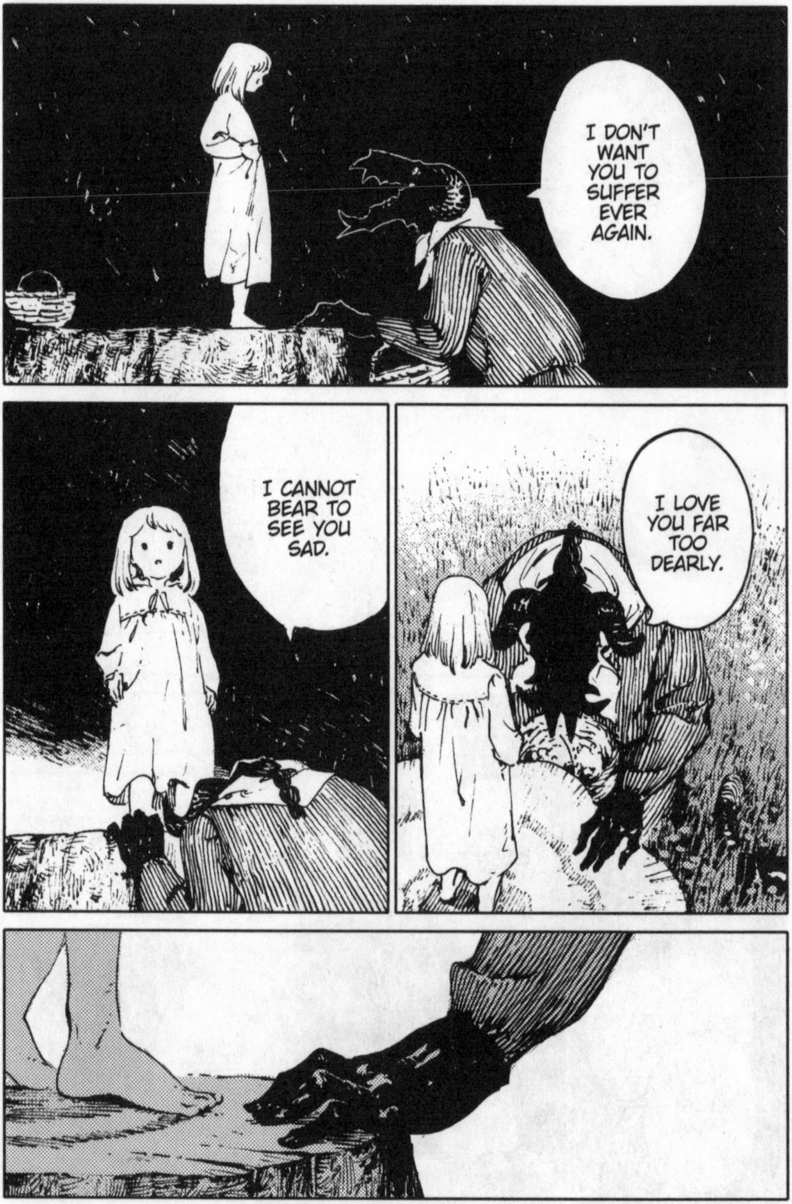
I DON'T WANT YOU TO SUFFER EVER AGAIN.
I CANNOT BEAR TO SEE YOU SAD.
I LOVE YOU FAR TOO DEARLY.

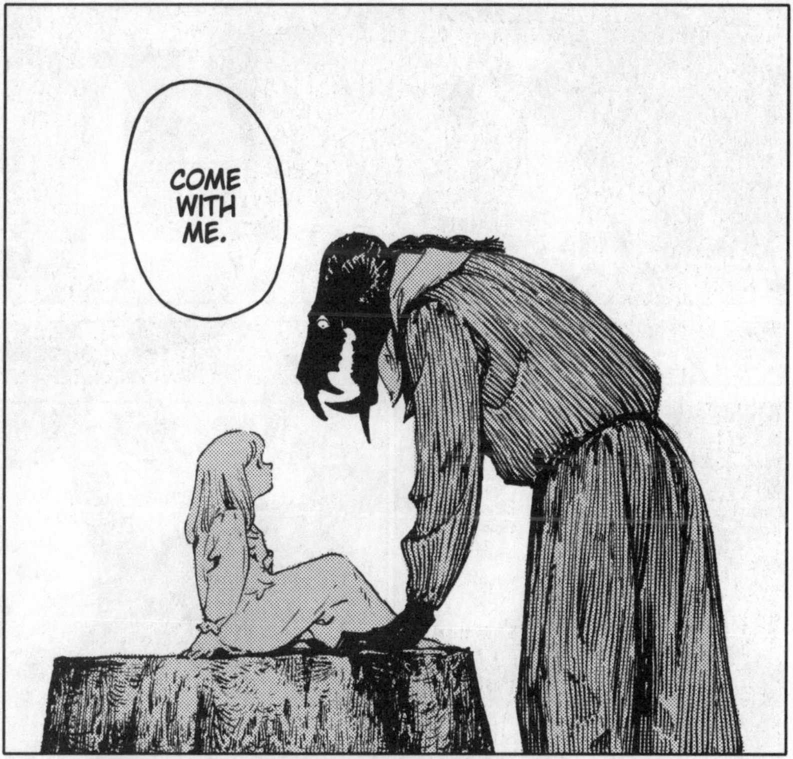
COME WITH ME.
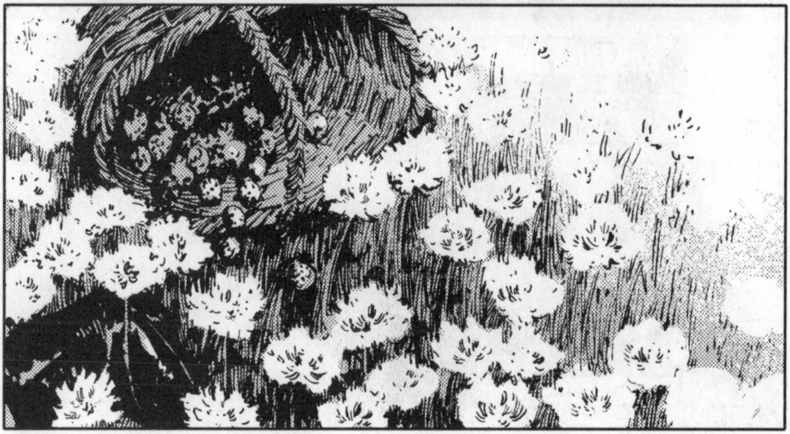

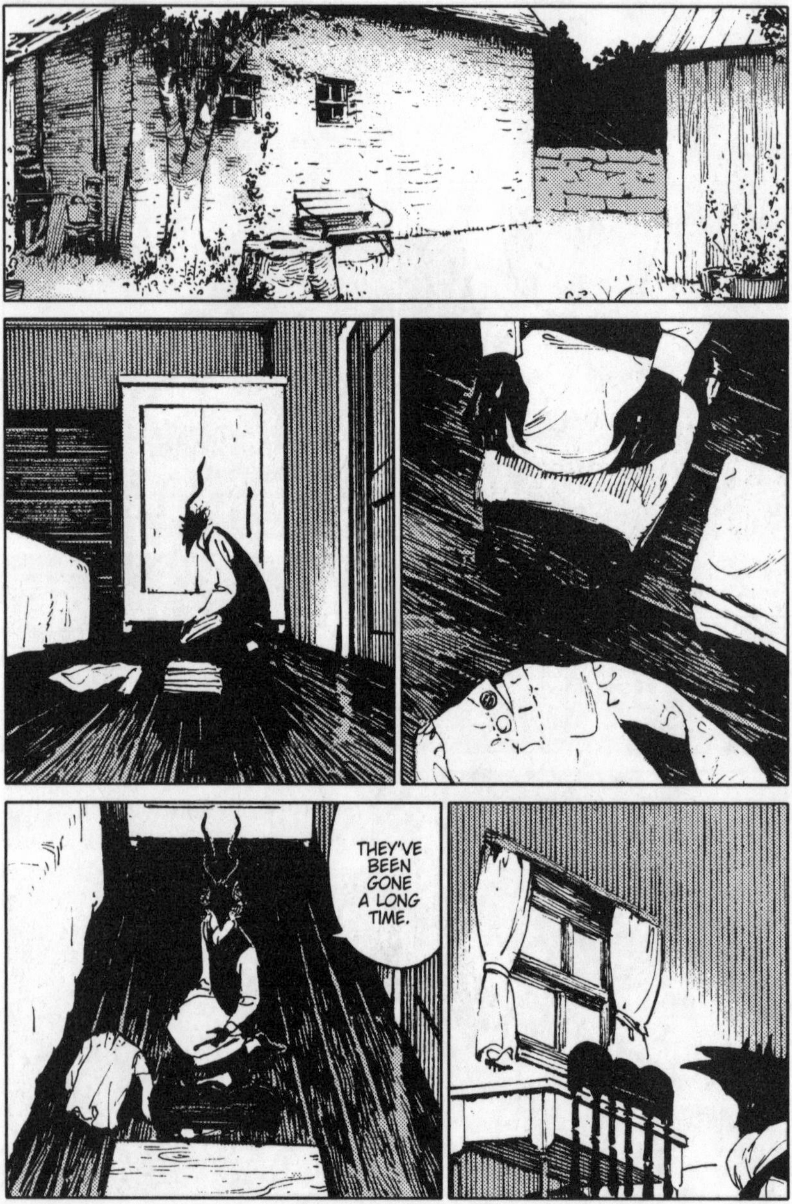
THEY'VE BEEN GONE A LONG TIME.

NO, NO. STOP WORRYING SO.

KREE

I EXPECT THEY'LL BE BACK SOON, BUT...

IF ANYTHING GOES WRONG, HER AUNT WILL PROTECT HER.

SHIVA IS WITH HER AUNT.

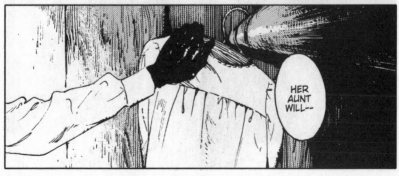

HER AUNT WILL--

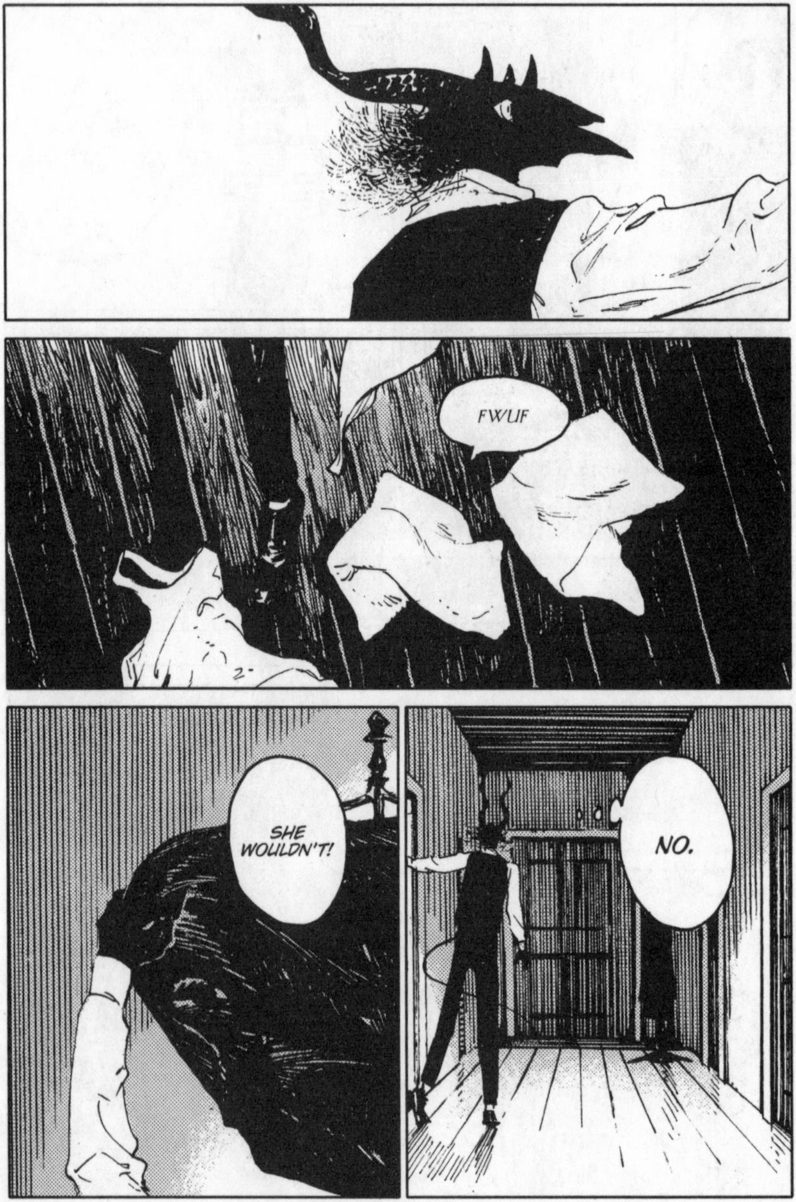
FWUF
NO.
SHE WOULDN'T!

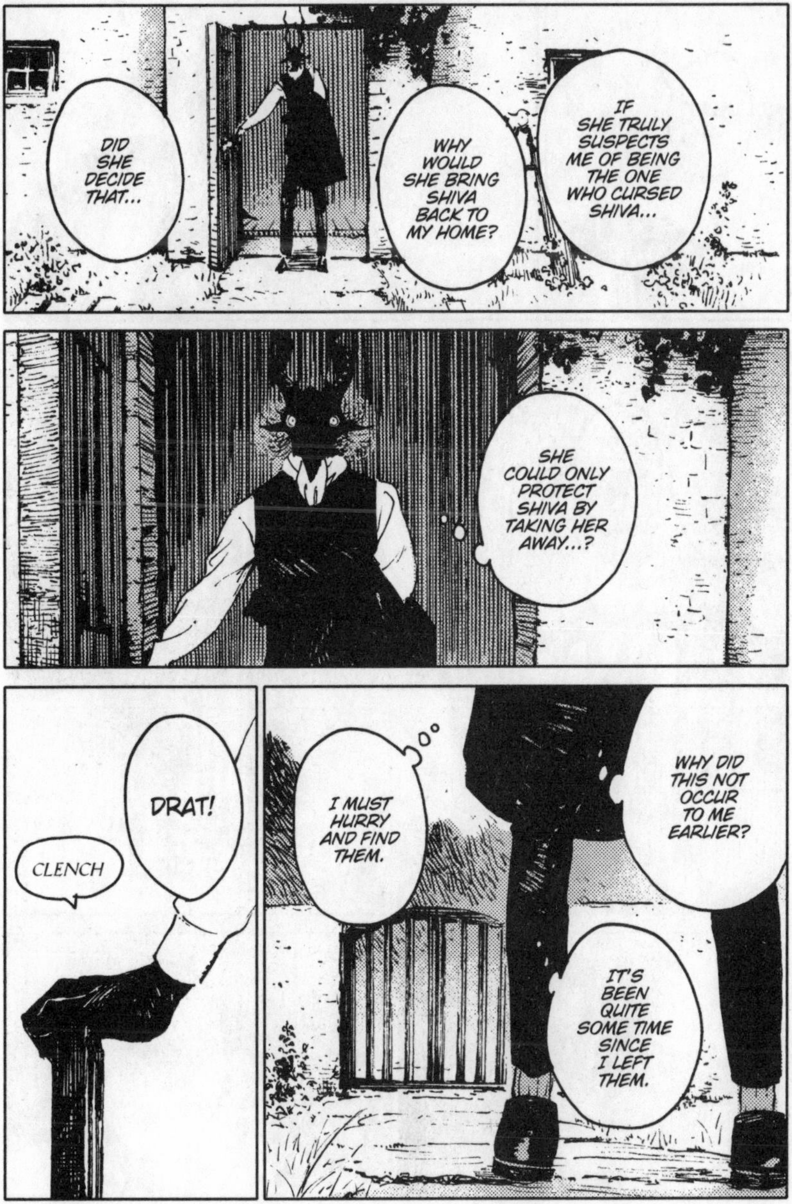
IF SHE TRULY SUSPECTS ME OF BEING THE ONE WHO CURSED SHIVA...
WHY WOULD SHE BRING SHIVA BACK TO MY HOME?
DID SHE DECIDE THAT...
SHE COULD ONLY PROTECT SHIVA BY TAKING HER AWAY...?
WHY DID THIS NOT OCCUR TO ME EARLIER?
IT'S BEEN QUITE SOME TIME SINCE I LEFT THEM.
I MUST HURRY AND FIND THEM.
DRAT!
CLENCH

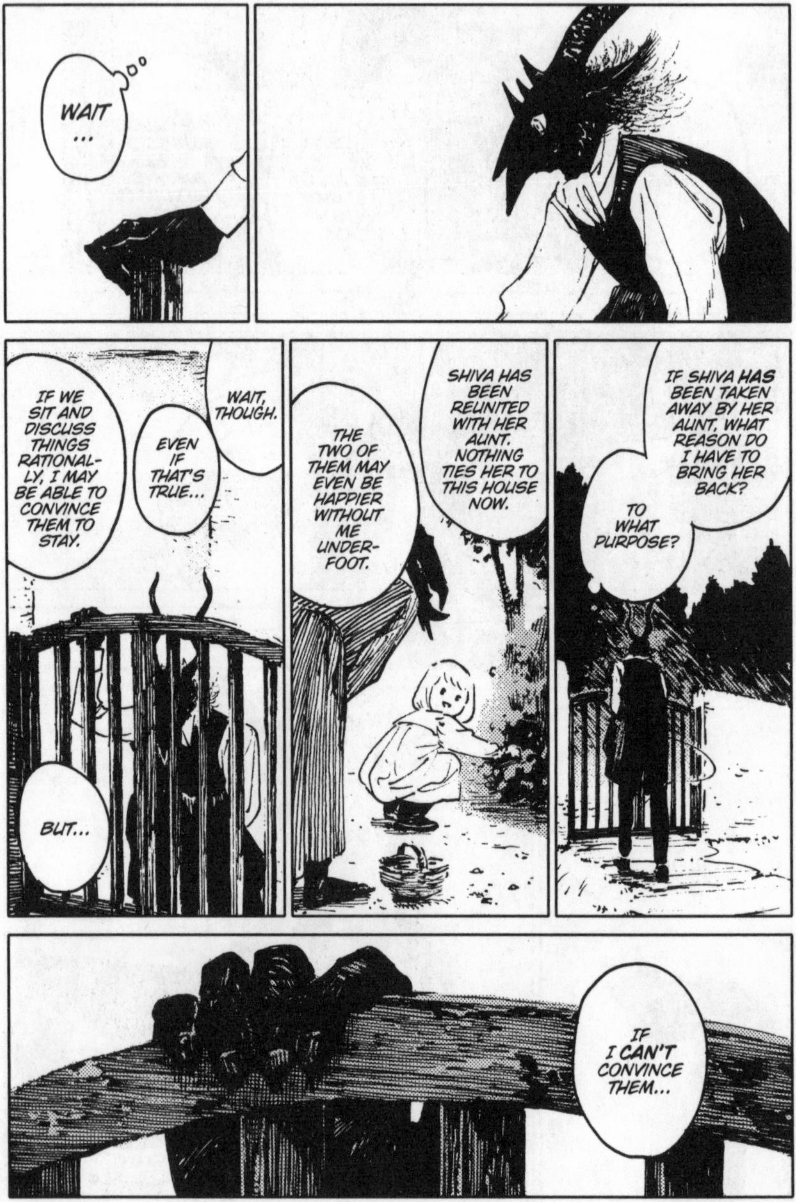
WAIT ...
IF SHIVA HAS BEEN TAKEN AWAY BY HER AUNT, WHAT REASON DO I HAVE TO BRING HER BACK?
TO WHAT PURPOSE?
SHIVA HAS BEEN REUNITED WITH HER AUNT. NOTHING TIES HER TO THIS HOUSE NOW.
THE TWO OF THEM MAY EVEN BE HAPPIER WITHOUT ME UNDER-FOOT.
WAIT, THOUGH.
EVEN IF THAT'S TRUE...
IF WE SIT AND DISCUSS THINGS RATIONAL-LY, I MAY BE ABLE TO CONVINCE THEM TO STAY.
BUT...
IF I CAN'T CONVINCE THEM...

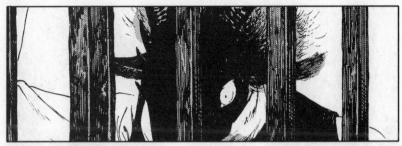

KREAK

SHIVA
....!

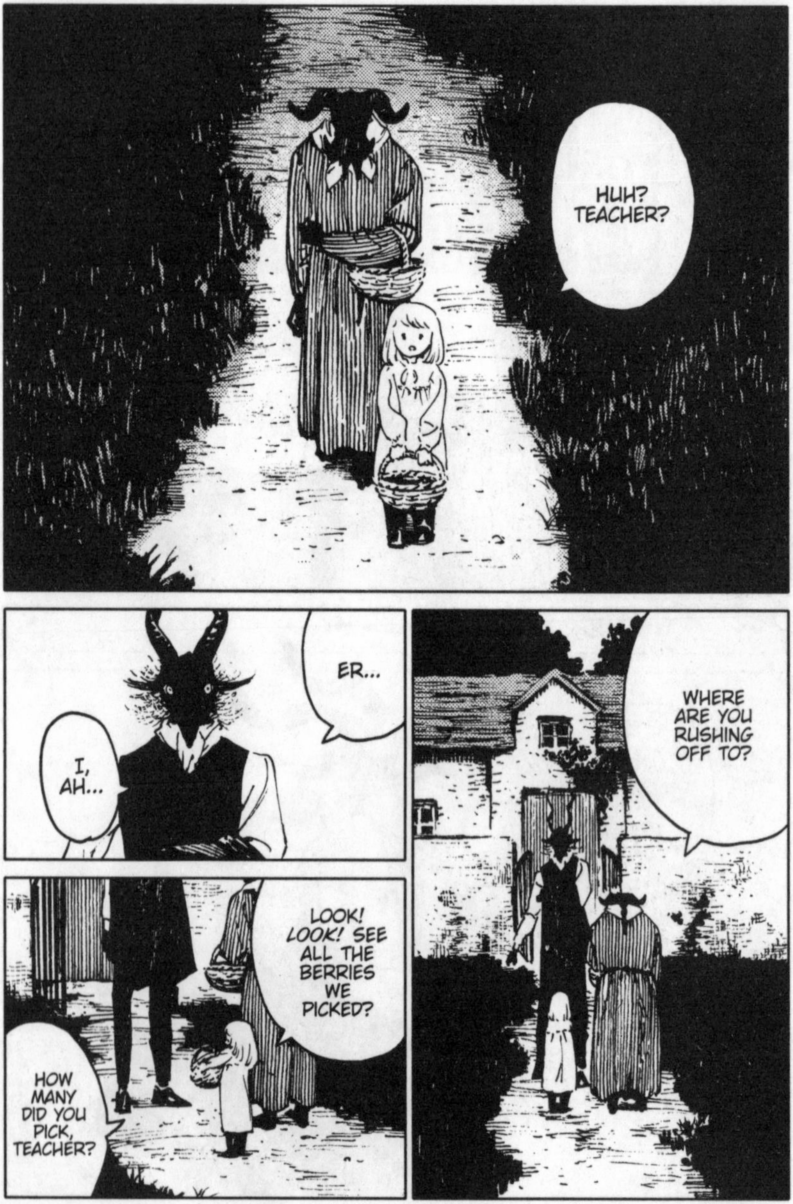
HUH? TEACHER?
WHERE ARE YOU RUSHING OFF TO?
ER...
I, AH...
LOOK! *LOOK!* SEE ALL THE BERRIES WE PICKED?
HOW MANY DID YOU PICK, TEACHER?

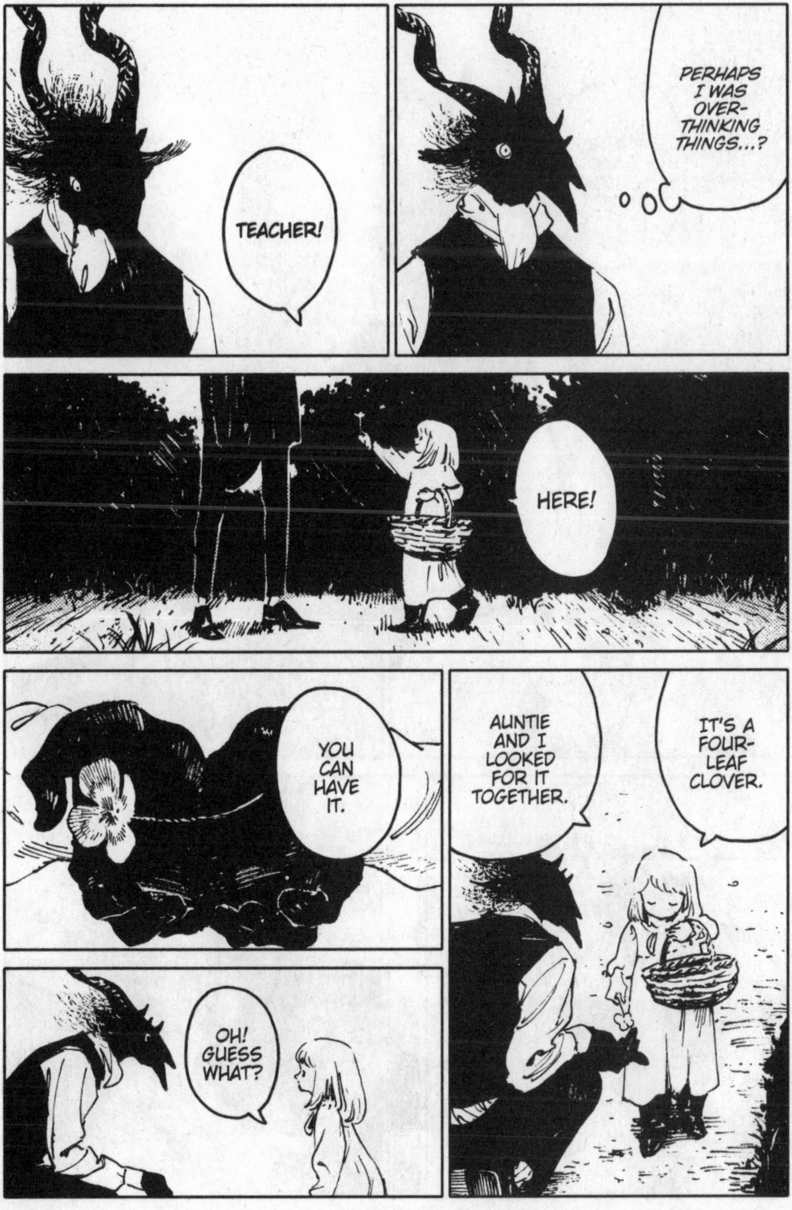
PERHAPS I WAS OVER-THINKING THINGS...?
TEACHER!
HERE!
IT'S A FOUR-LEAF CLOVER.
AUNTIE AND I LOOKED FOR IT TOGETHER.
YOU CAN HAVE IT.
OH! GUESS WHAT?

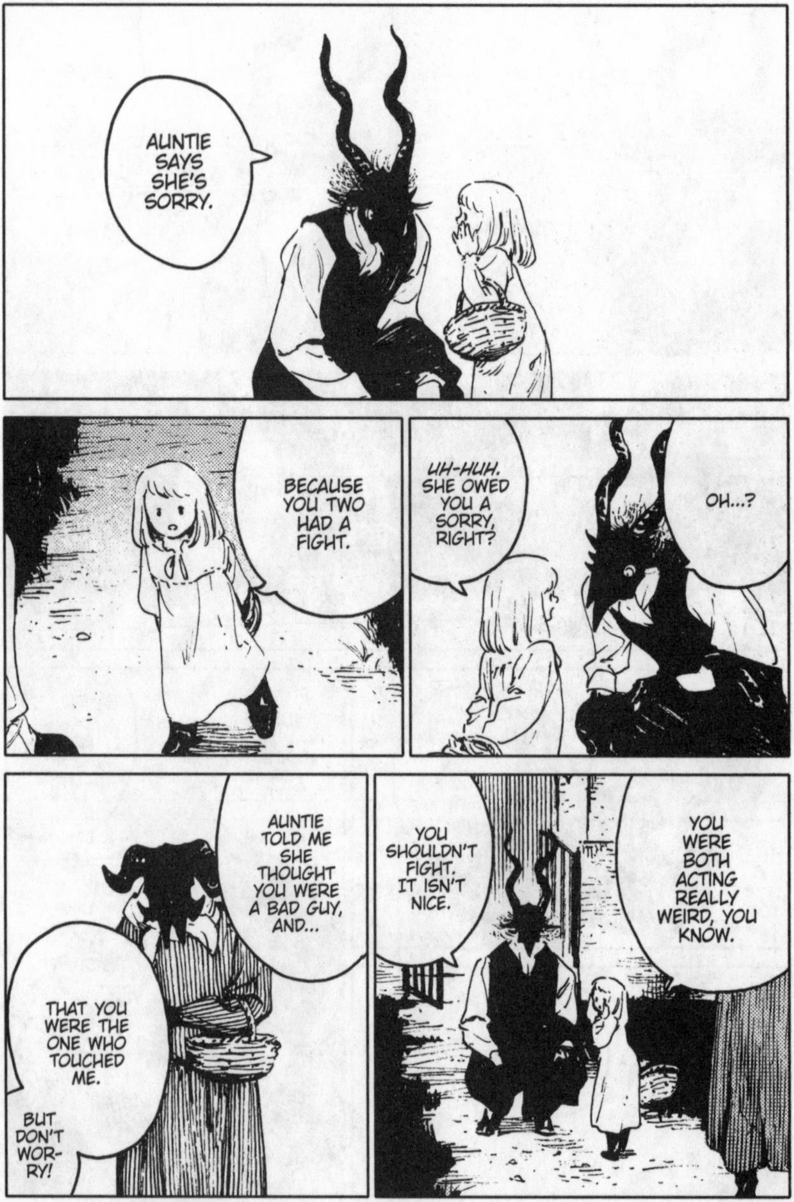
AUNTIE SAYS SHE'S SORRY.
BECAUSE YOU TWO HAD A FIGHT.
UH-HUH. SHE OWED YOU A SORRY, RIGHT?
OH...?
AUNTIE TOLD ME SHE THOUGHT YOU WERE A BAD GUY, AND...
THAT YOU WERE THE ONE WHO TOUCHED ME.
BUT DON'T WOR-RY!
YOU SHOULDN'T FIGHT. IT ISN'T NICE.
YOU WERE BOTH ACTING REALLY WEIRD, YOU KNOW.

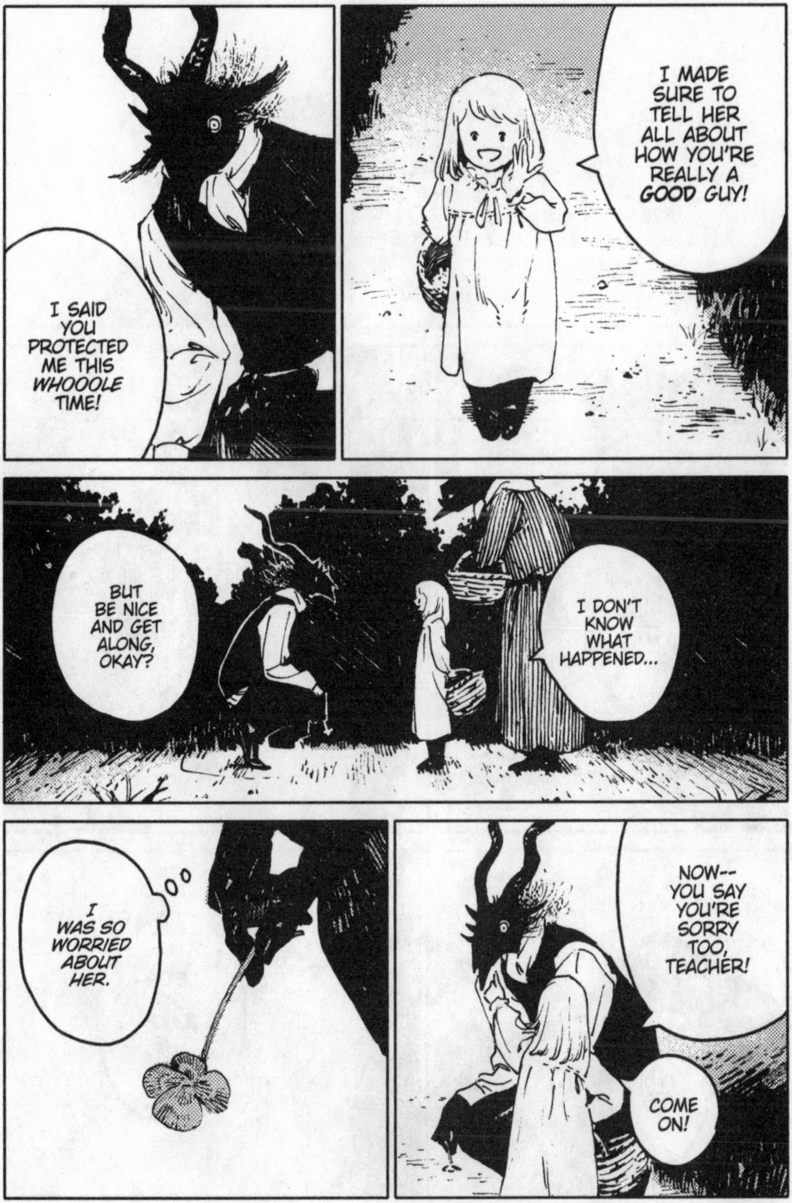
I MADE SURE TO TELL HER ALL ABOUT HOW YOU'RE REALLY A GOOD GUY!
I SAID YOU PROTECTED ME THIS WHOOOLE TIME!
I DON'T KNOW WHAT HAPPENED...
BUT BE NICE AND GET ALONG, OKAY?
NOW-- YOU SAY YOU'RE SORRY TOO, TEACHER!
COME ON!
I WAS SO WORRIED ABOUT HER.

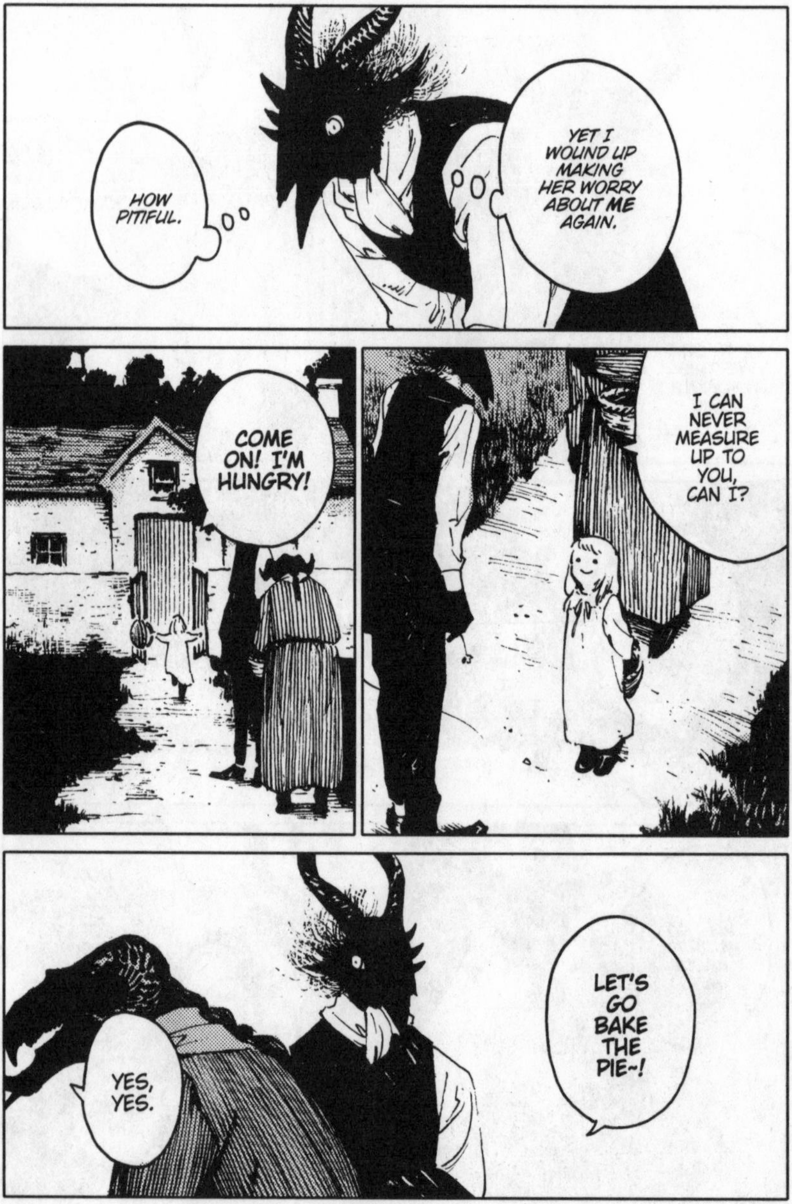
YET I WOUND UP MAKING HER WORRY ABOUT ME AGAIN.
HOW PITIFUL.
I CAN NEVER MEASURE UP TO YOU, CAN I?
COME ON! I'M HUNGRY!
LET'S GO BAKE THE PIE~!
YES, YES.

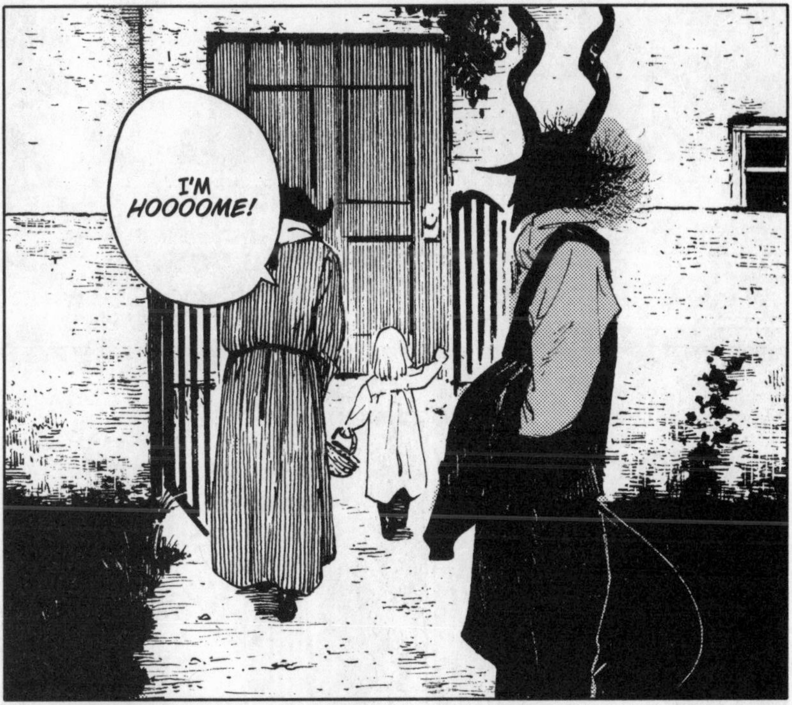
I'M HOOOOME!
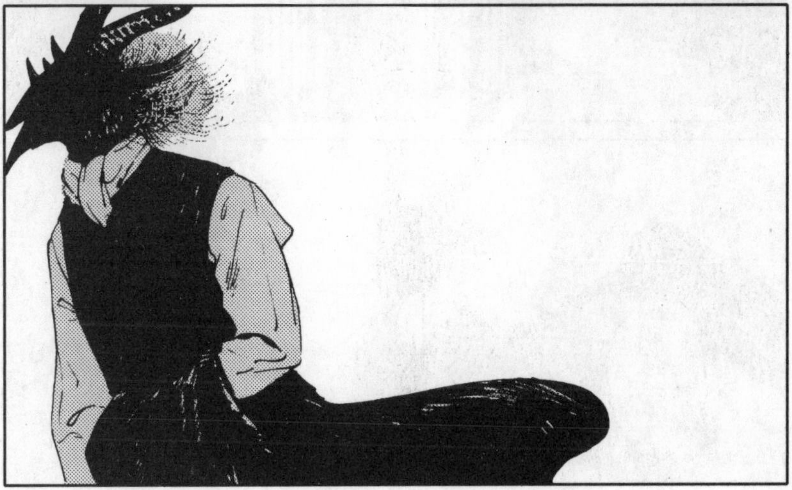

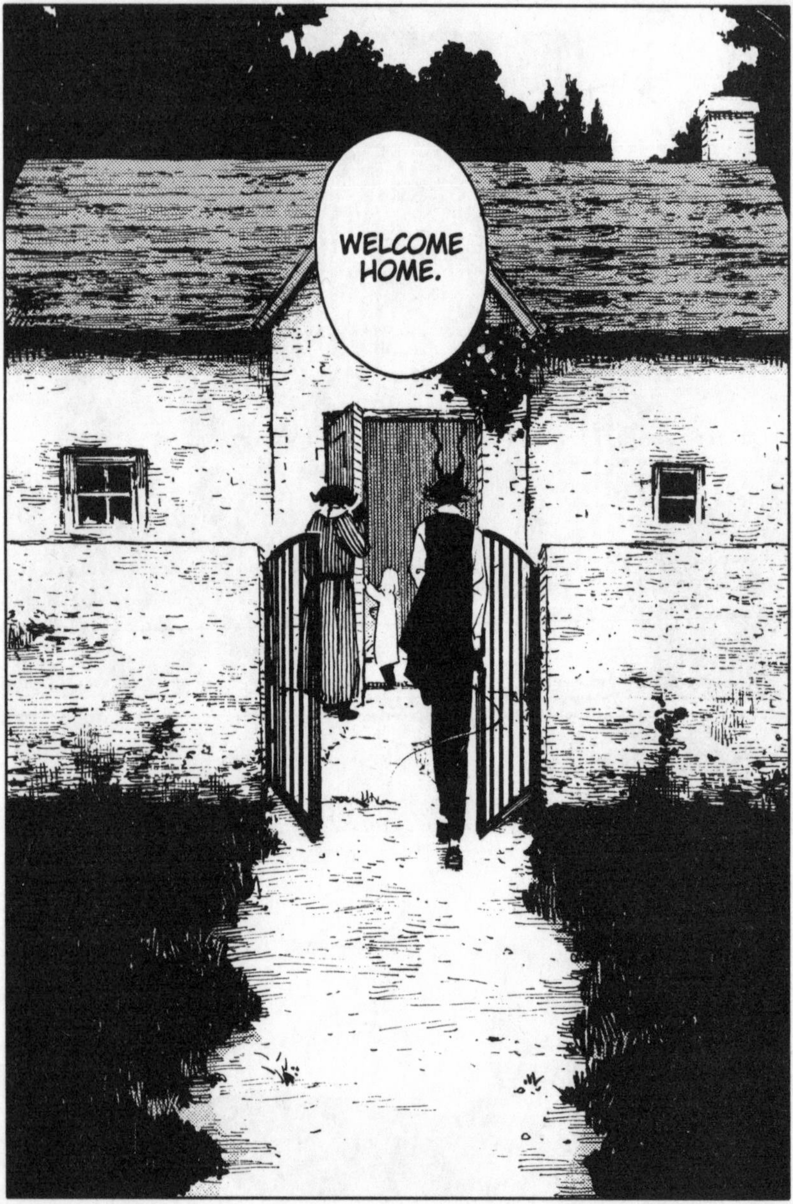
WELCOME HOME.

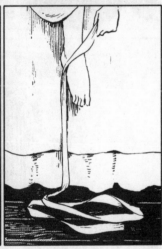

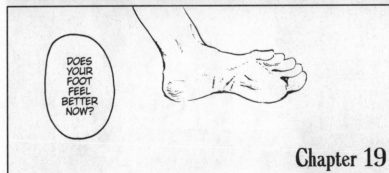

DOES YOUR FOOT FEEL BETTER NOW?

Chapter 19

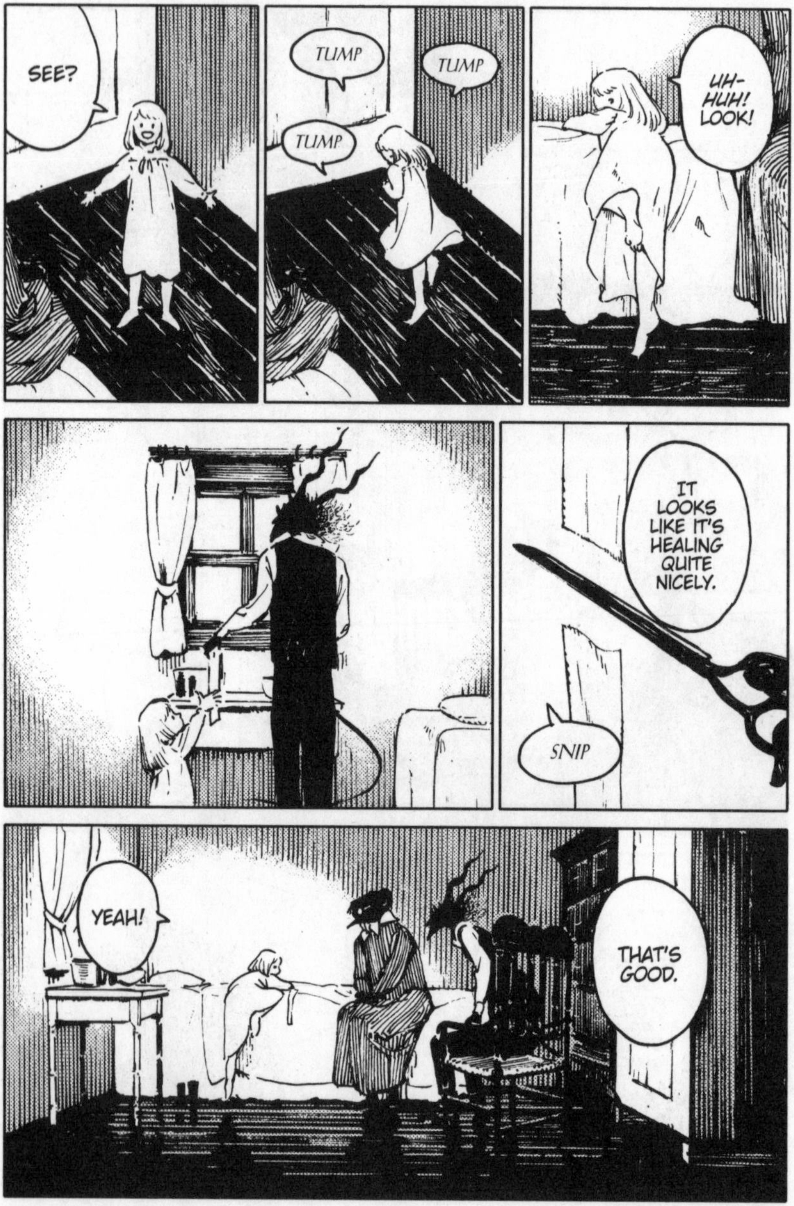
SEE?
TUMP
TUMP
TUMP
UH-HUH! LOOK!
IT LOOKS LIKE IT'S HEALING QUITE NICELY.
SNIP
YEAH!
THAT'S GOOD.

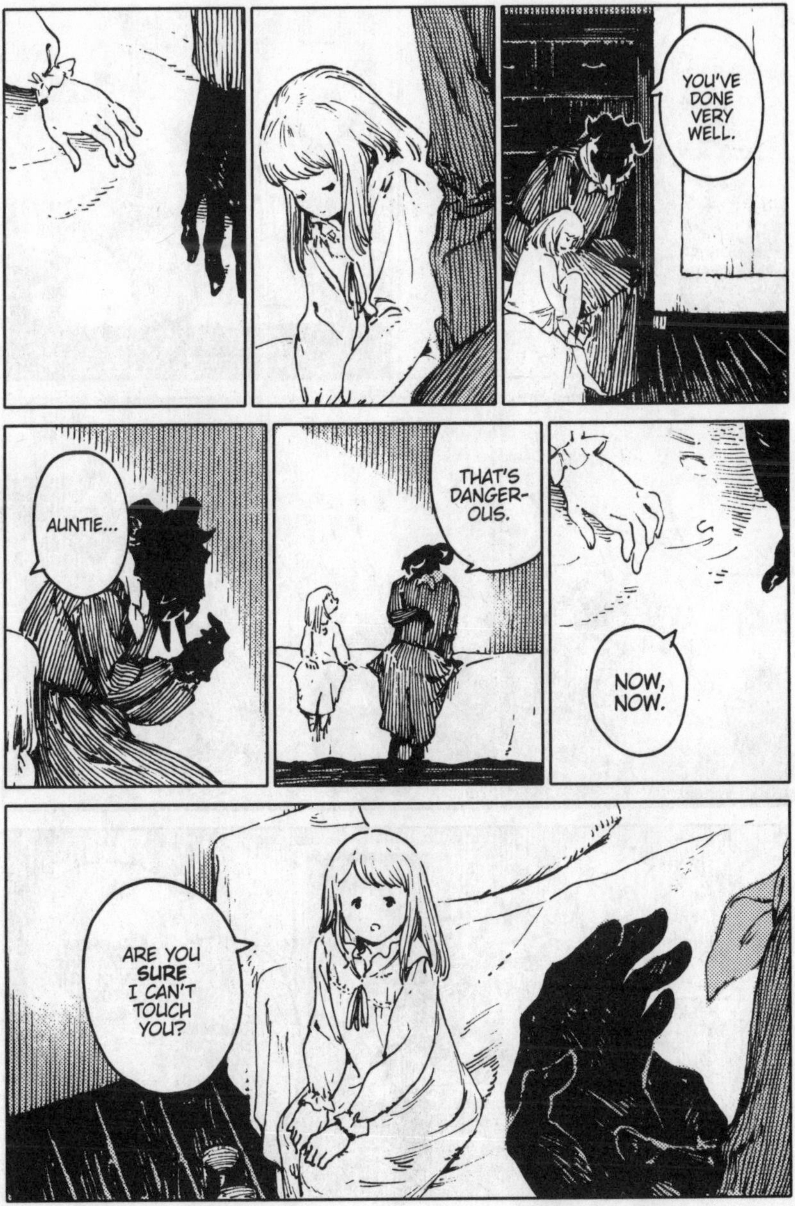
YOU'VE DONE VERY WELL.
AUNTIE...
THAT'S DANGER-OUS.
NOW, NOW.
ARE YOU SURE I CAN'T TOUCH YOU?

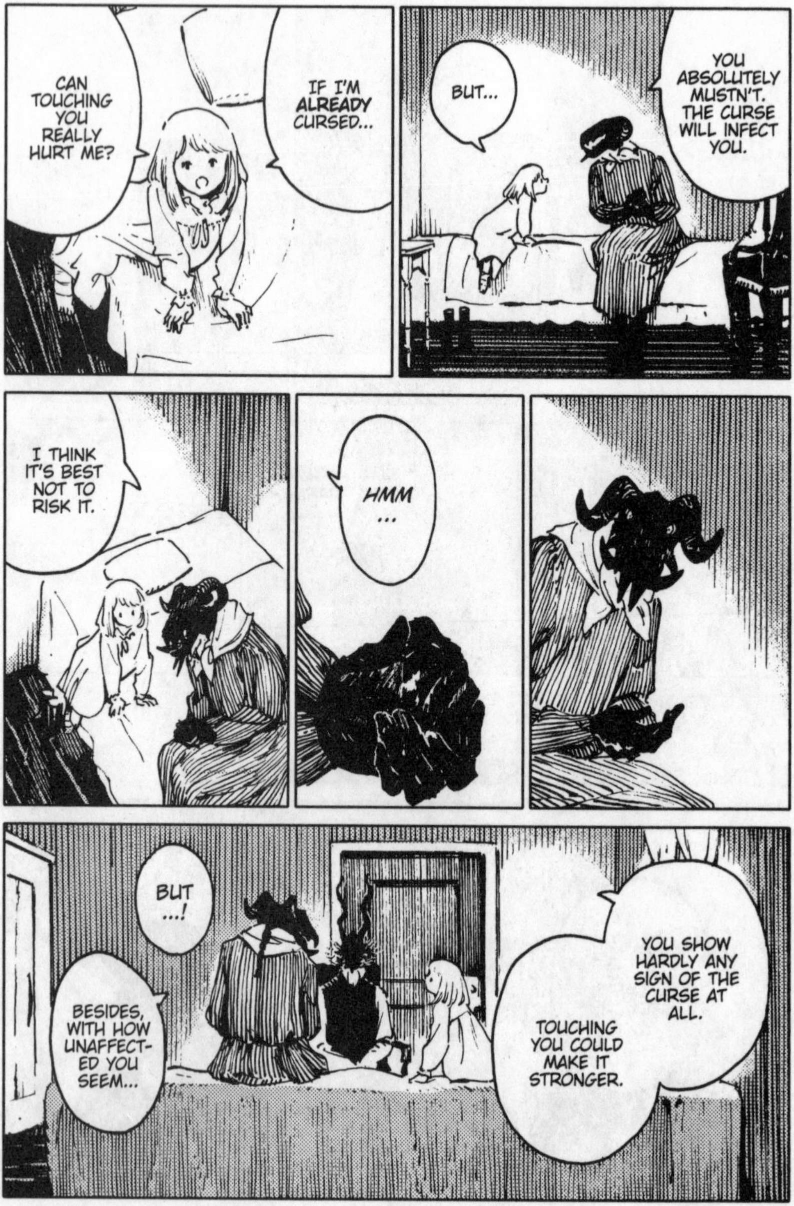
CAN TOUCHING YOU REALLY HURT ME?
IF I'M **ALREADY** CURSED...
BUT...
YOU ABSOLUTELY MUSTN'T. THE CURSE WILL INFECT YOU.
I THINK IT'S BEST NOT TO RISK IT.
HMM ...
BUT ...!
BESIDES, WITH HOW UNAFFECT-ED YOU SEEM...
YOU SHOW HARDLY ANY SIGN OF THE CURSE AT ALL.
TOUCHING YOU COULD MAKE IT STRONGER.

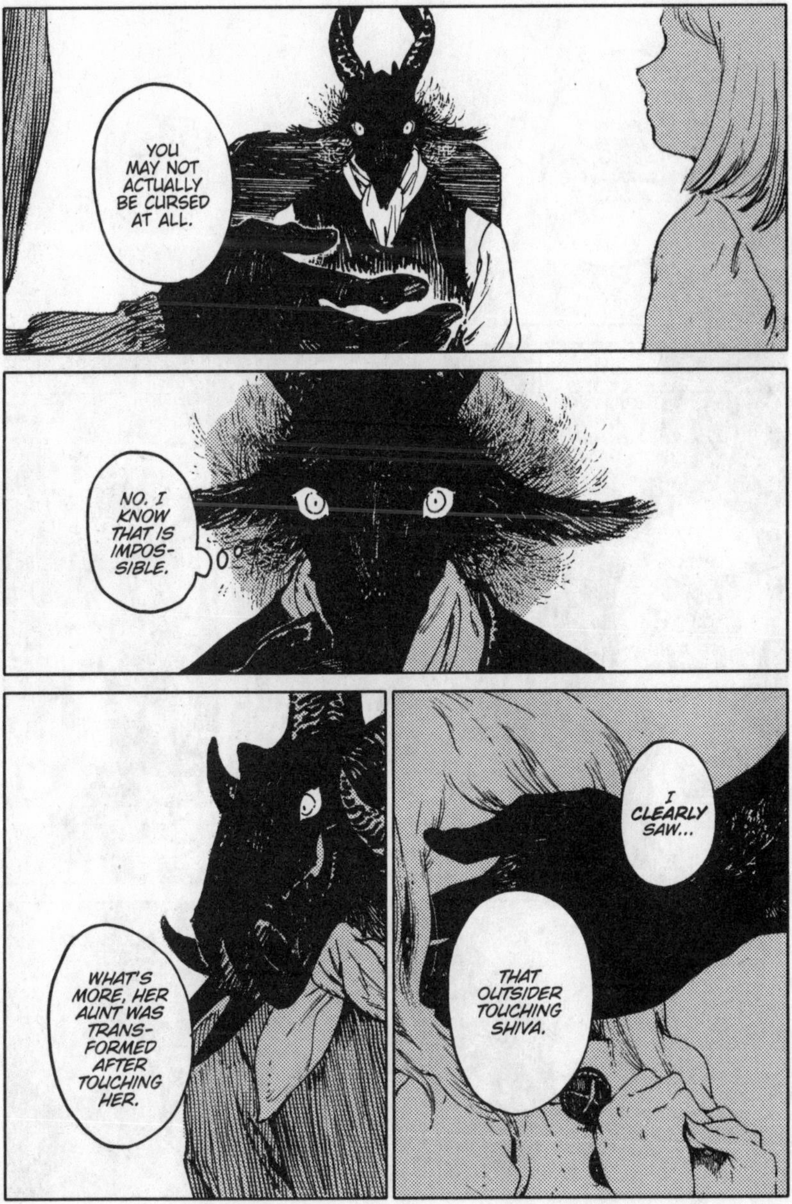
YOU MAY NOT ACTUALLY BE CURSED AT ALL.
NO. I KNOW THAT IS IMPOSSIBLE.
I CLEARLY SAW...
THAT OUTSIDER TOUCHING SHIVA.
WHAT'S MORE, HER AUNT WAS TRANSFORMED AFTER TOUCHING HER.

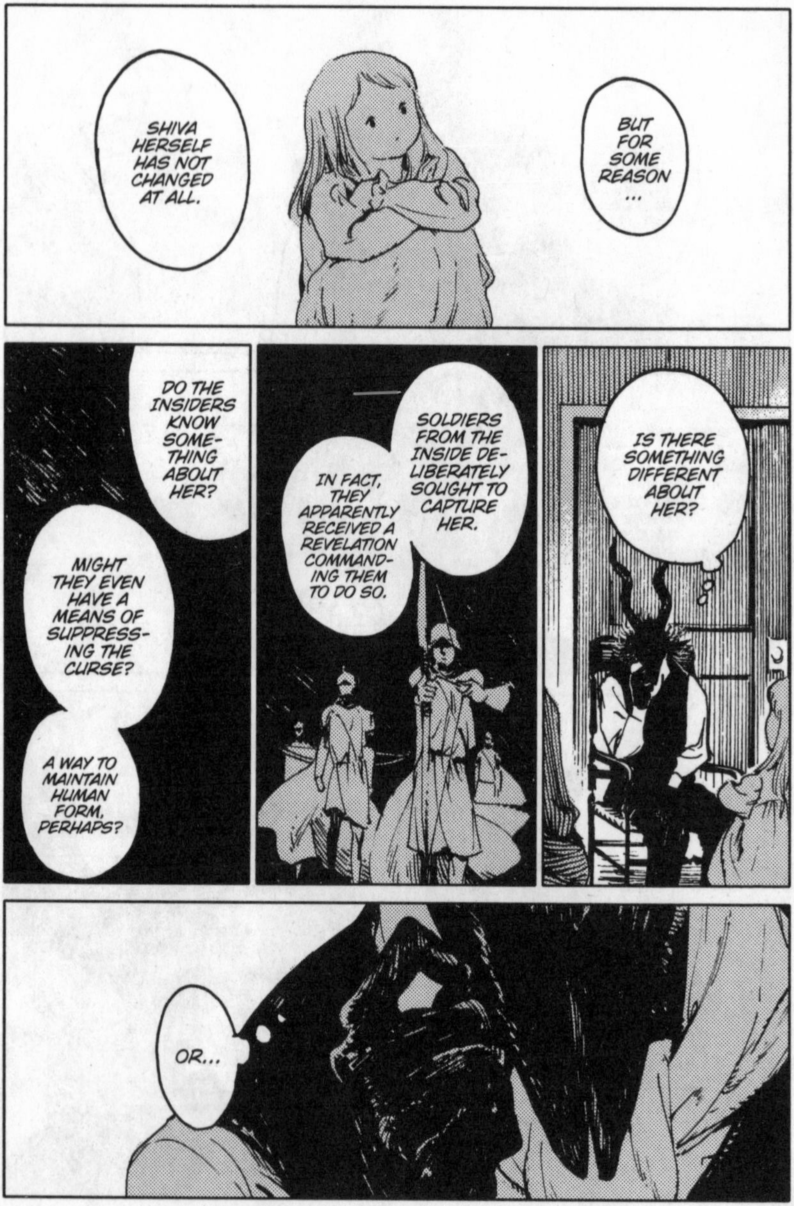
BUT FOR SOME REASON...
SHIVA HERSELF HAS NOT CHANGED AT ALL.
IS THERE SOMETHING DIFFERENT ABOUT HER?
SOLDIERS FROM THE INSIDE DELIBERATELY SOUGHT TO CAPTURE HER.
IN FACT, THEY APPARENTLY RECEIVED A REVELATION COMMANDING THEM TO DO SO.
DO THE INSIDERS KNOW SOMETHING ABOUT HER?
MIGHT THEY EVEN HAVE A MEANS OF SUPPRESSING THE CURSE?
A WAY TO MAINTAIN HUMAN FORM, PERHAPS?
OR...

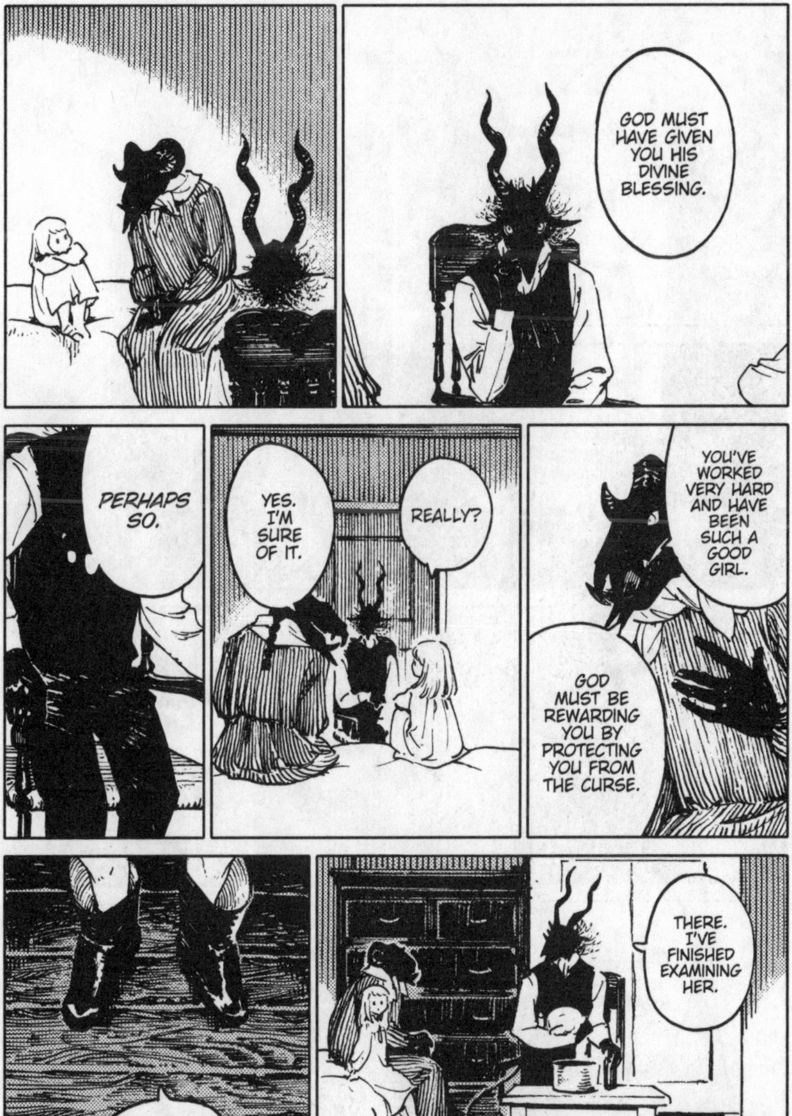
GOD MUST HAVE GIVEN YOU HIS DIVINE BLESSING.
YOU'VE WORKED VERY HARD AND HAVE BEEN SUCH A GOOD GIRL.
GOD MUST BE REWARDING YOU BY PROTECTING YOU FROM THE CURSE.
REALLY?
YES. I'M SURE OF IT.
PERHAPS SO.
THERE. I'VE FINISHED EXAMINING HER.
TUMP

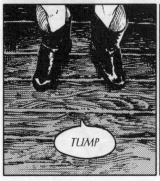

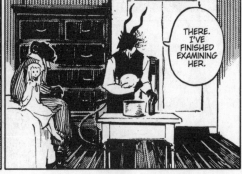

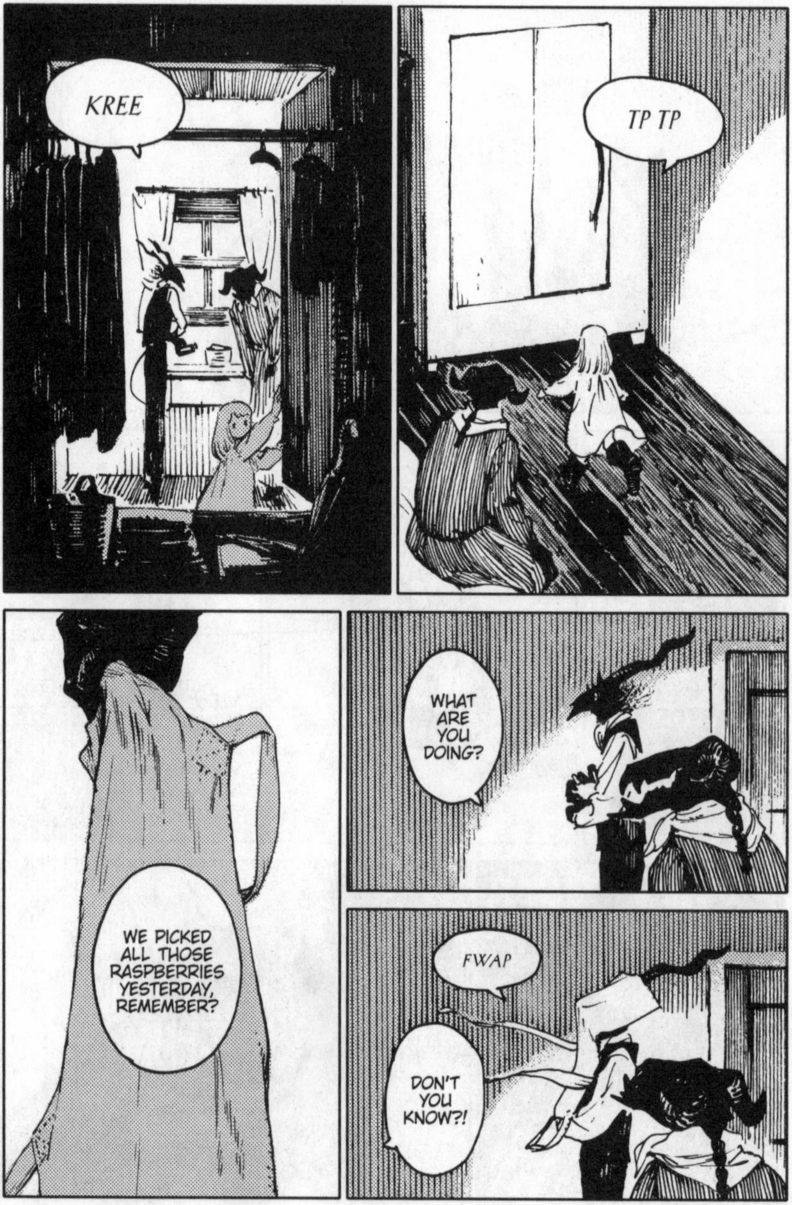
KREE
TP TP
WE PICKED ALL THOSE RASPBERRIES YESTERDAY, REMEMBER?
WHAT ARE YOU DOING?
FWAP
DON'T YOU KNOW?!

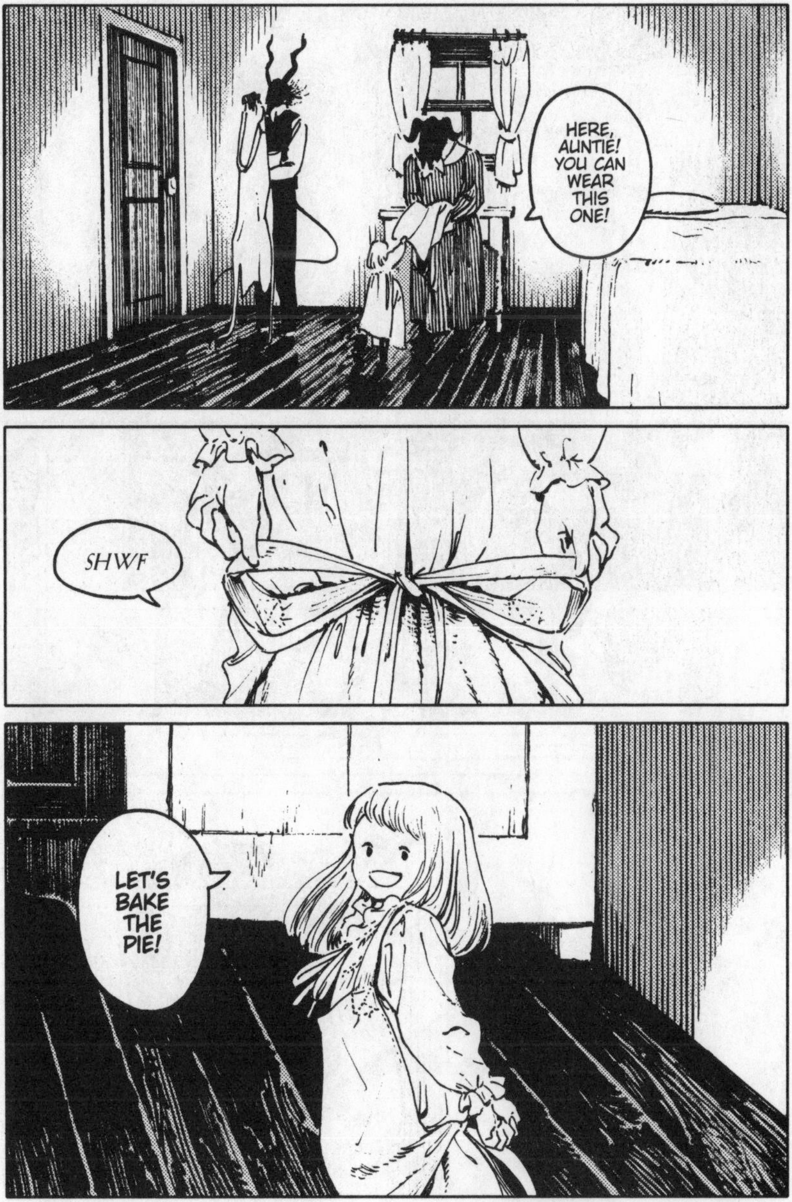
HERE, AUNTIE! YOU CAN WEAR THIS ONE!
SHWF
LET'S BAKE THE PIE!

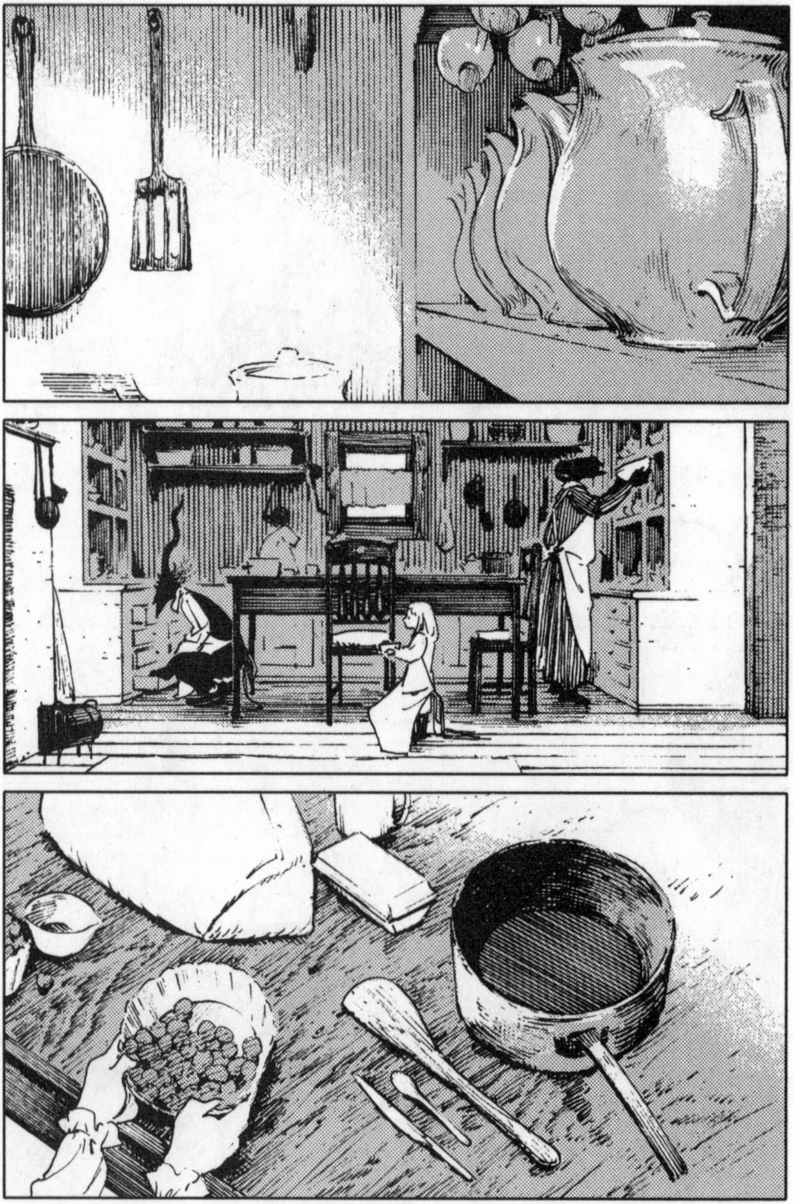

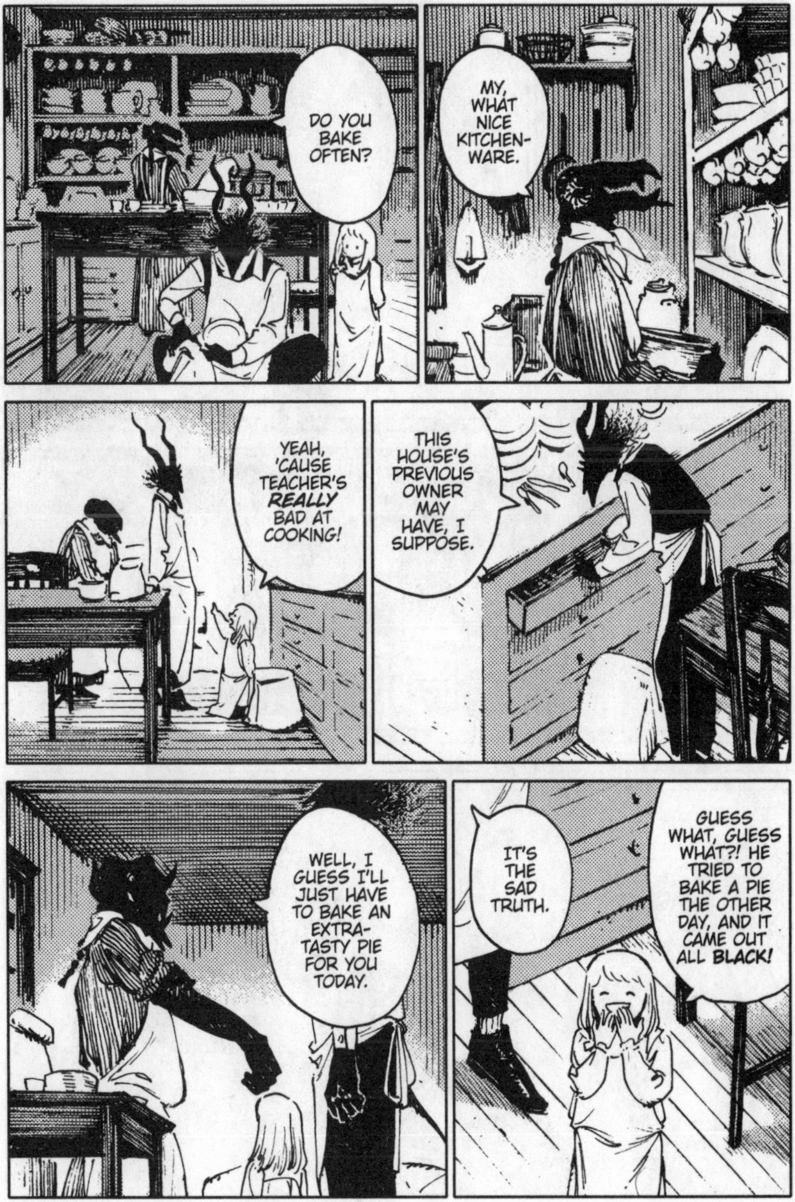
MY, WHAT NICE KITCHEN-WARE.
DO YOU BAKE OFTEN?
THIS HOUSE'S PREVIOUS OWNER MAY HAVE, I SUPPOSE.
YEAH, 'CAUSE TEACHER'S *REALLY* BAD AT COOKING!
GUESS WHAT, GUESS WHAT?! HE TRIED TO BAKE A PIE THE OTHER DAY, AND IT CAME OUT ALL **BLACK!**
IT'S THE SAD TRUTH.
WELL, I GUESS I'LL JUST HAVE TO BAKE AN EXTRA-TASTY PIE FOR YOU TODAY.

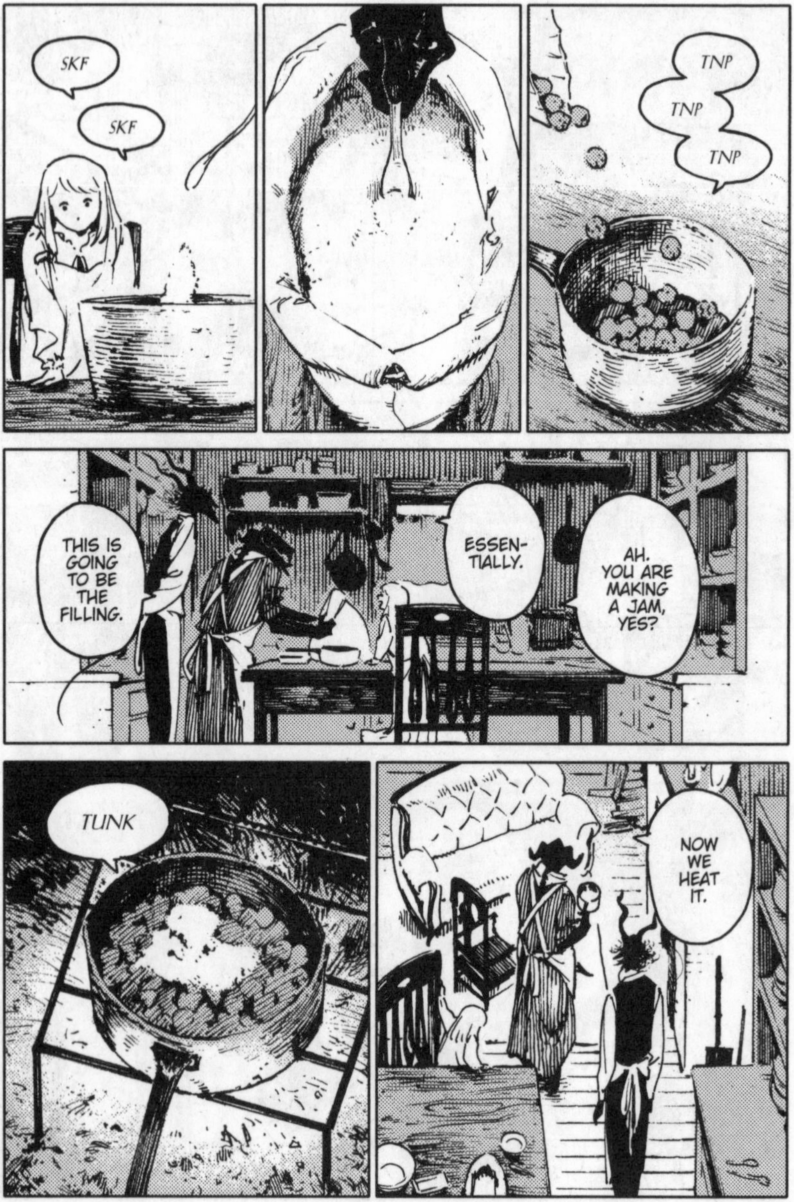
SKF
SKF
TNP
TNP
TNP
THIS IS GOING TO BE THE FILLING.
ESSEN-TIALLY.
AH. YOU ARE MAKING A JAM, YES?
TUNK
NOW WE HEAT IT.

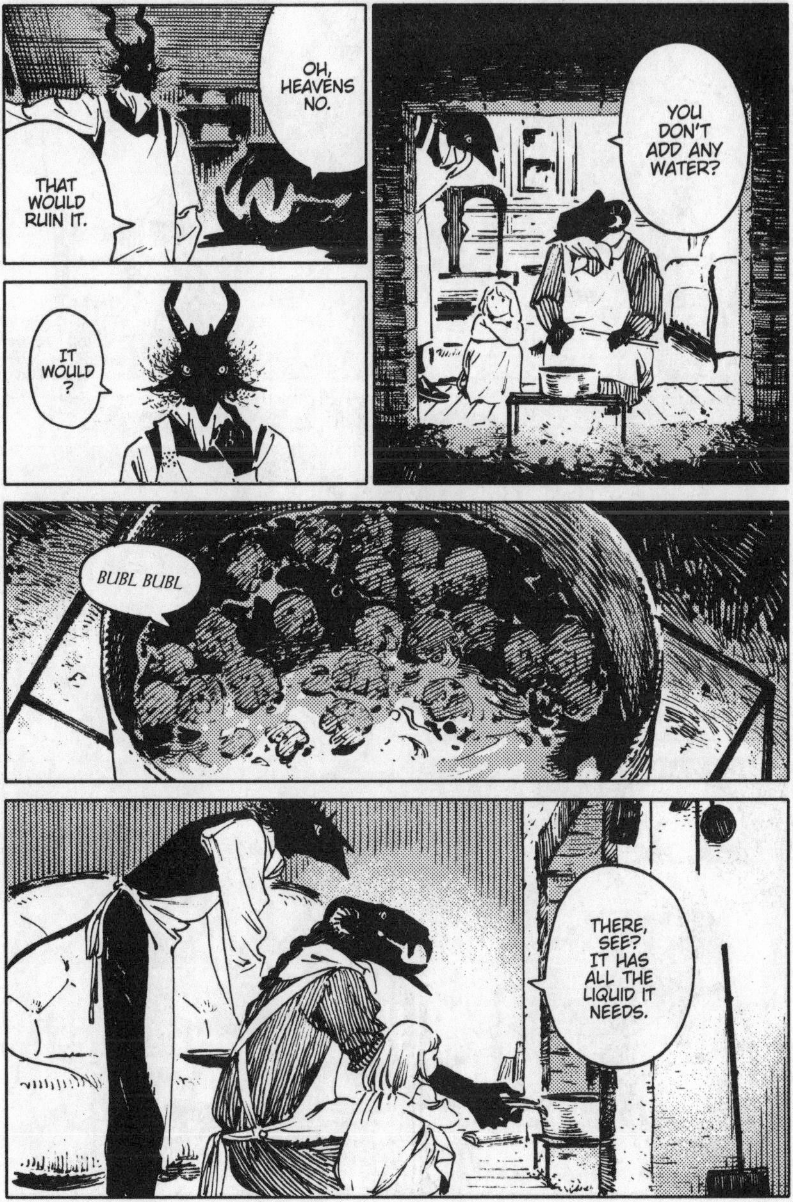
YOU DON'T ADD ANY WATER?
OH, HEAVENS NO.
THAT WOULD RUIN IT.
IT WOULD?
BUBL BUBL
THERE, SEE? IT HAS ALL THE LIQUID IT NEEDS.

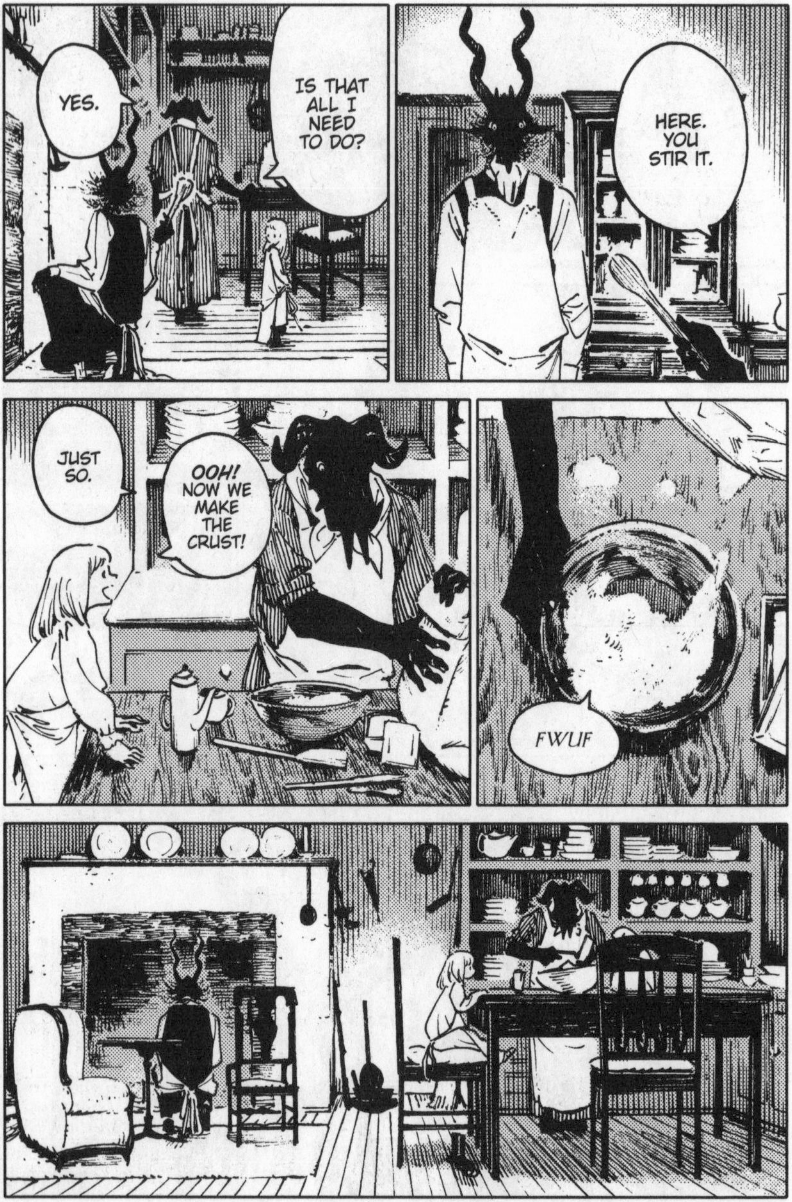
YES.
IS THAT ALL I NEED TO DO?
HERE. YOU STIR IT.
JUST SO.
OOH! NOW WE MAKE THE CRUST!
FWUF

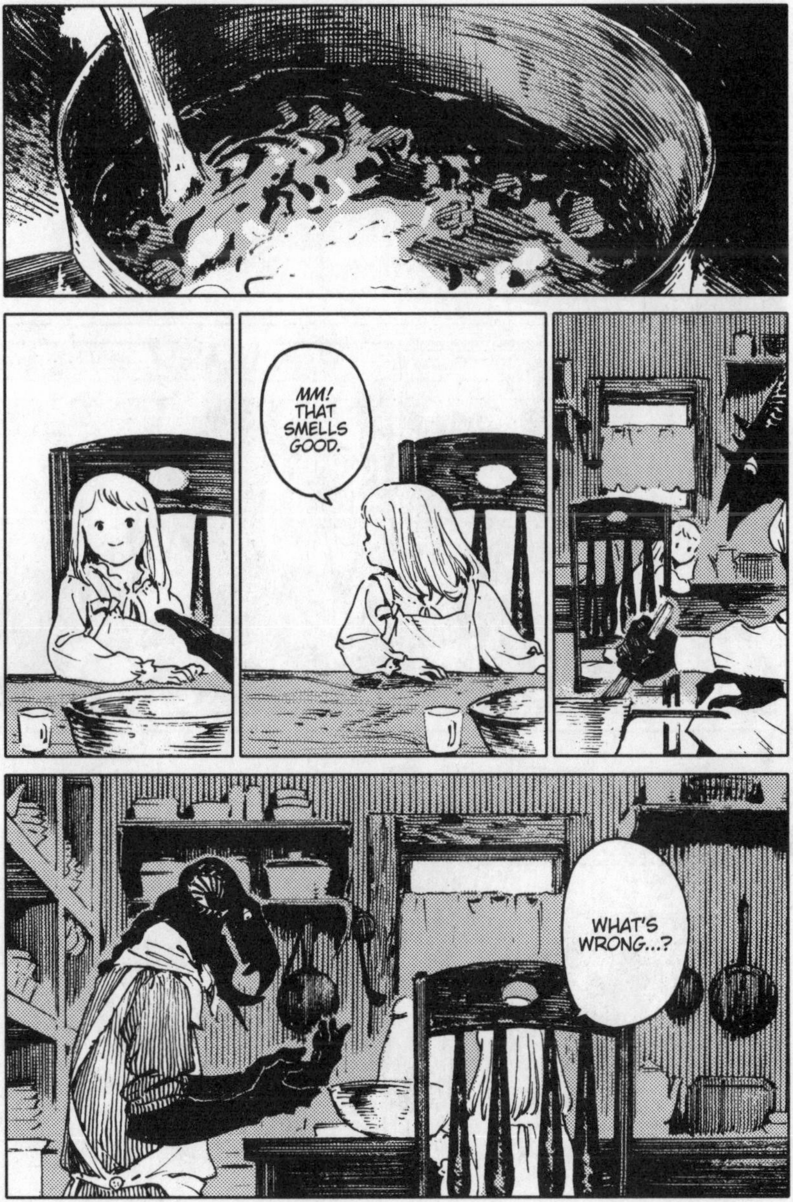
MM! THAT SMELLS GOOD.
WHAT'S WRONG...?

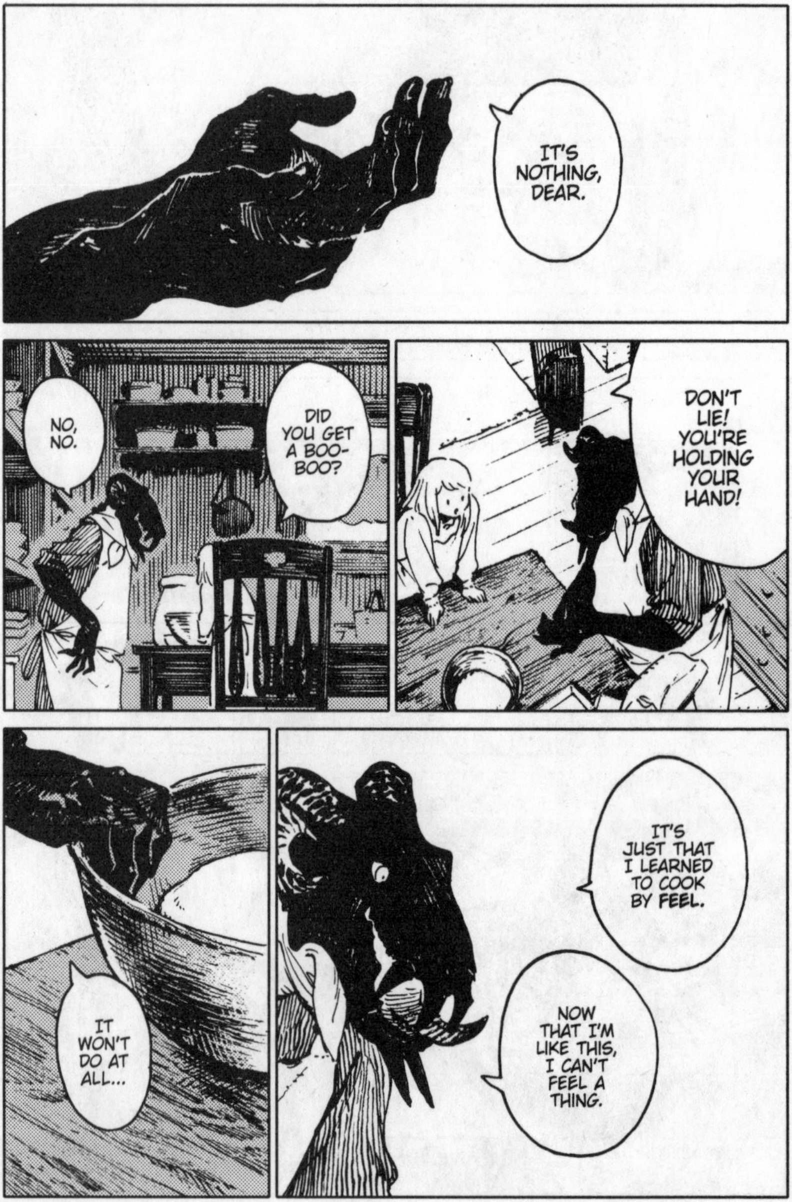
IT'S NOTHING, DEAR.
DID YOU GET A BOO-BOO?
NO, NO.
DON'T LIE! YOU'RE HOLDING YOUR HAND!
IT'S JUST THAT I LEARNED TO COOK BY FEEL.
NOW THAT I'M LIKE THIS, I CAN'T FEEL A THING.
IT WON'T DO AT ALL...

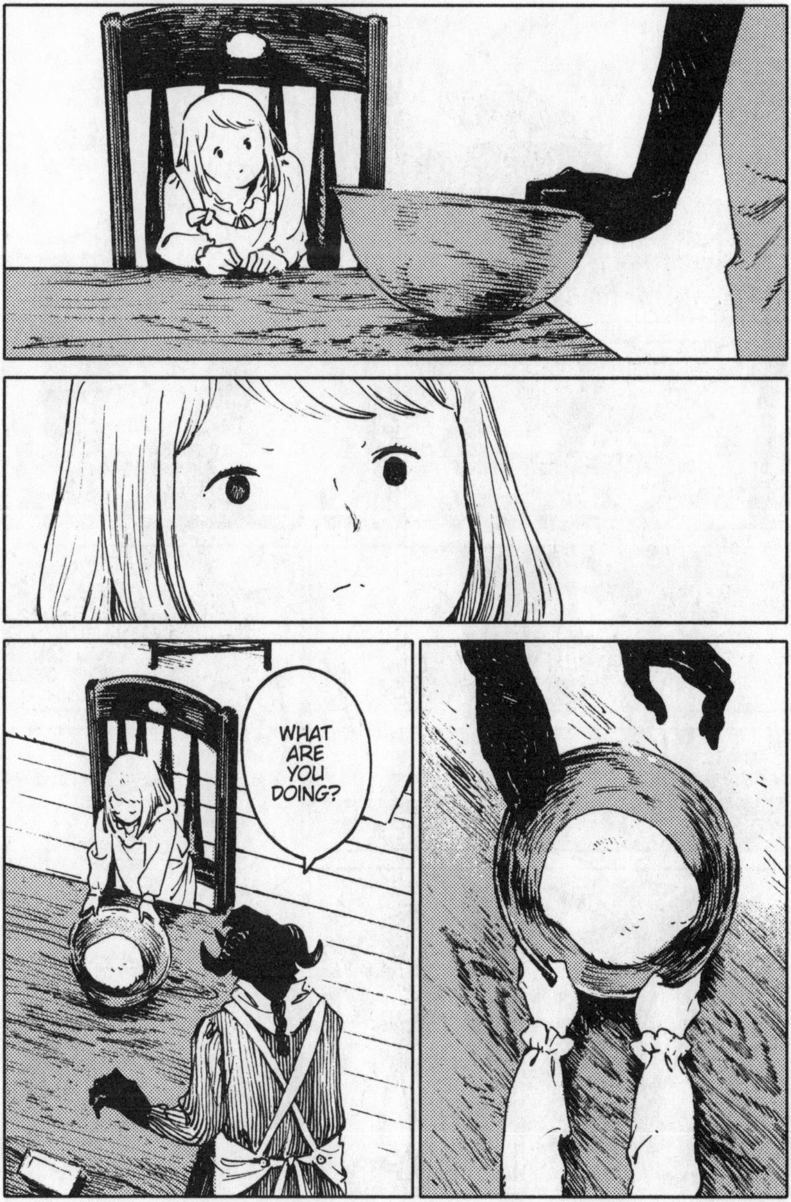
WHAT ARE YOU DOING?

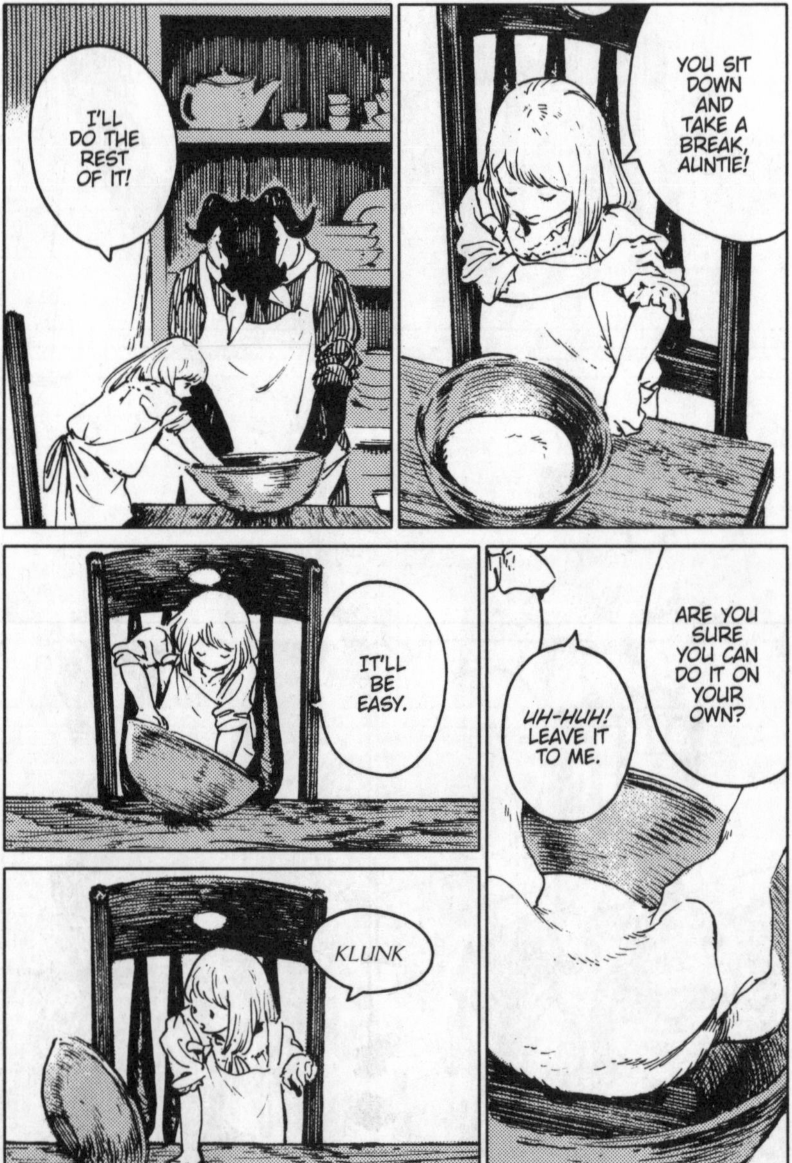
I'LL DO THE REST OF IT!
YOU SIT DOWN AND TAKE A BREAK, AUNTIE!
IT'LL BE EASY.
ARE YOU SURE YOU CAN DO IT ON YOUR OWN?
UH-HUH! LEAVE IT TO ME.
KLUNK

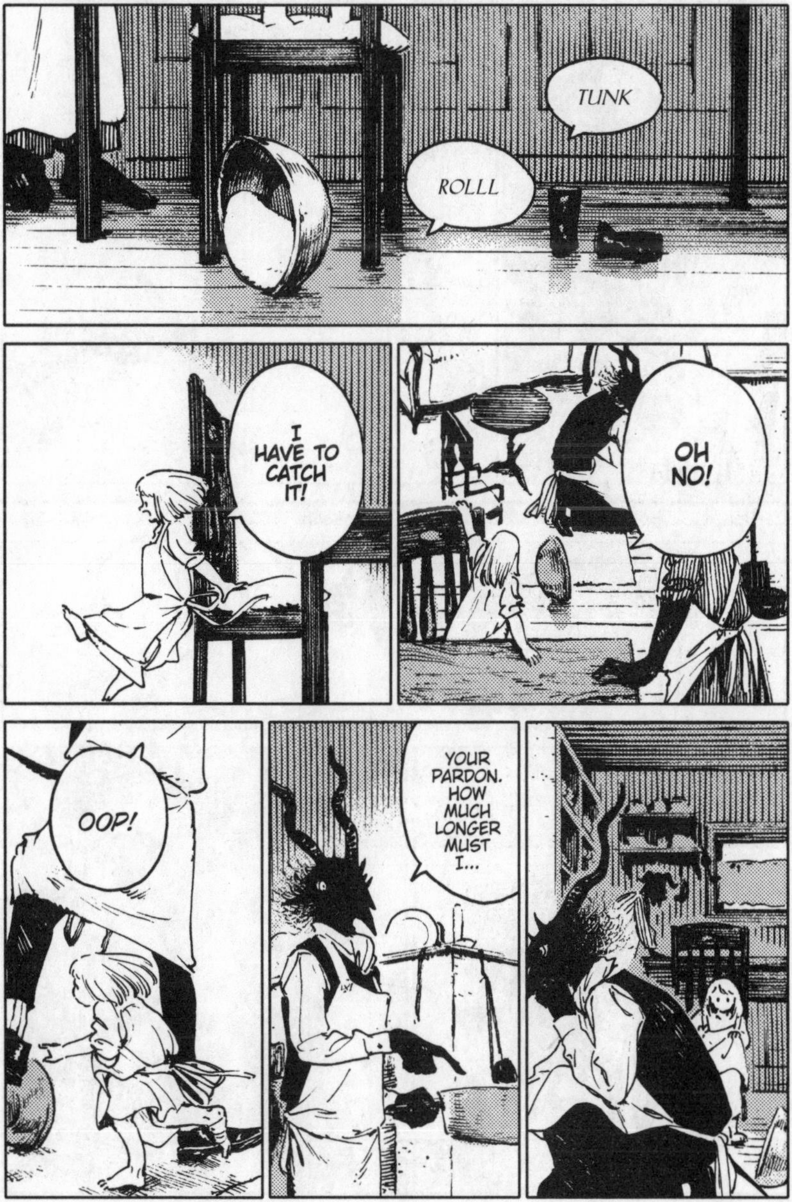
TUNK
ROLLL
I HAVE TO CATCH IT!
OH NO!
OOP!
YOUR PARDON. HOW MUCH LONGER MUST I...

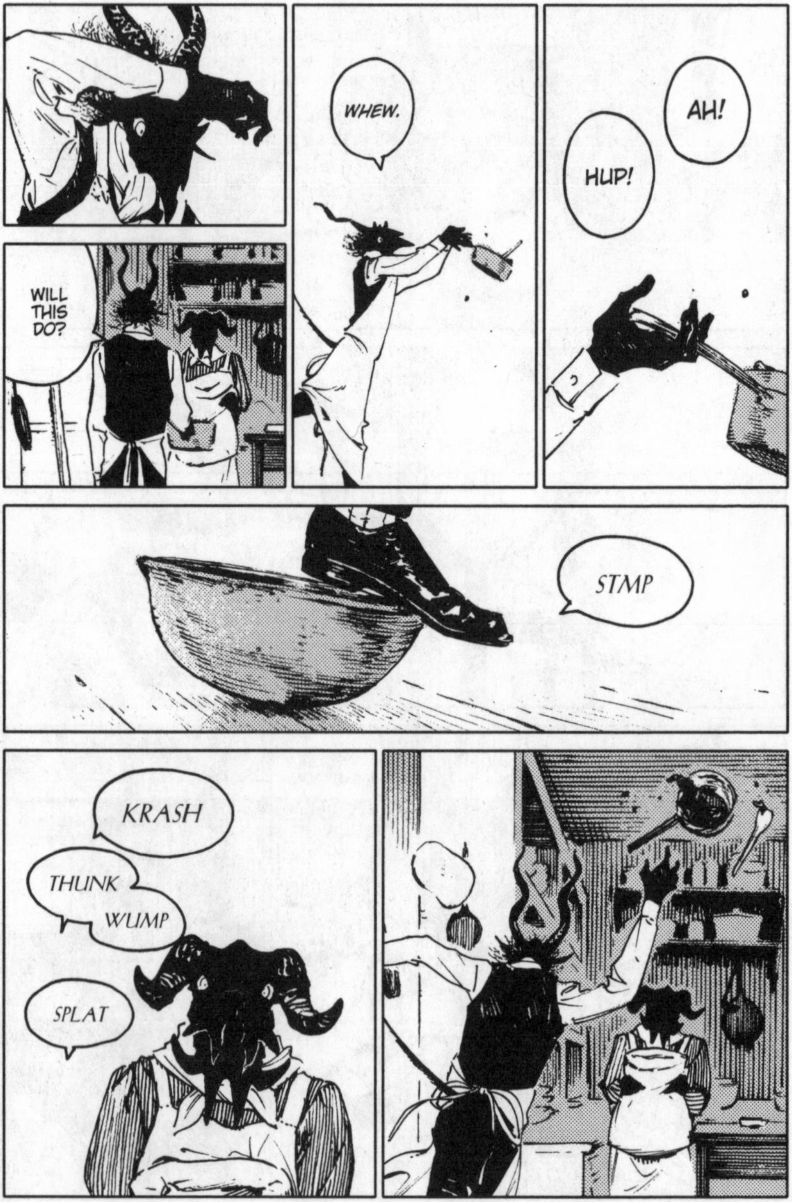
WHEW.
AH!
HUP!
WILL THIS DO?
STMP
KRASH
THUNK
WUMP
SPLAT

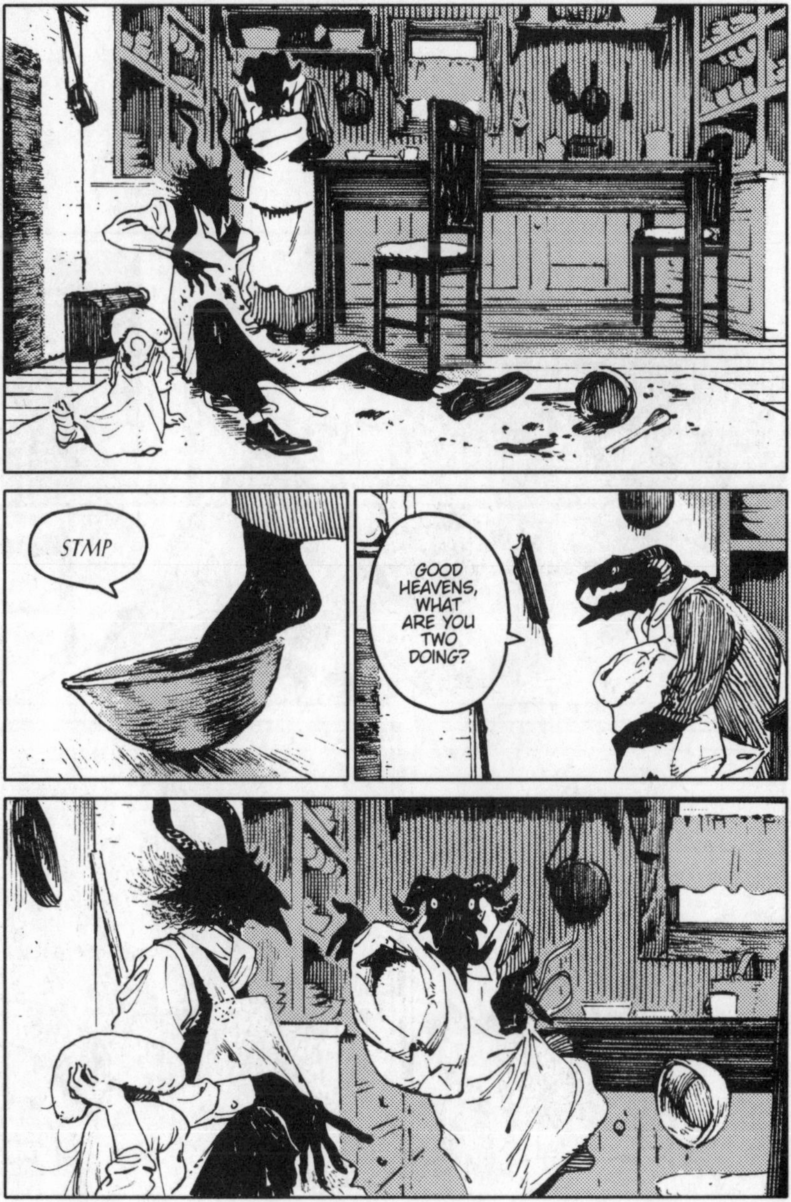
STMP
GOOD HEAVENS, WHAT ARE YOU TWO DOING?

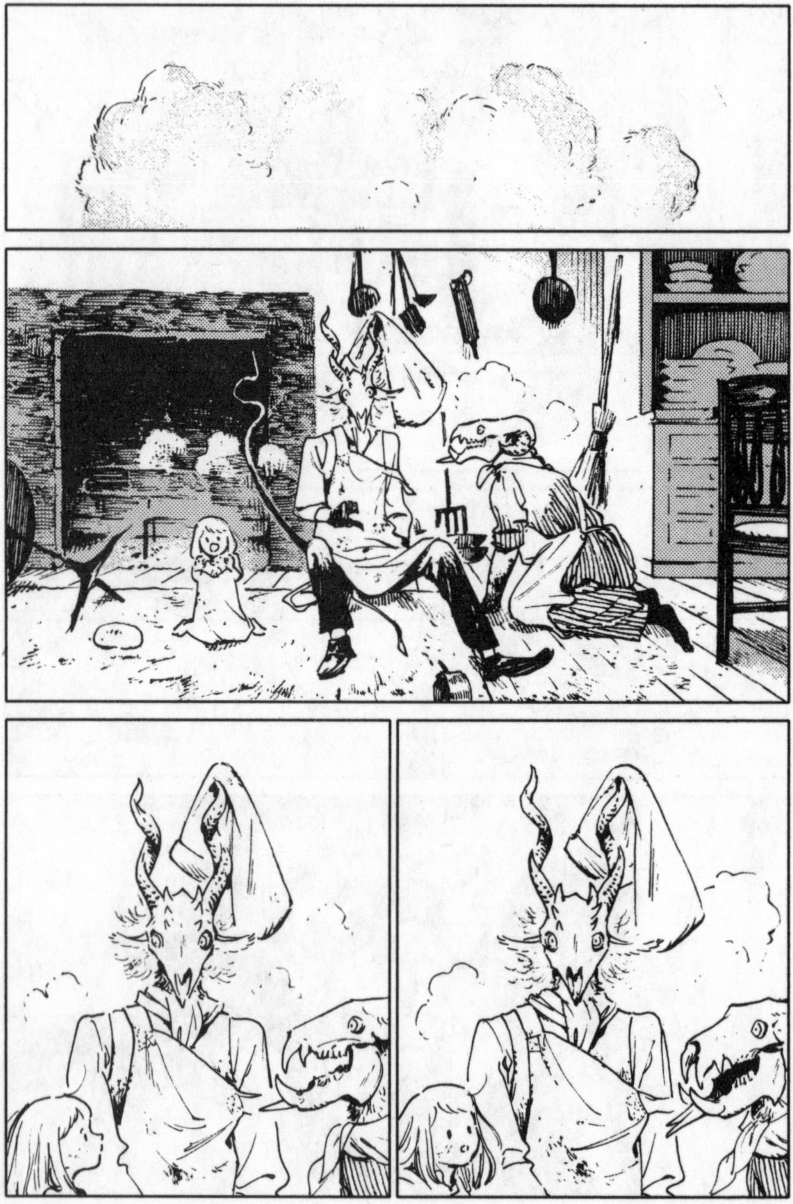

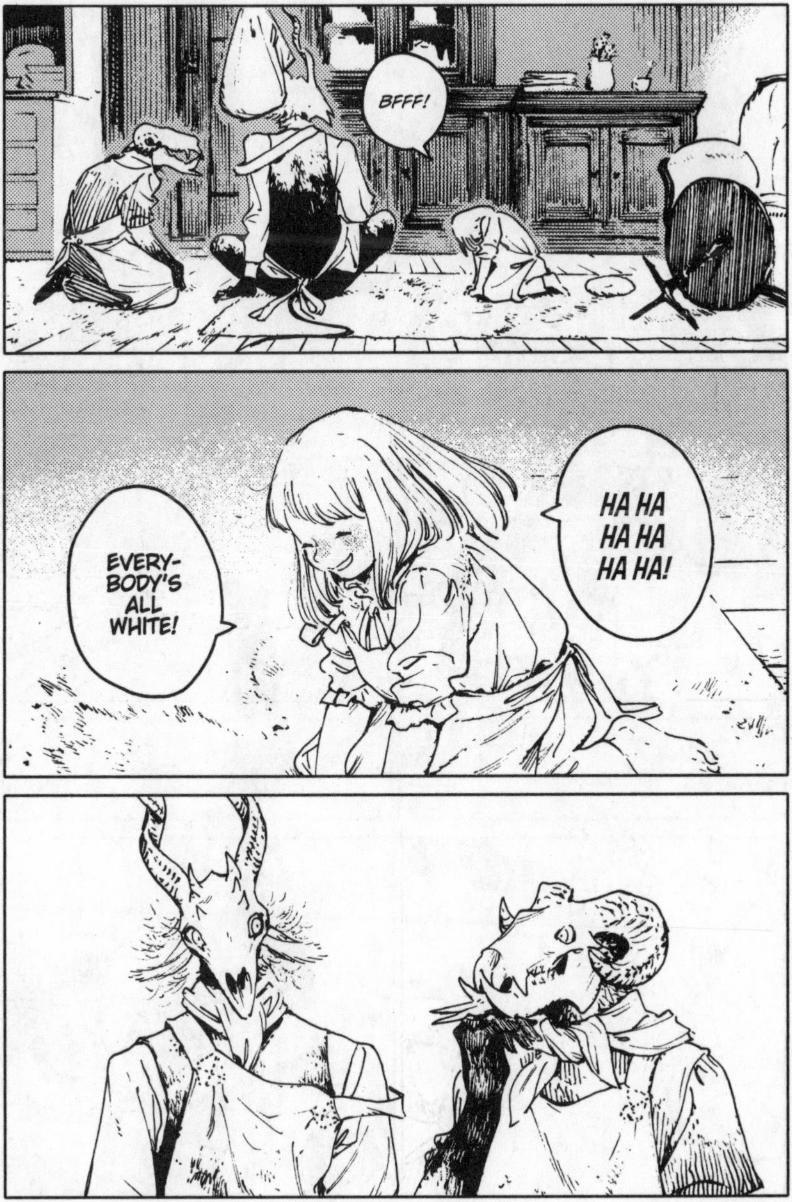
BFFF!
HA HA HA HA HA HA!
EVERY-BODY'S ALL WHITE!

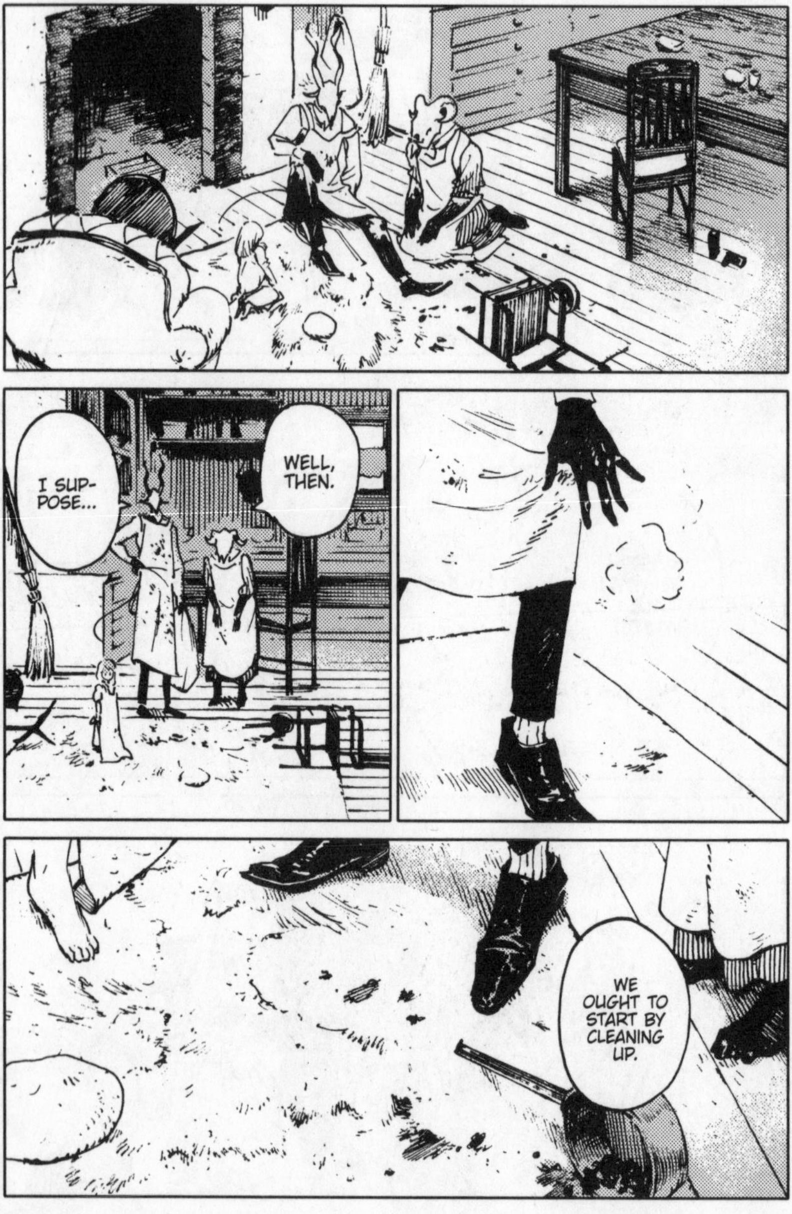
WELL, THEN.
I SUPPOSE...
WE OUGHT TO START BY CLEANING UP.

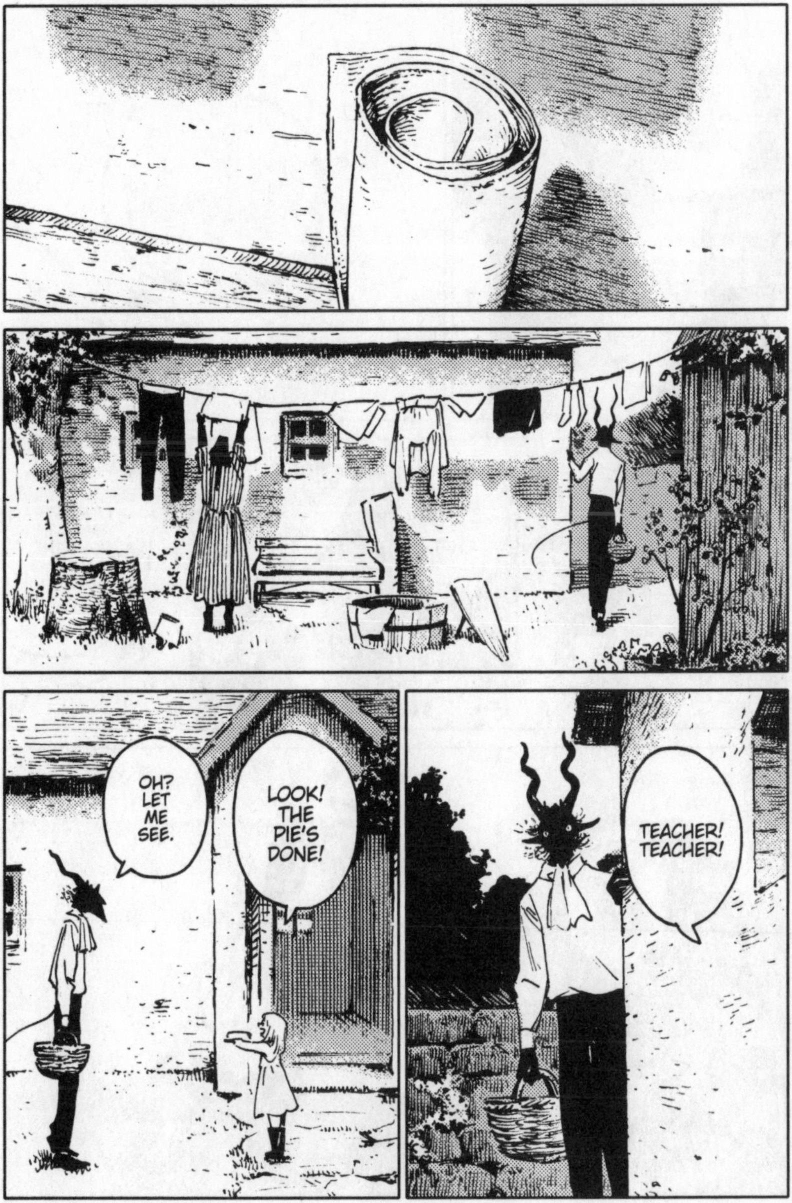
TEACHER! TEACHER!
LOOK! THE PIE'S DONE!
OH? LET ME SEE.

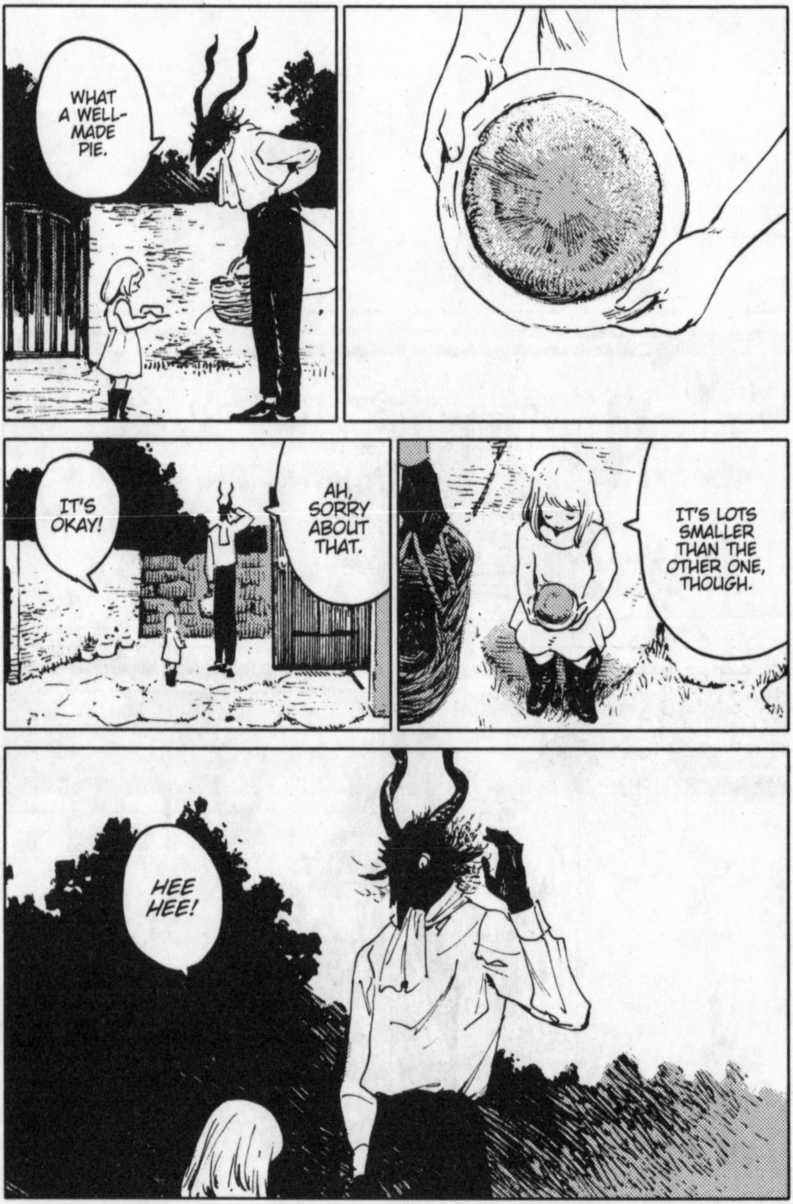
WHAT A WELL-MADE PIE.
IT'S LOTS SMALLER THAN THE OTHER ONE, THOUGH.
AH, SORRY ABOUT THAT.
IT'S OKAY!
HEE HEE!

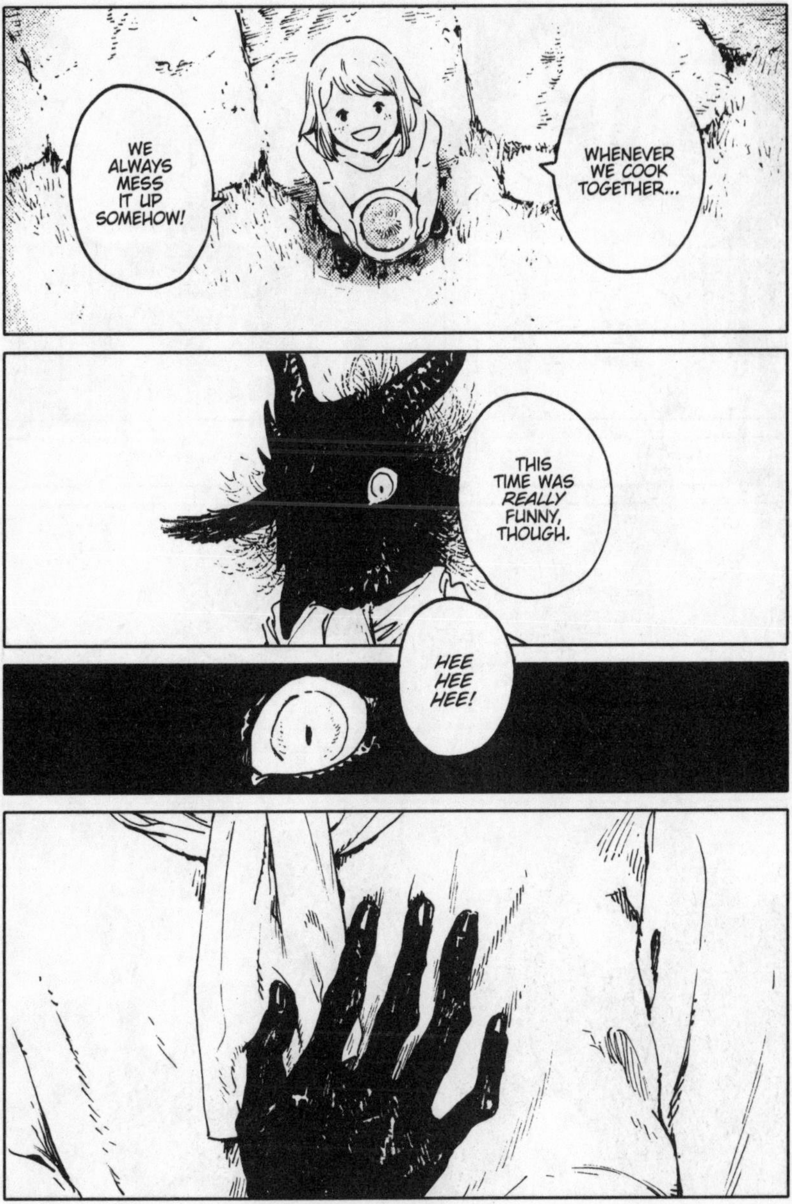
WHENEVER WE COOK TOGETHER...
WE ALWAYS MESS IT UP SOMEHOW!
THIS TIME WAS *REALLY* FUNNY, THOUGH.
HEE HEE HEE!

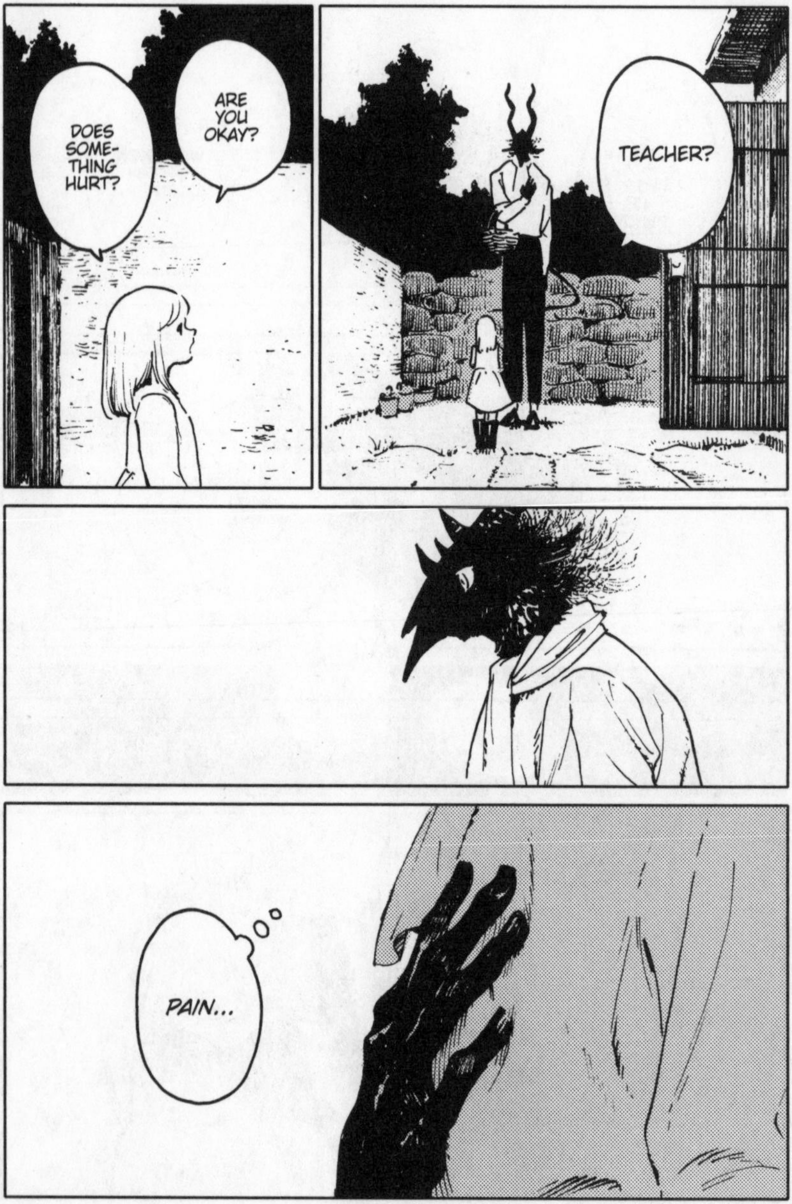
TEACHER?
ARE YOU OKAY?
DOES SOME-THING HURT?
PAIN...

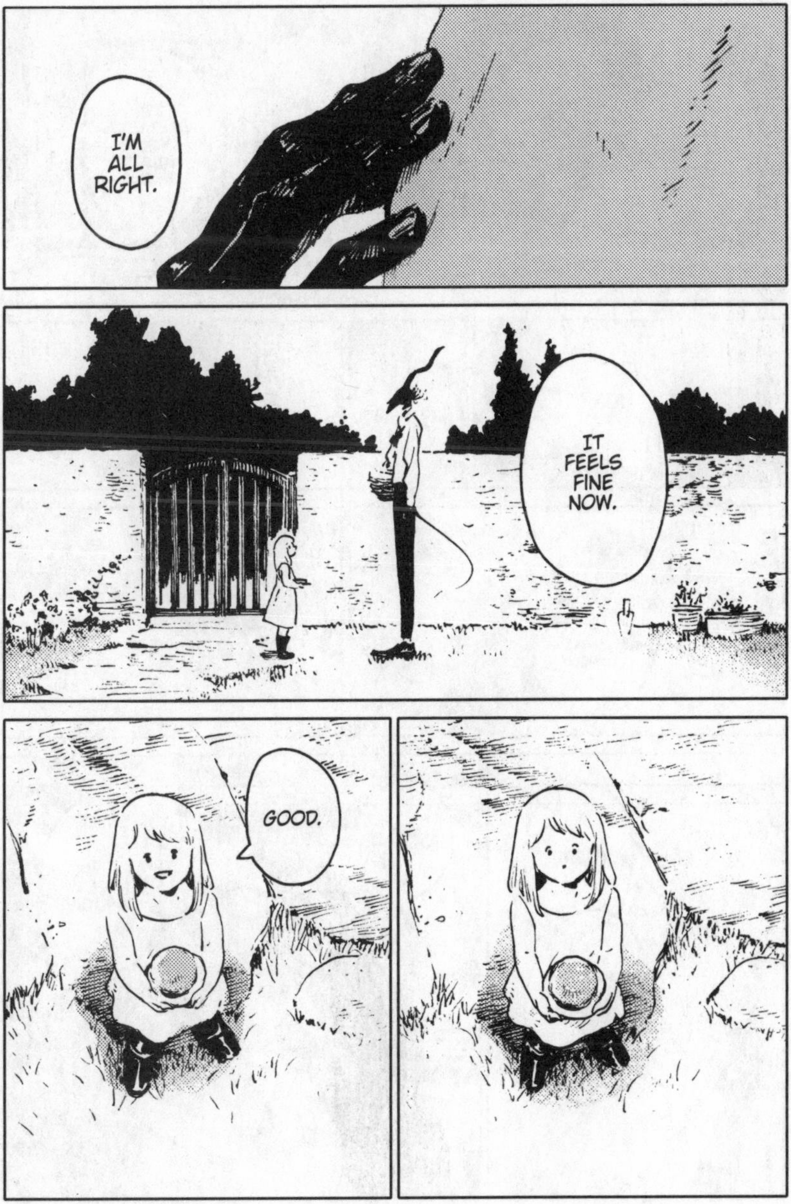
I'M ALL RIGHT.
IT FEELS FINE NOW.
GOOD.

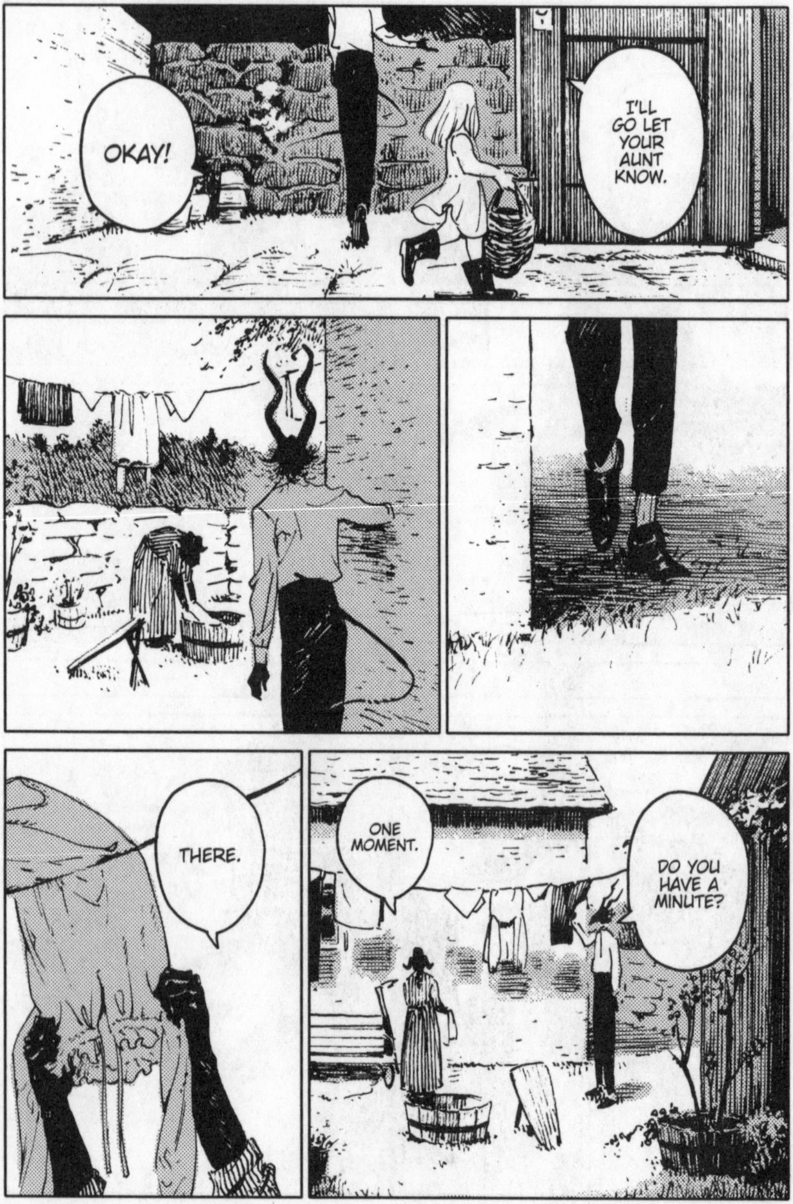
I'LL GO LET YOUR AUNT KNOW.
OKAY!
DO YOU HAVE A MINUTE?
ONE MOMENT.
THERE.

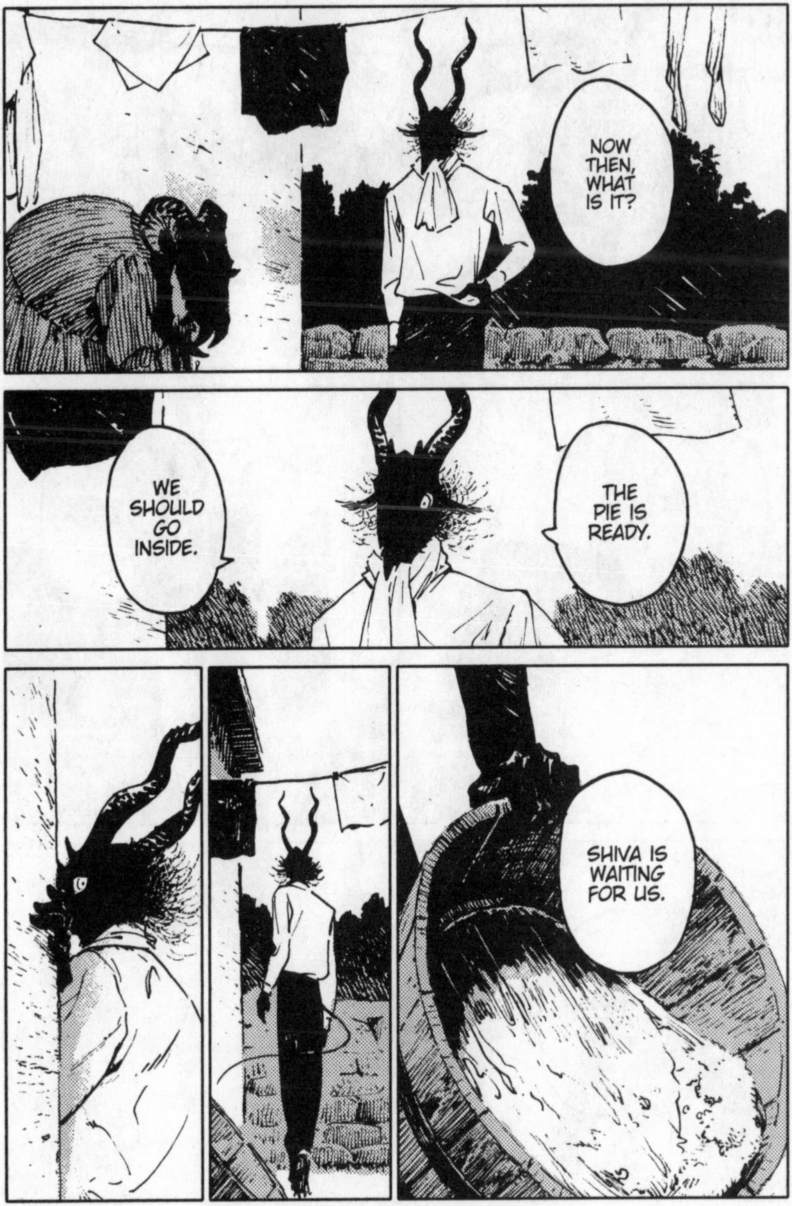
NOW THEN, WHAT IS IT?
WE SHOULD GO INSIDE.
THE PIE IS READY.
SHIVA IS WAITING FOR US.

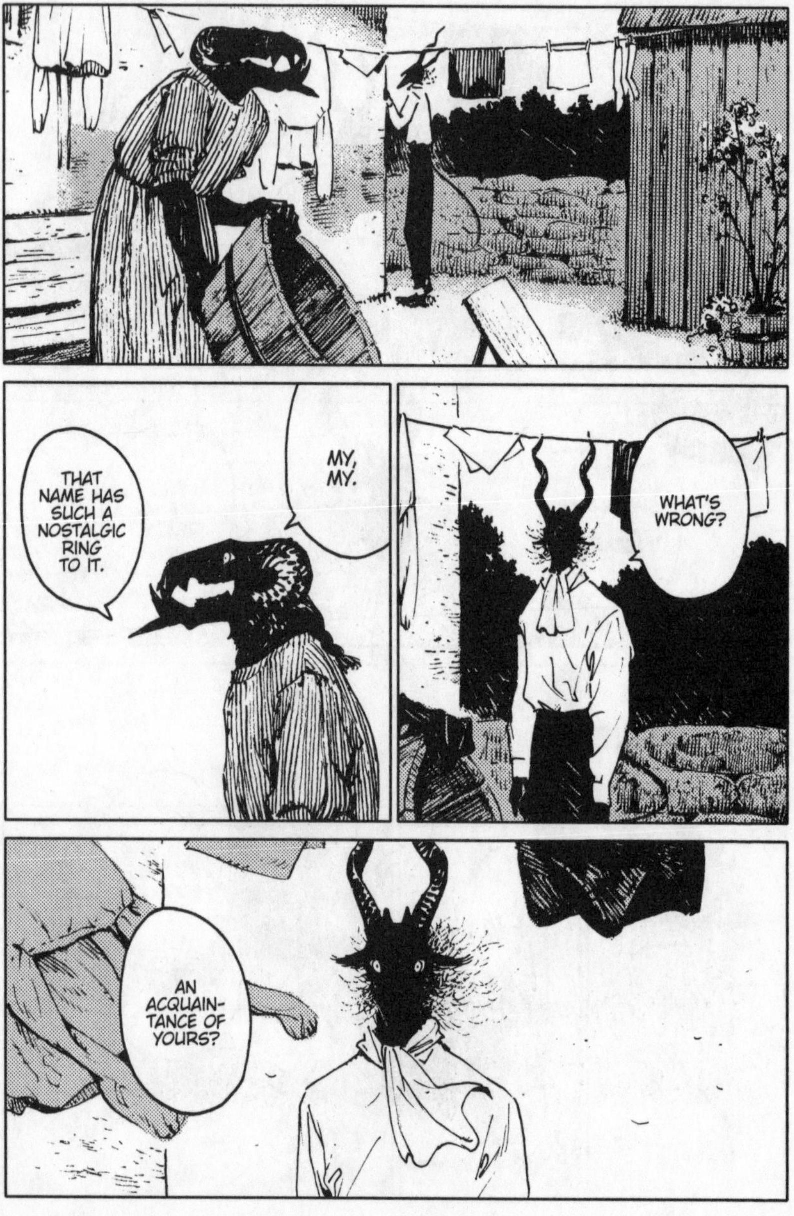
WHAT'S WRONG?
MY, MY.
THAT NAME HAS SUCH A NOSTALGIC RING TO IT.
AN ACQUAIN-TANCE OF YOURS?

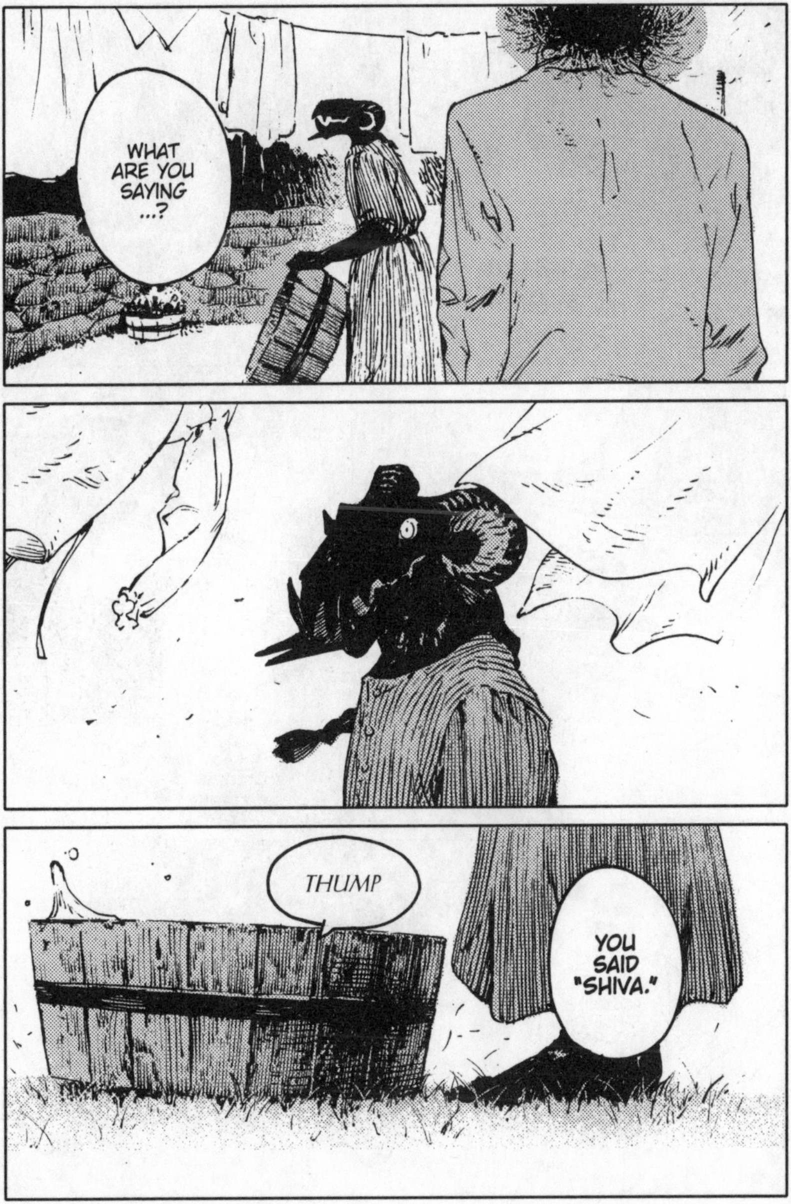
WHAT ARE YOU SAYING ...?
THUMP
YOU SAID "SHIVA."

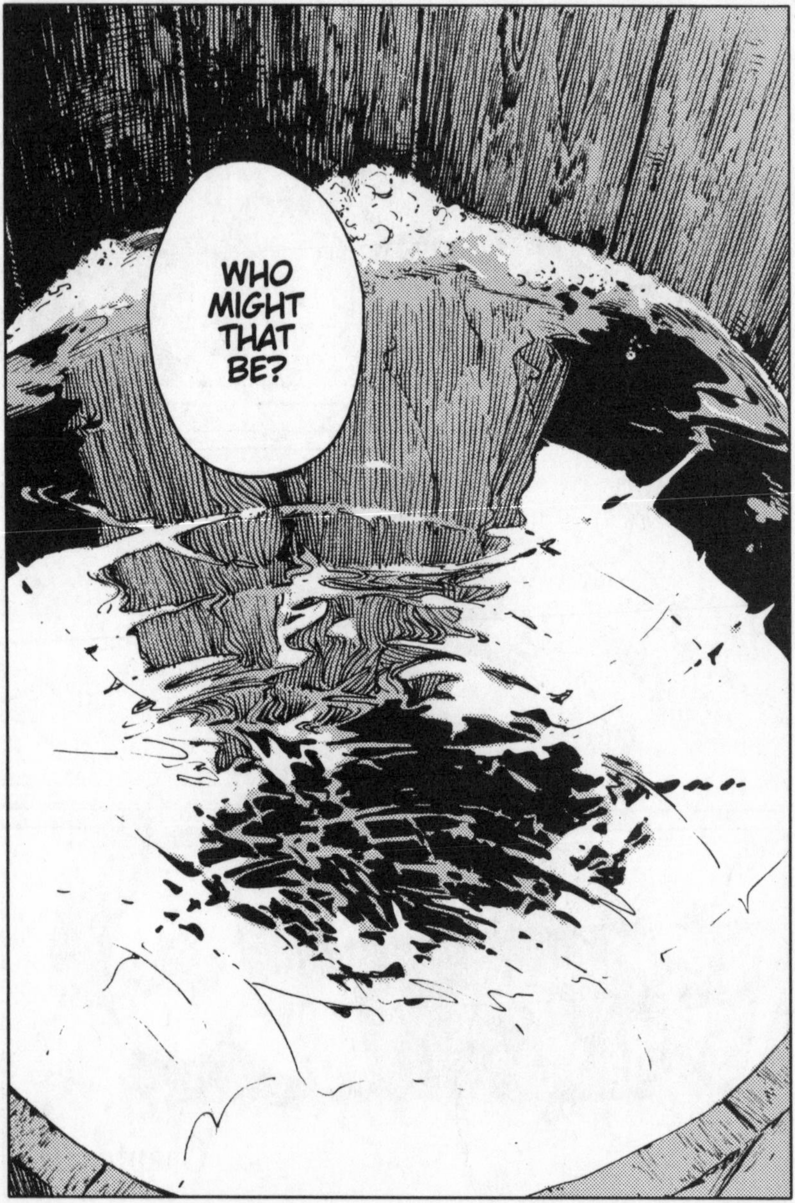
WHO MIGHT THAT BE?

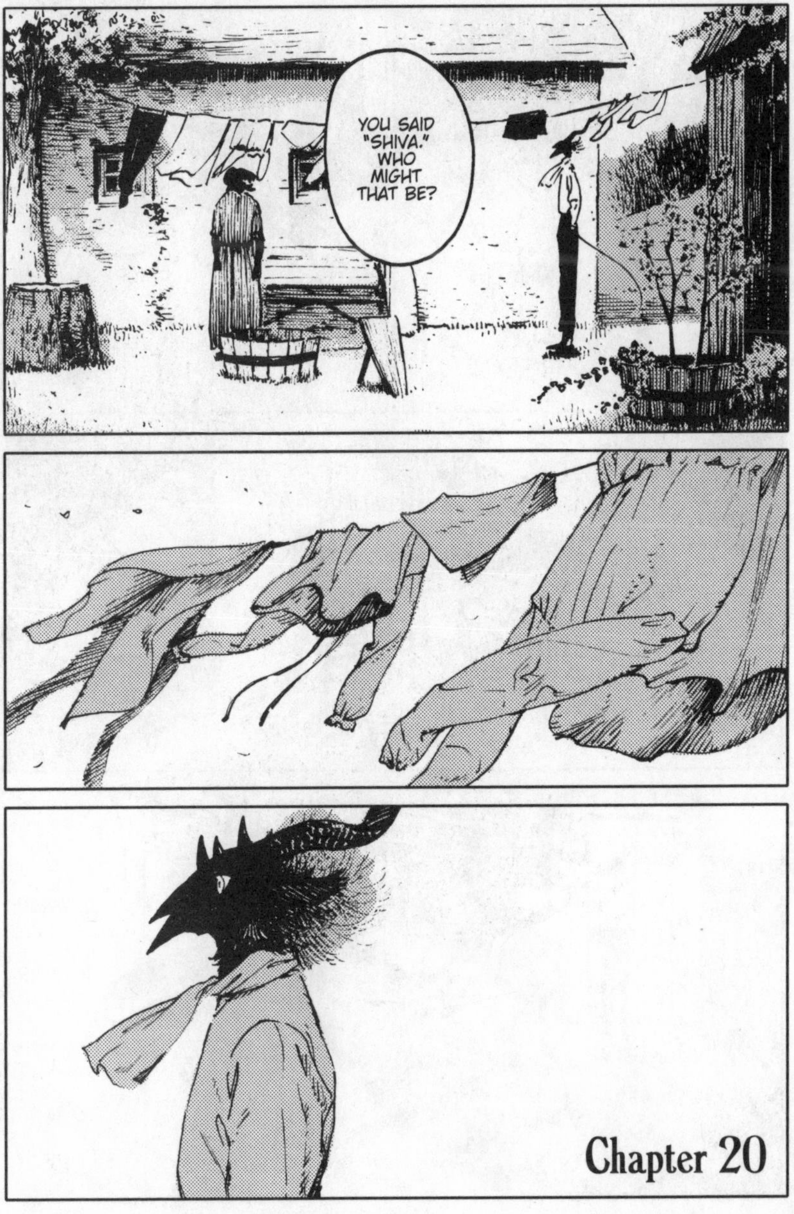
YOU SAID "SHIVA." WHO MIGHT THAT BE?
Chapter 20

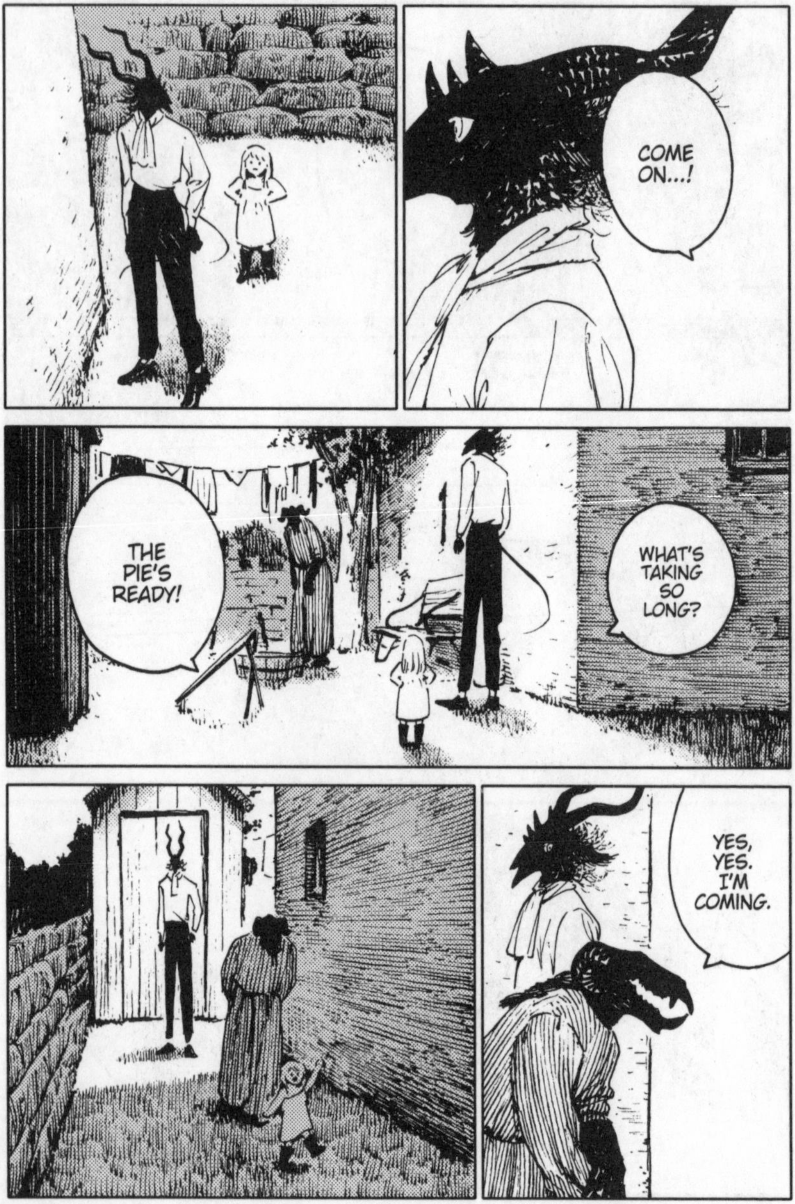
COME ON...!
THE PIE'S READY!
WHAT'S TAKING SO LONG?
YES, YES. I'M COMING.

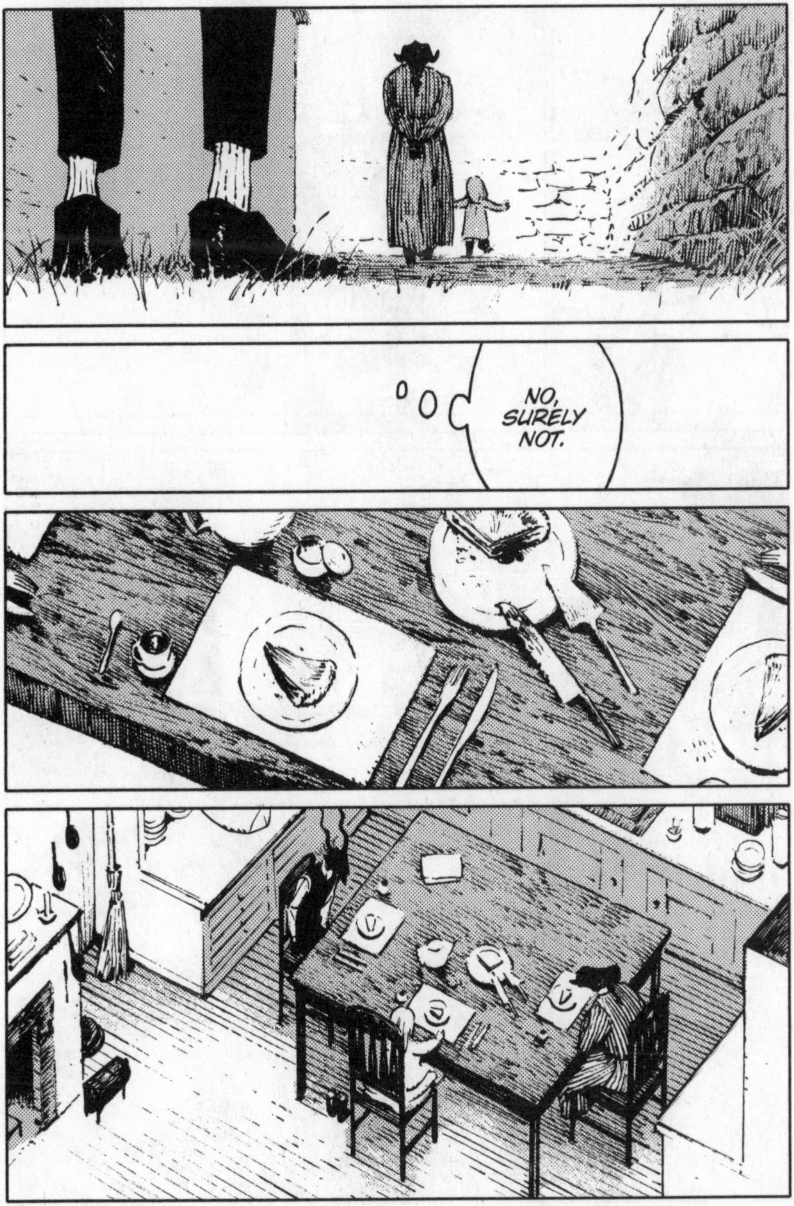
NO, SURELY NOT.

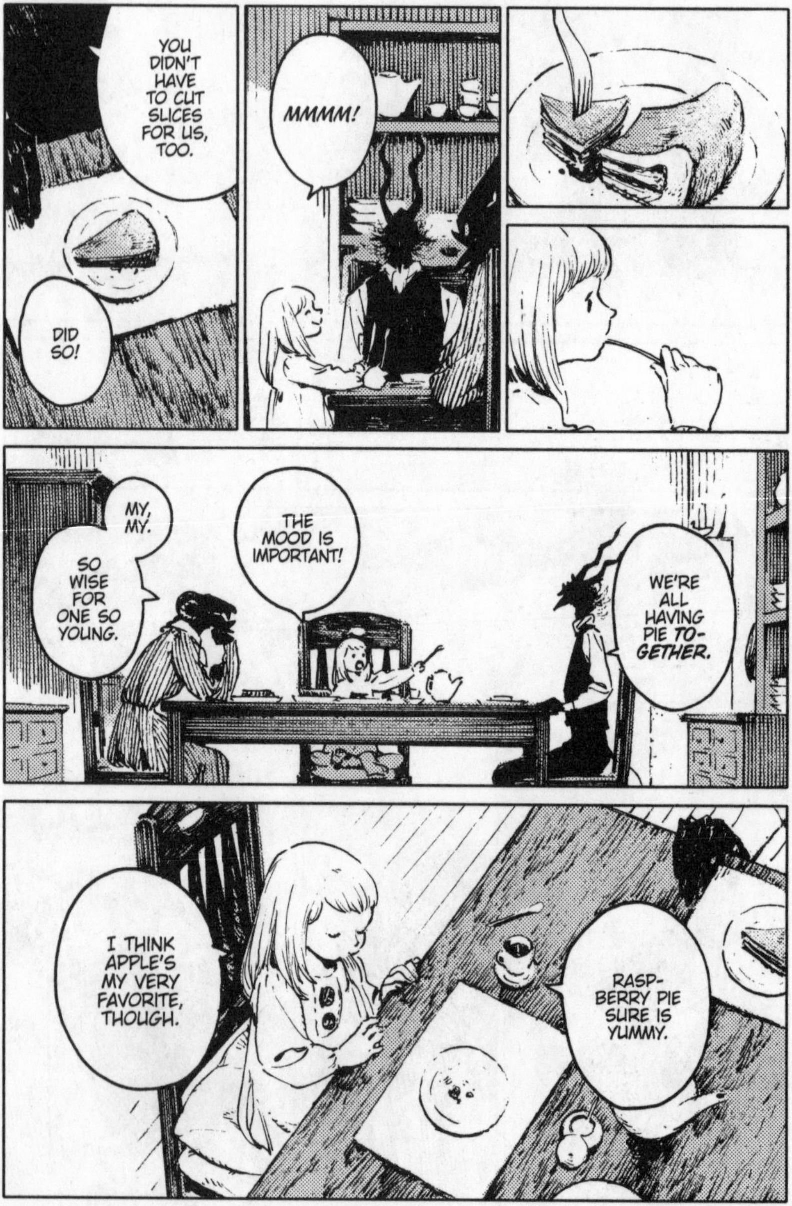
YOU DIDN'T HAVE TO CUT SLICES FOR US, TOO.
DID SO!
MMMM!
MY, MY.
SO WISE FOR ONE SO YOUNG.
THE MOOD IS IMPORTANT!
WE'RE ALL HAVING PIE TO-GETHER.
RASP-BERRY PIE SURE IS YUMMY.
I THINK APPLE'S MY VERY FAVORITE, THOUGH.

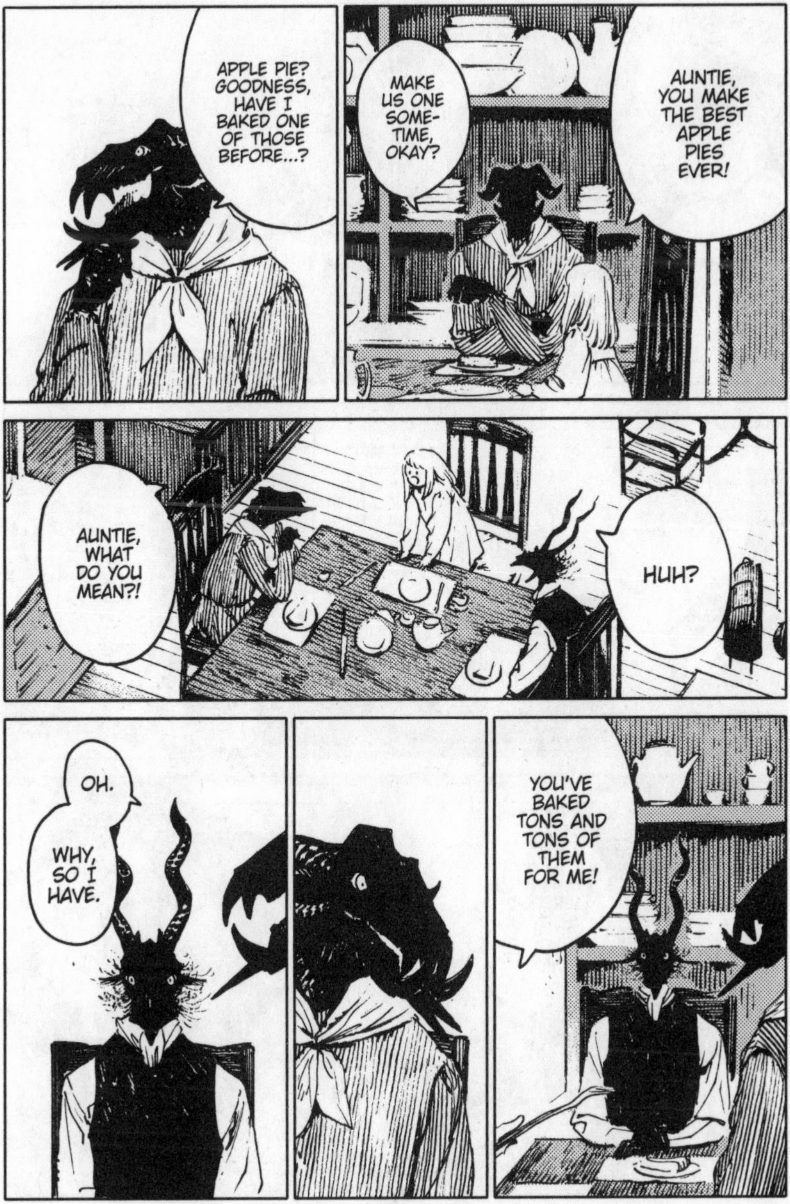
APPLE PIE? GOODNESS, HAVE I BAKED ONE OF THOSE BEFORE...?
MAKE US ONE SOME-TIME, OKAY?
AUNTIE, YOU MAKE THE BEST APPLE PIES EVER!
AUNTIE, WHAT DO YOU MEAN?!
HUH?
OH.
WHY, SO I HAVE.
YOU'VE BAKED TONS AND TONS OF THEM FOR ME!

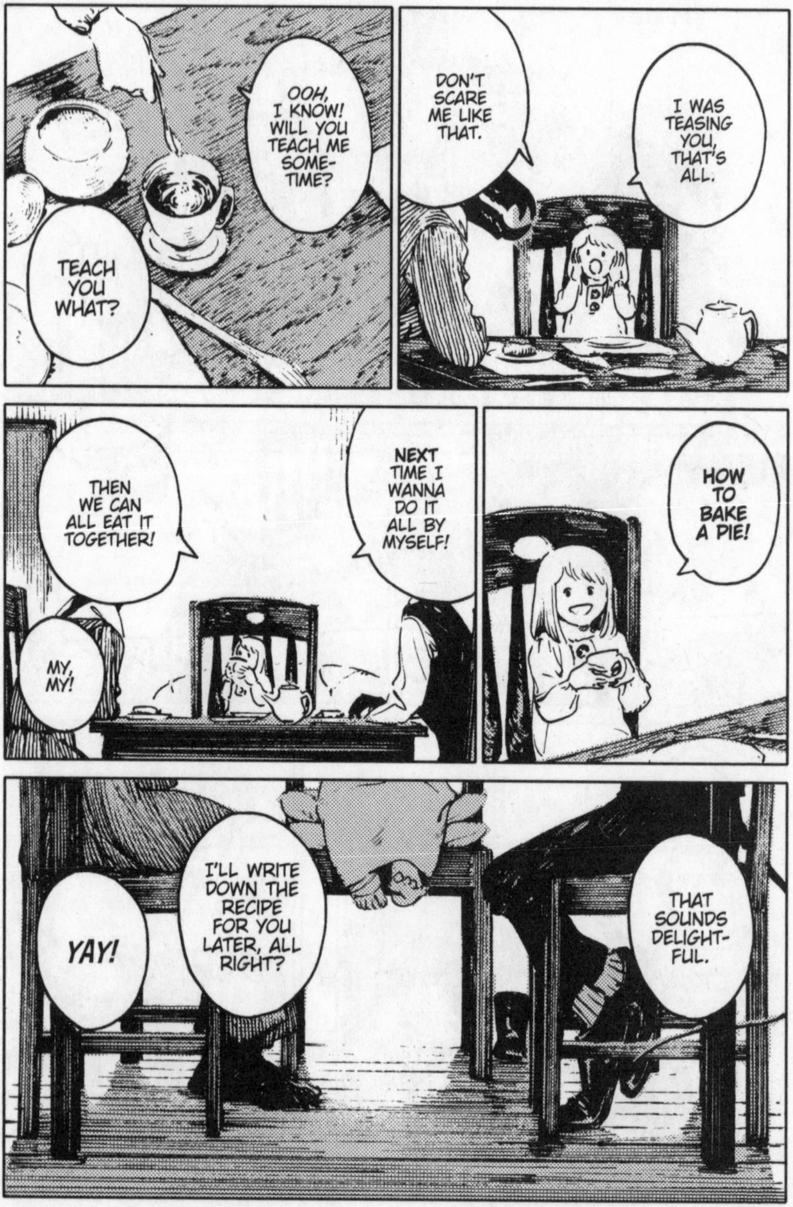
DON'T SCARE ME LIKE THAT.
I WAS TEASING YOU, THAT'S ALL.
OOH, I KNOW! WILL YOU TEACH ME SOME-TIME?
TEACH YOU WHAT?
HOW TO BAKE A PIE!
NEXT TIME I WANNA DO IT ALL BY MYSELF!
THEN WE CAN ALL EAT IT TOGETHER!
MY, MY!
THAT SOUNDS DELIGHT-FUL.
I'LL WRITE DOWN THE RECIPE FOR YOU LATER, ALL RIGHT?
YAY!

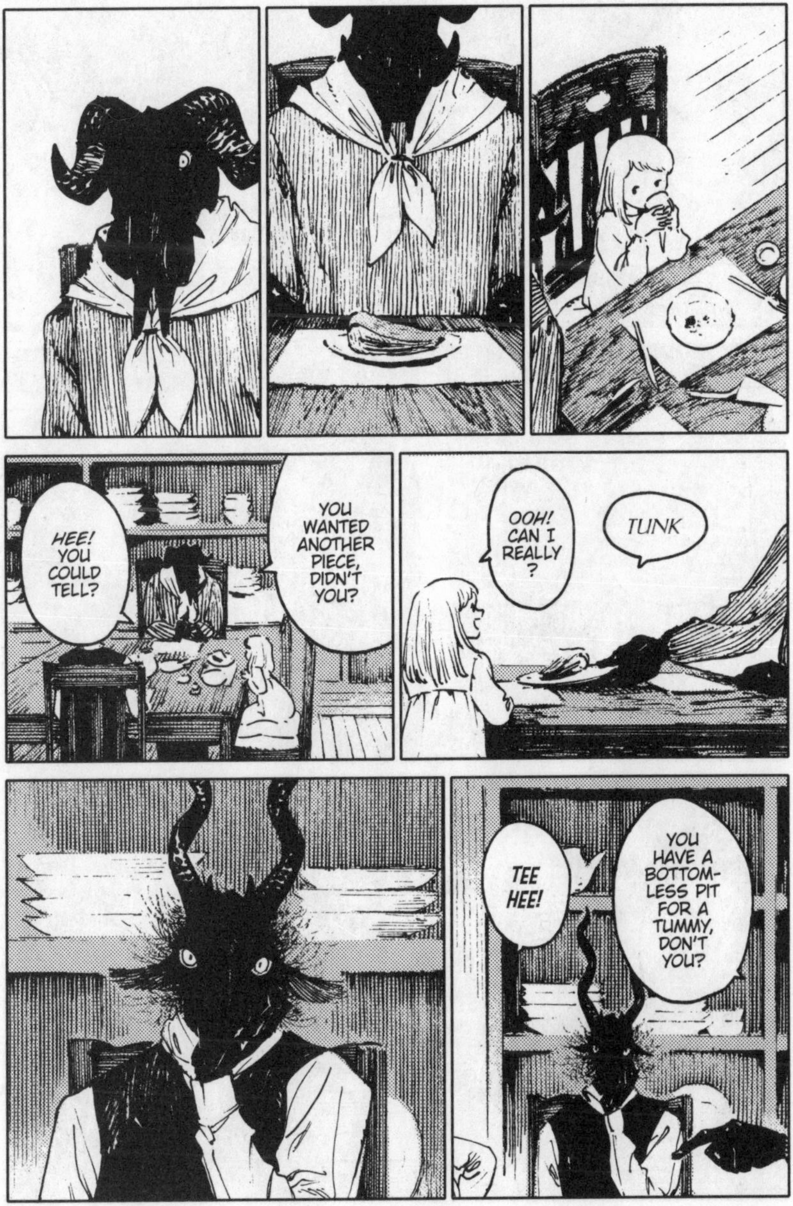
HEE! YOU COULD TELL?
YOU WANTED ANOTHER PIECE, DIDN'T YOU?
OOH! CAN I REALLY?
TUNK
TEE HEE!
YOU HAVE A BOTTOMLESS PIT FOR A TUMMY, DON'T YOU?

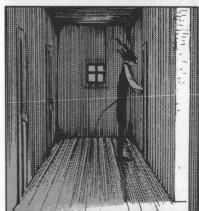

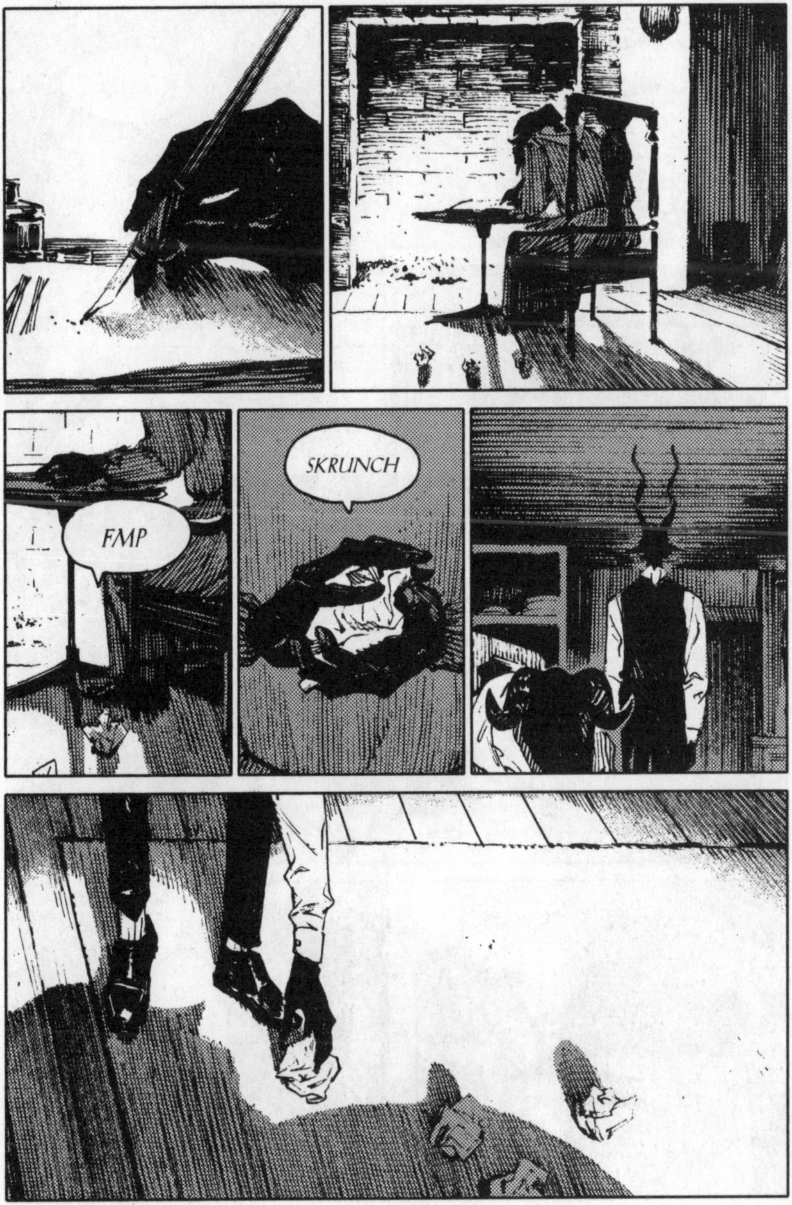
FMP
SKRUNCH

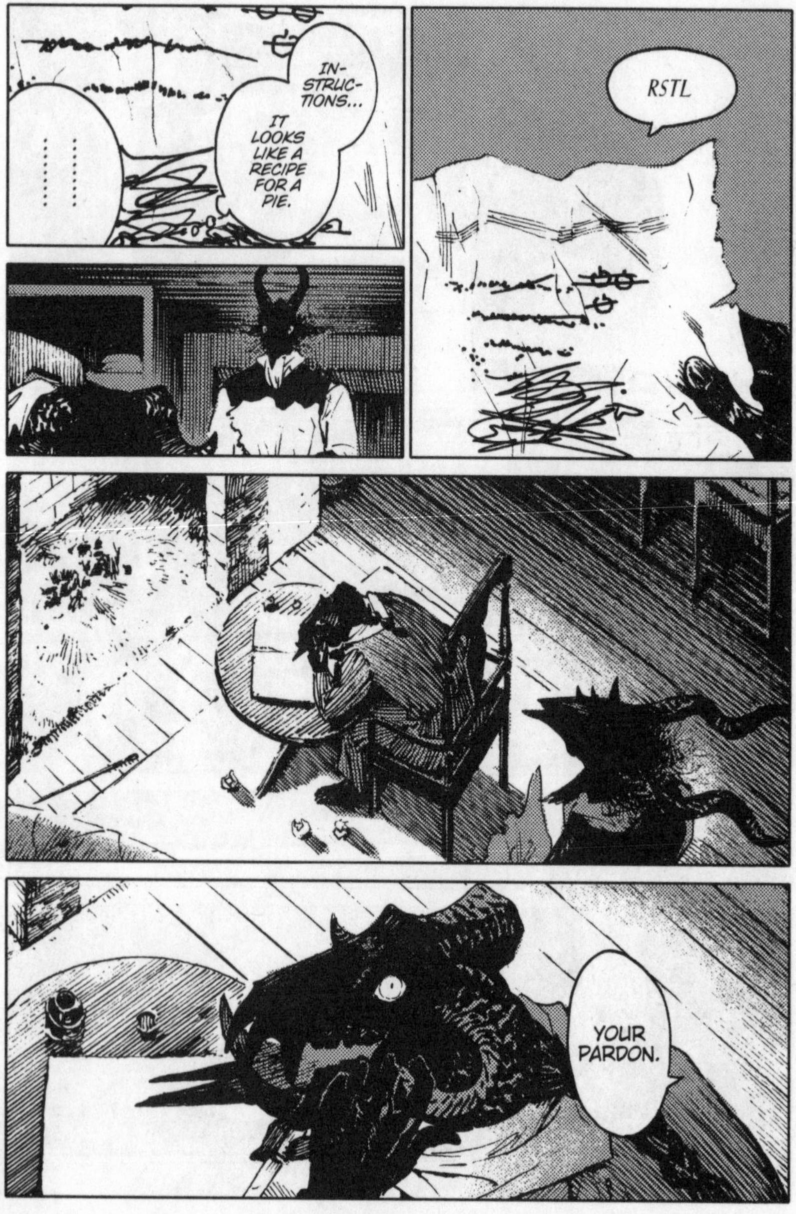
RSTL
IN-STRUC-TIONS... IT LOOKS LIKE A RECIPE FOR A PIE.
......
YOUR PARDON.

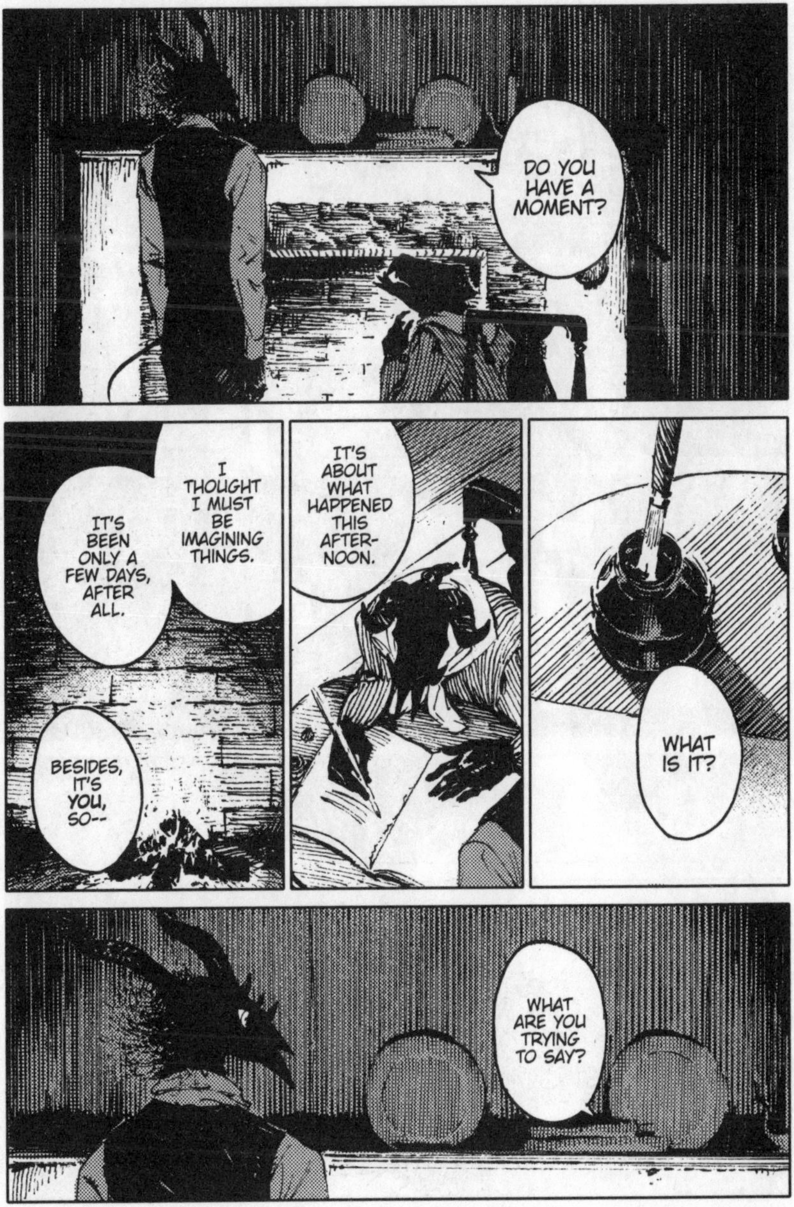
DO YOU HAVE A MOMENT?
WHAT IS IT?
IT'S ABOUT WHAT HAPPENED THIS AFTER-NOON.
I THOUGHT I MUST BE IMAGINING THINGS.
IT'S BEEN ONLY A FEW DAYS, AFTER ALL.
BESIDES, IT'S YOU, SO--
WHAT ARE YOU TRYING TO SAY?

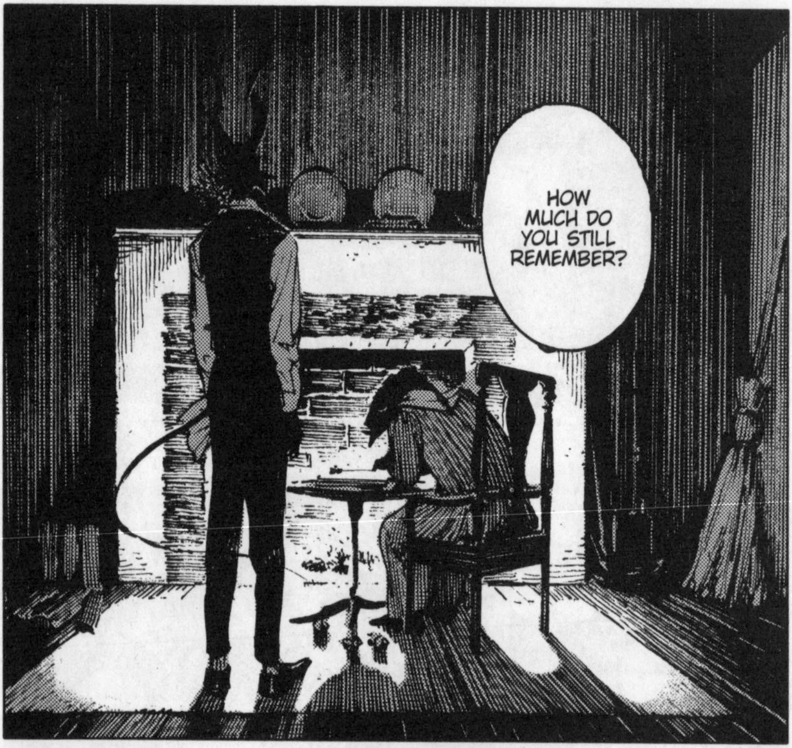
HOW MUCH DO YOU STILL REMEMBER?

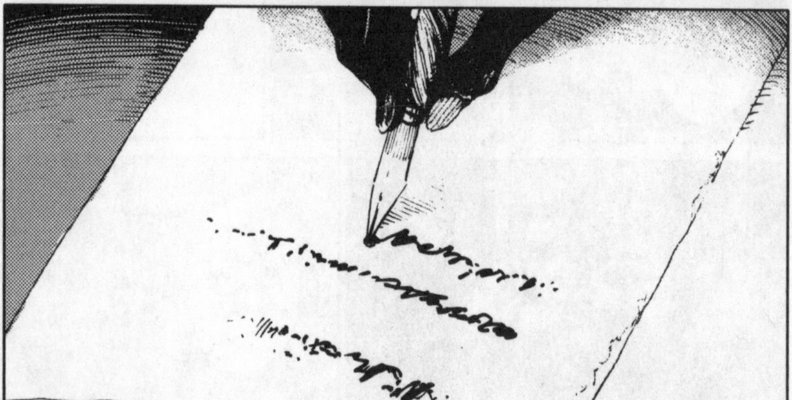

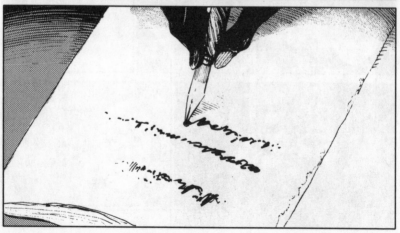

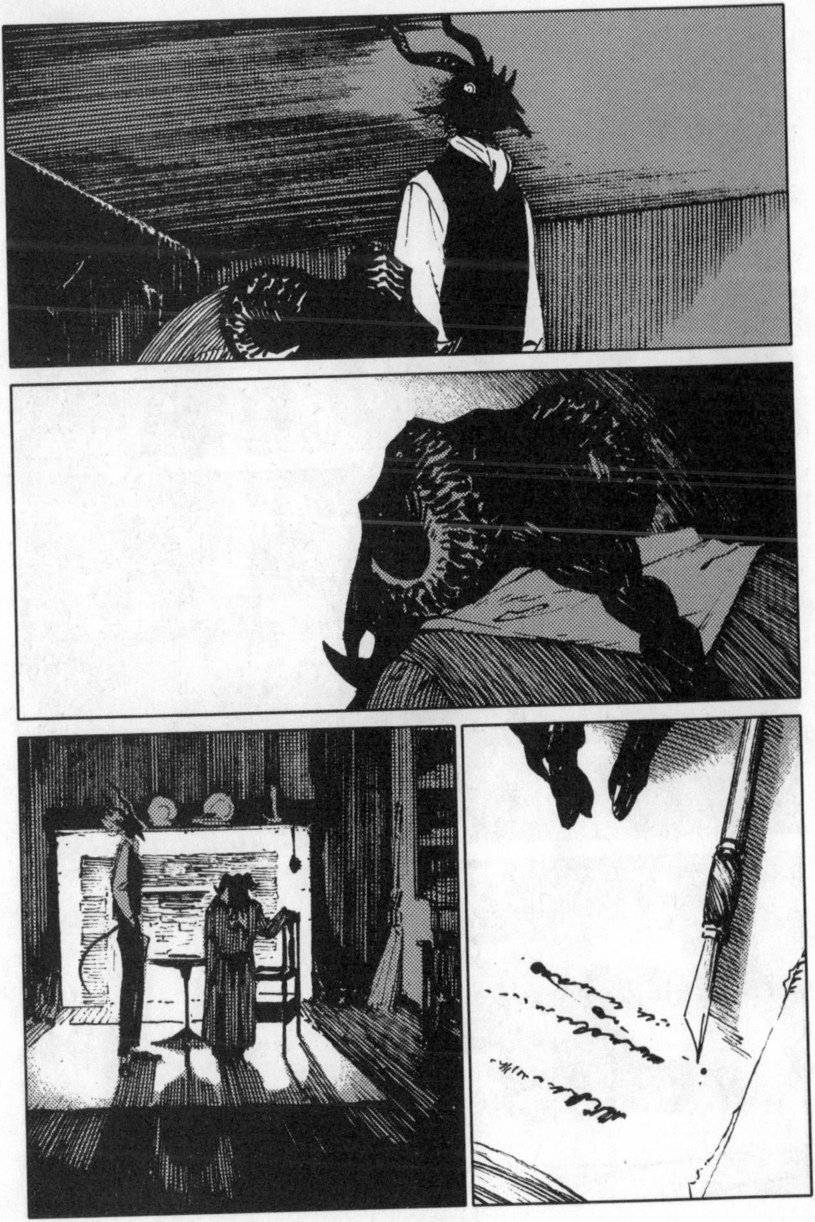

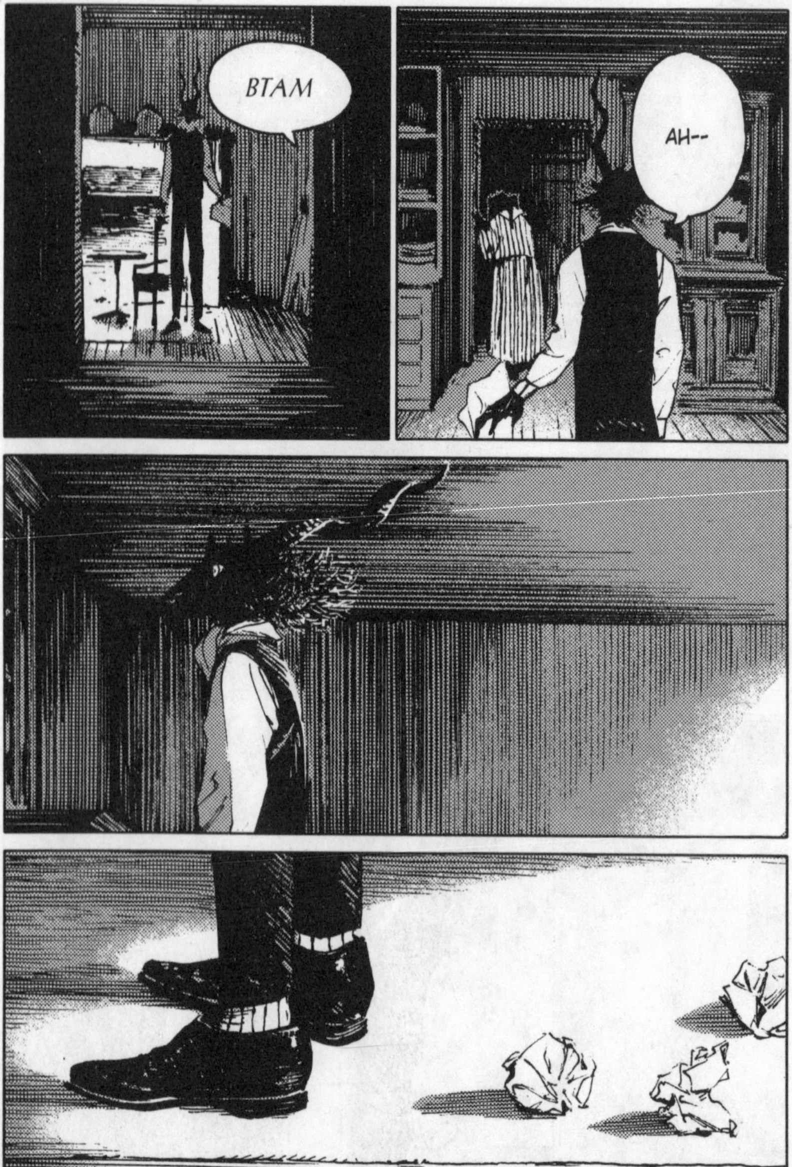
BTAM
AH--

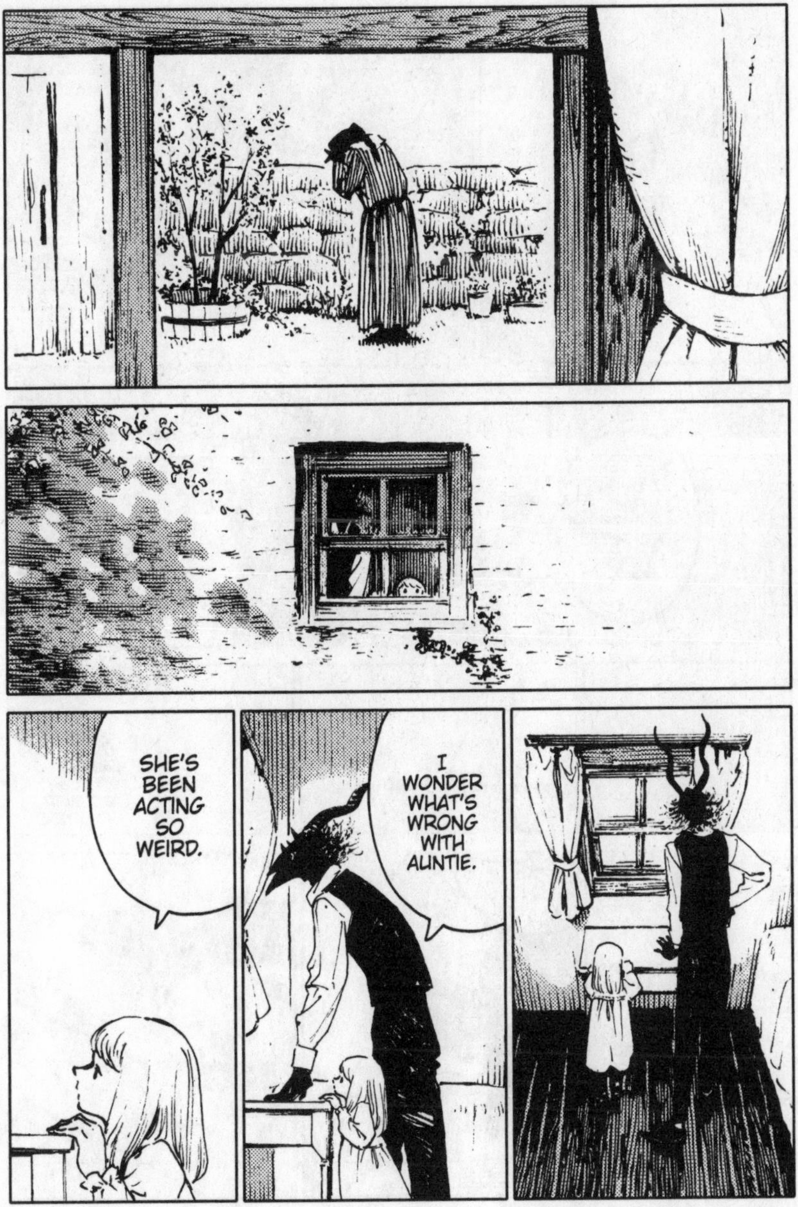
I WONDER WHAT'S WRONG WITH AUNTIE.
SHE'S BEEN ACTING SO WEIRD.

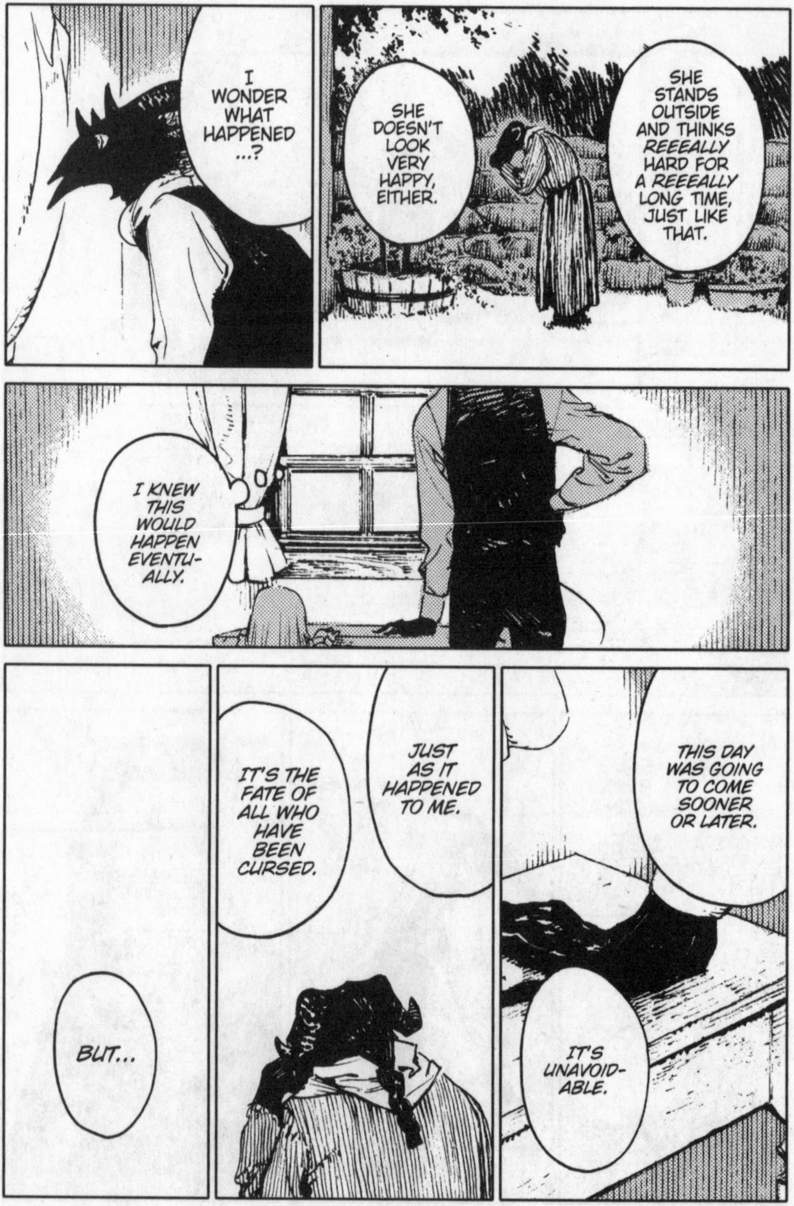
SHE STANDS OUTSIDE AND THINKS REEEALLY HARD FOR A REEEALLY LONG TIME, JUST LIKE THAT.
SHE DOESN'T LOOK VERY HAPPY, EITHER.
I WONDER WHAT HAPPENED ...?
I KNEW THIS WOULD HAPPEN EVENTUALLY.
THIS DAY WAS GOING TO COME SOONER OR LATER.
IT'S UNAVOIDABLE.
JUST AS IT HAPPENED TO ME.
IT'S THE FATE OF ALL WHO HAVE BEEN CURSED.
BUT...

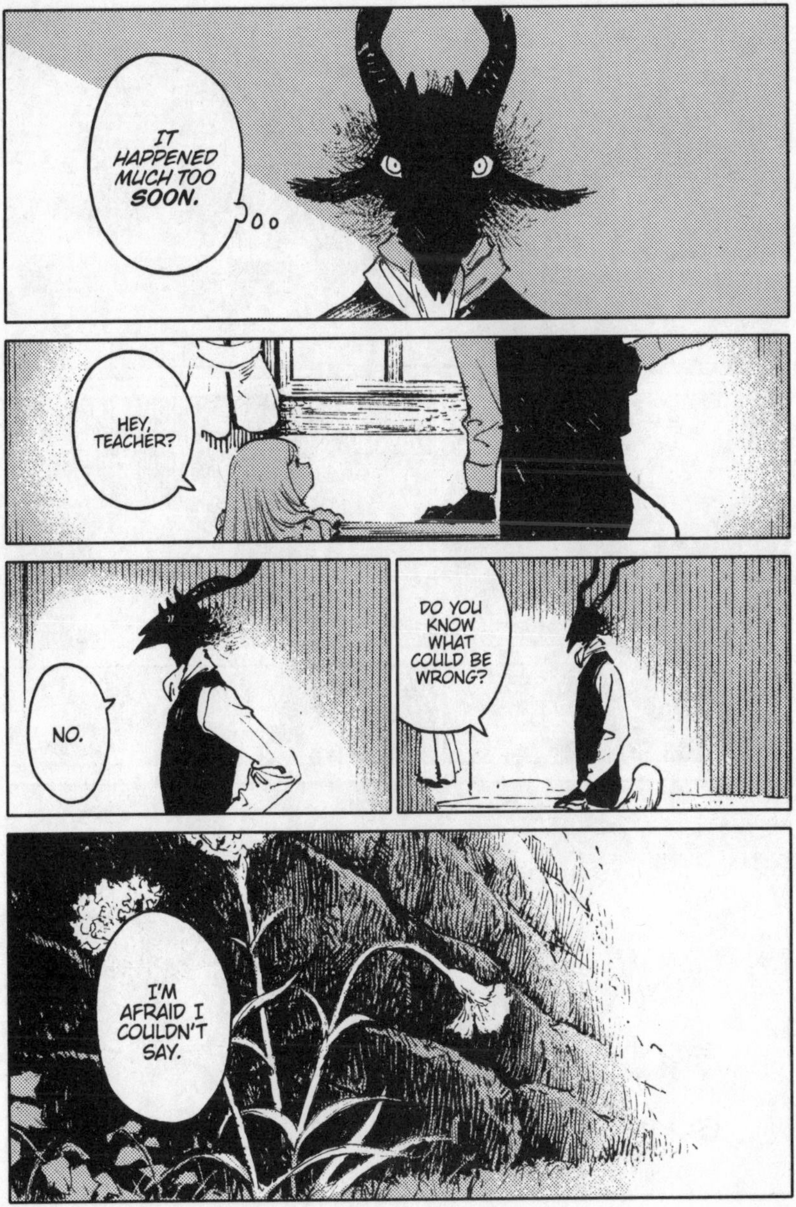
IT HAPPENED MUCH TOO SOON.
HEY, TEACHER?
DO YOU KNOW WHAT COULD BE WRONG?
NO.
I'M AFRAID I COULDN'T SAY.

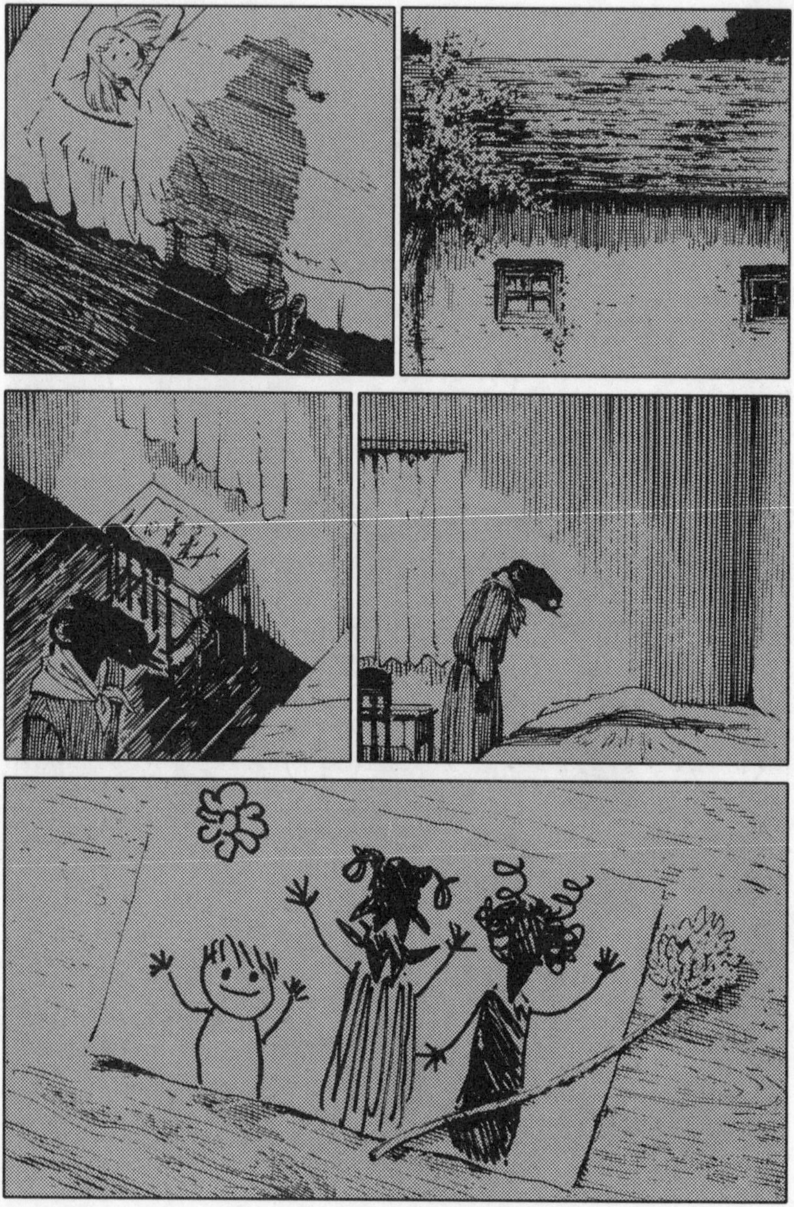

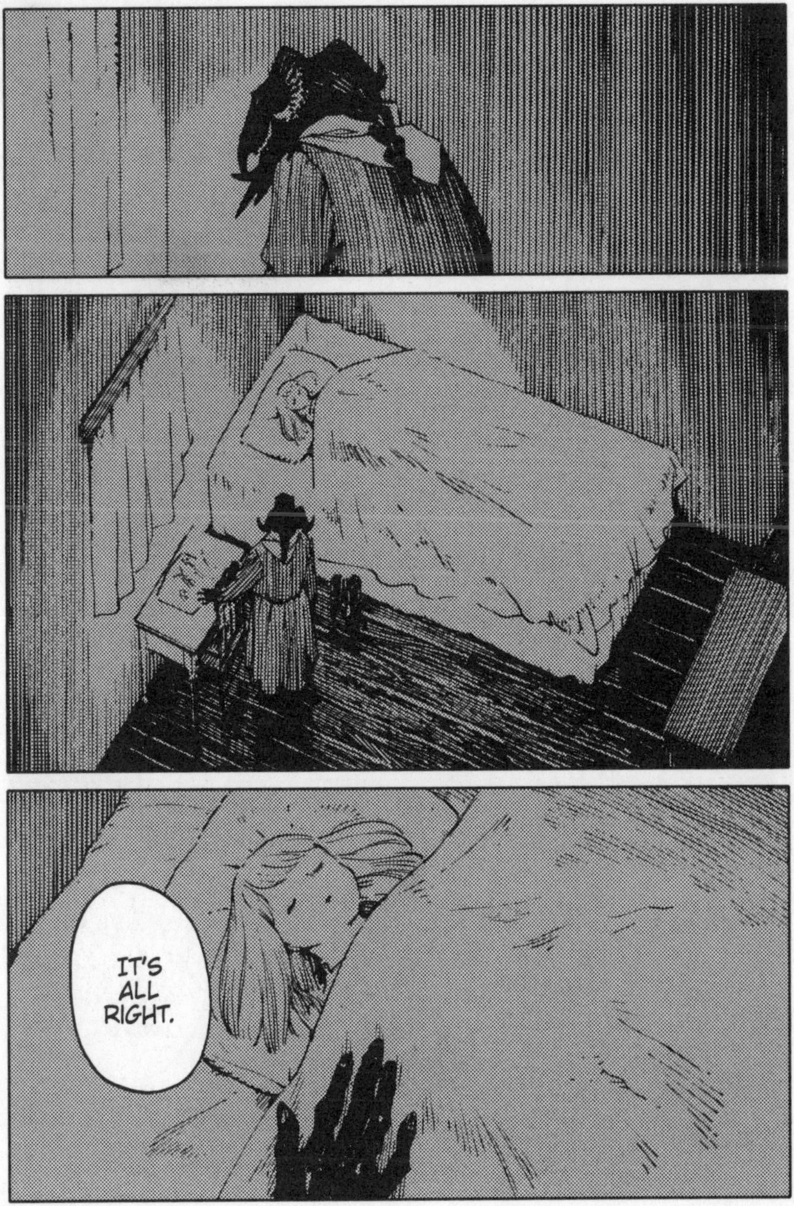
IT'S ALL RIGHT.

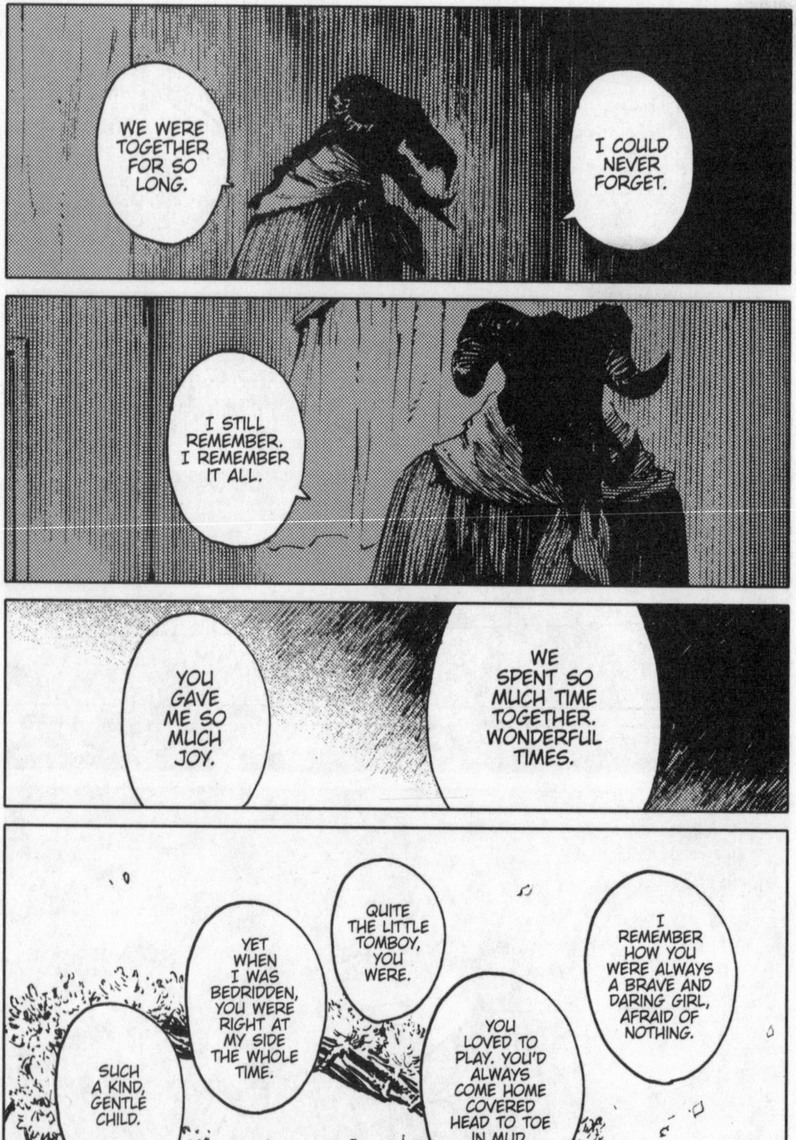
I COULD NEVER FORGET.
WE WERE TOGETHER FOR SO LONG.
I STILL REMEMBER. I REMEMBER IT ALL.
WE SPENT SO MUCH TIME TOGETHER. WONDERFUL TIMES.
YOU GAVE ME SO MUCH JOY.
I REMEMBER HOW YOU WERE ALWAYS A BRAVE AND DARING GIRL, AFRAID OF NOTHING.
YOU LOVED TO PLAY. YOU'D ALWAYS COME HOME COVERED HEAD TO TOE IN MUD.
QUITE THE LITTLE TOMBOY, YOU WERE.
YET WHEN I WAS BEDRIDDEN, YOU WERE RIGHT AT MY SIDE THE WHOLE TIME.
SUCH A KIND, GENTLE CHILD.

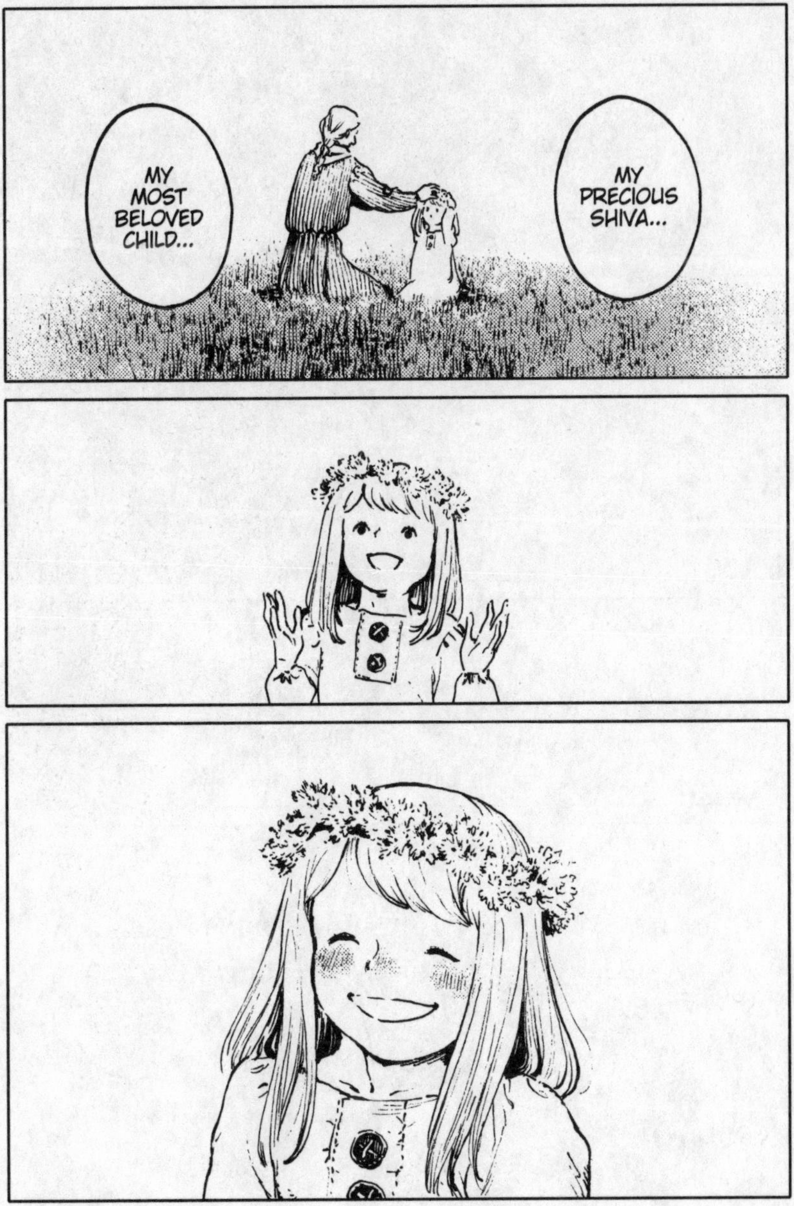
MY PRECIOUS SHIVA...
MY MOST BELOVED CHILD...

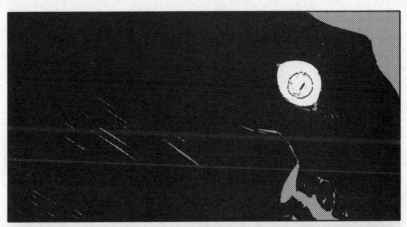

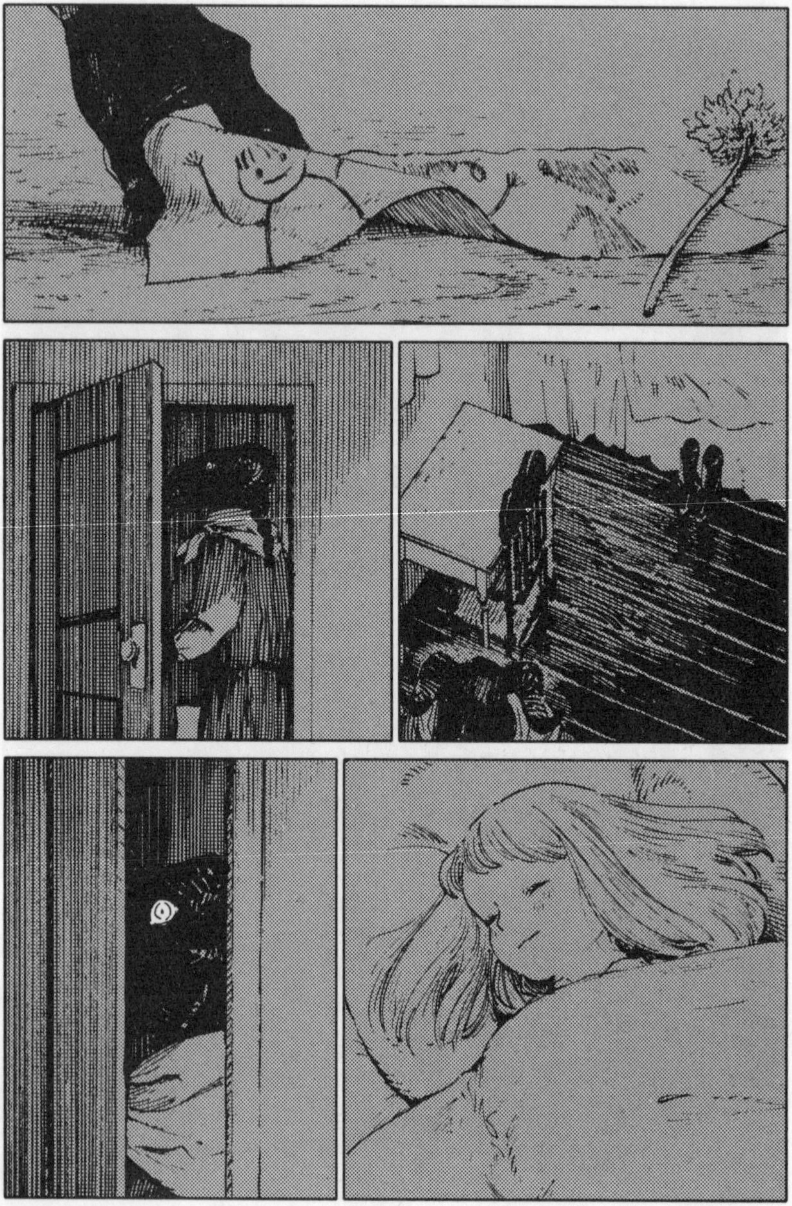

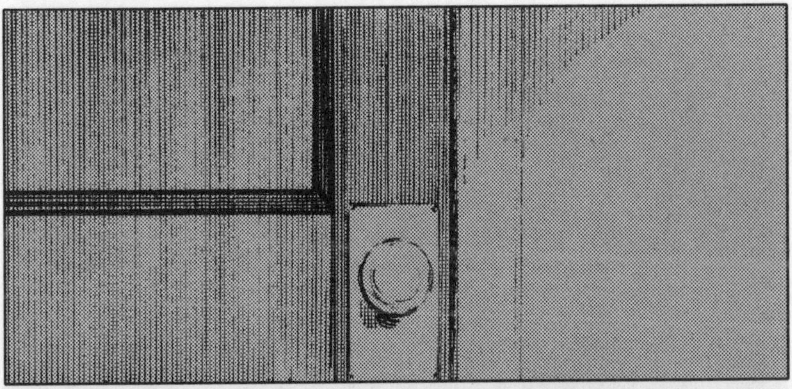
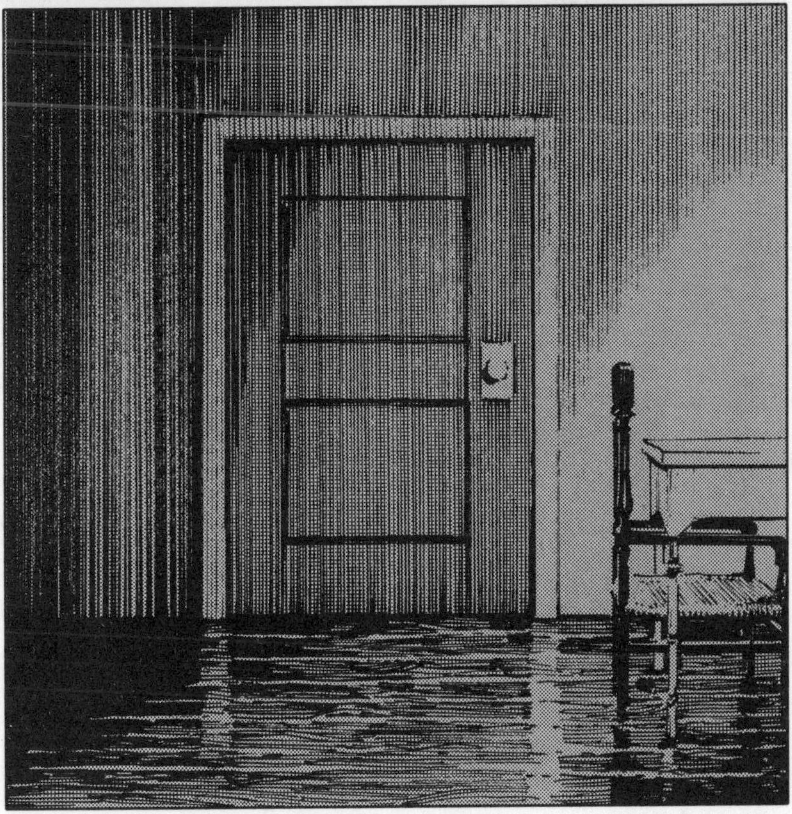

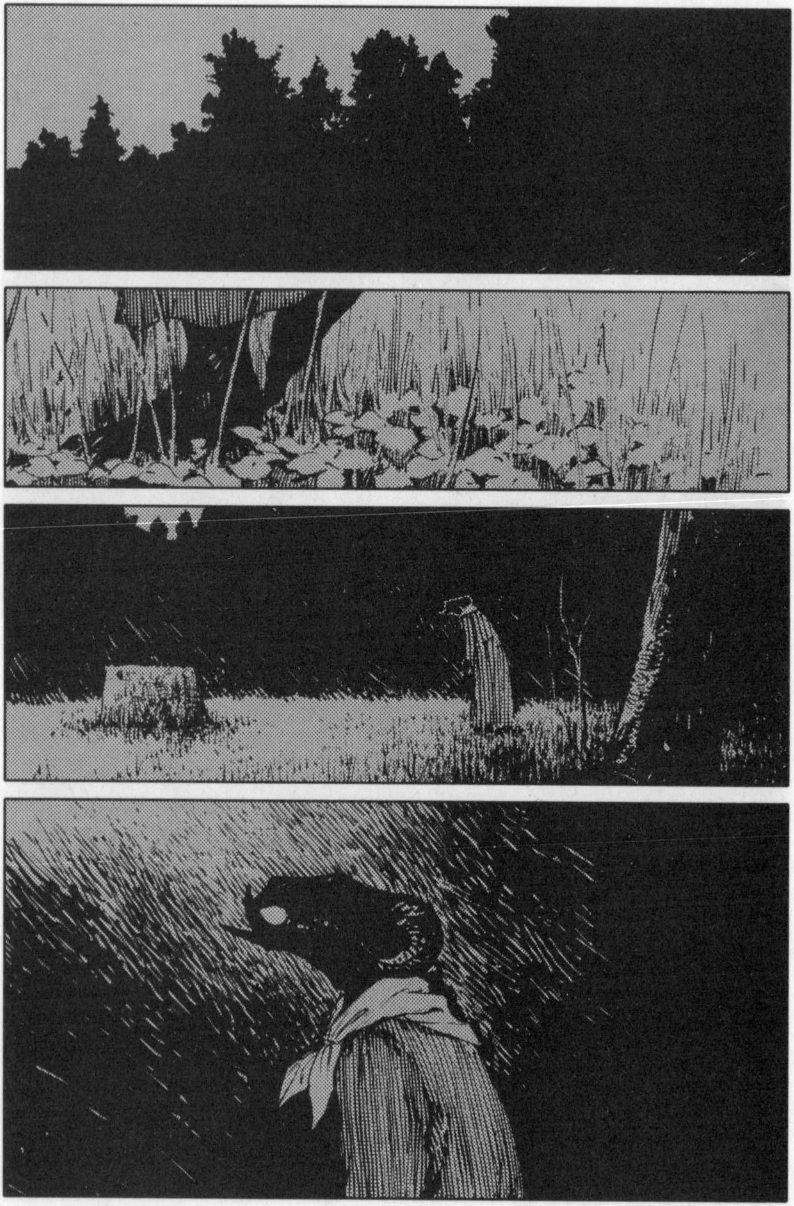

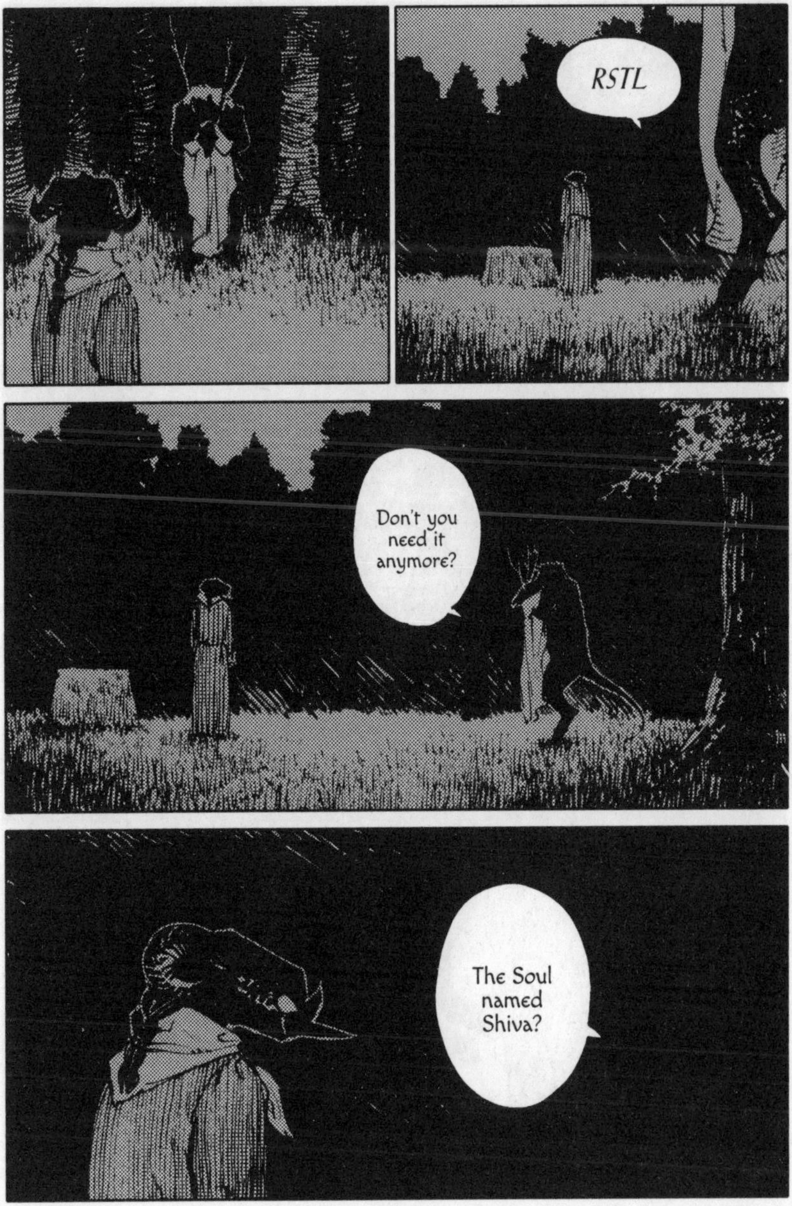
RSTL
Don't you need it anymore?
The Soul named Shiva?

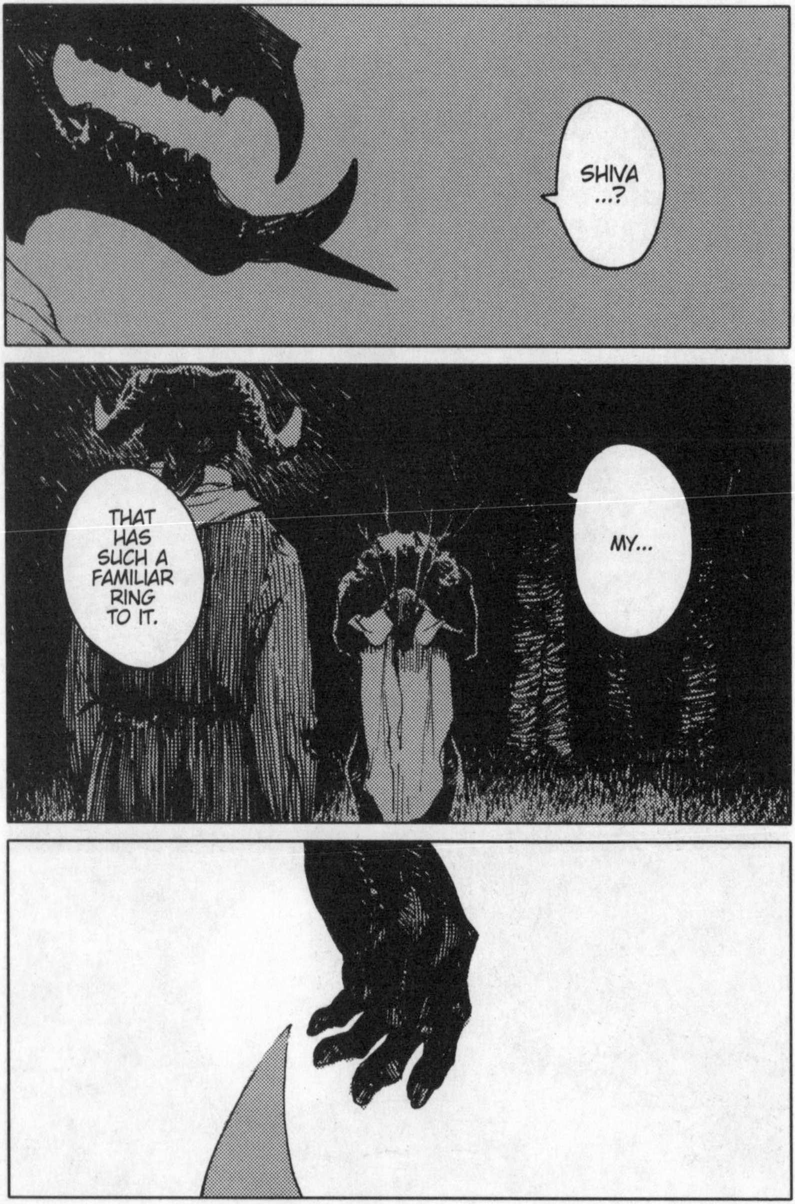
SHIVA ...?
MY...
THAT HAS SUCH A FAMILIAR RING TO IT.

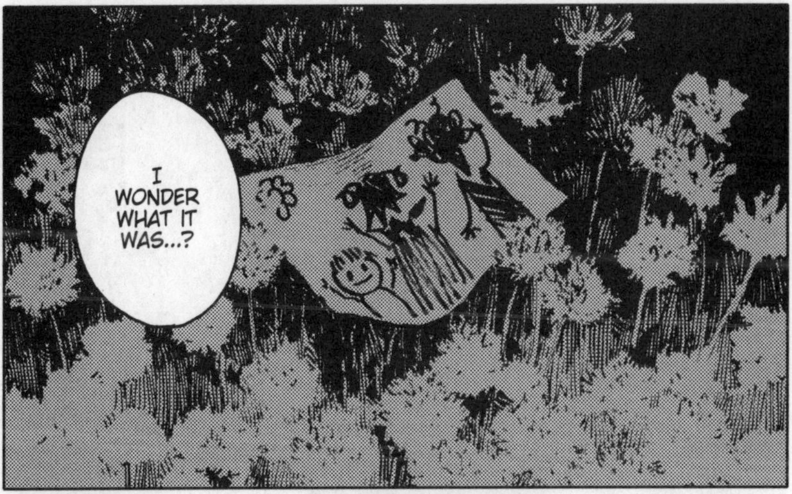
I WONDER WHAT IT WAS...?

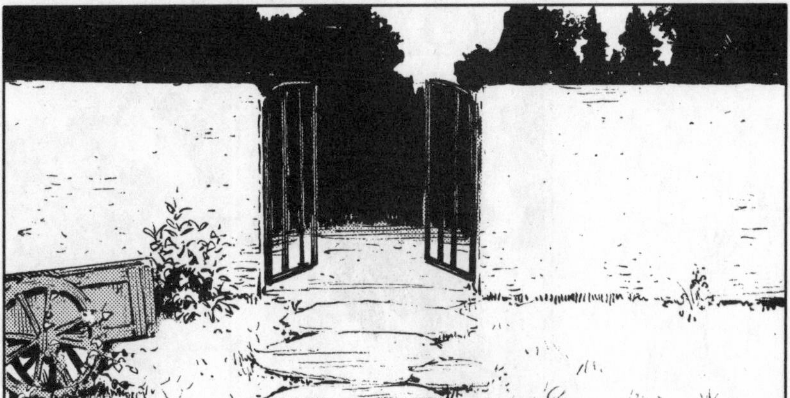

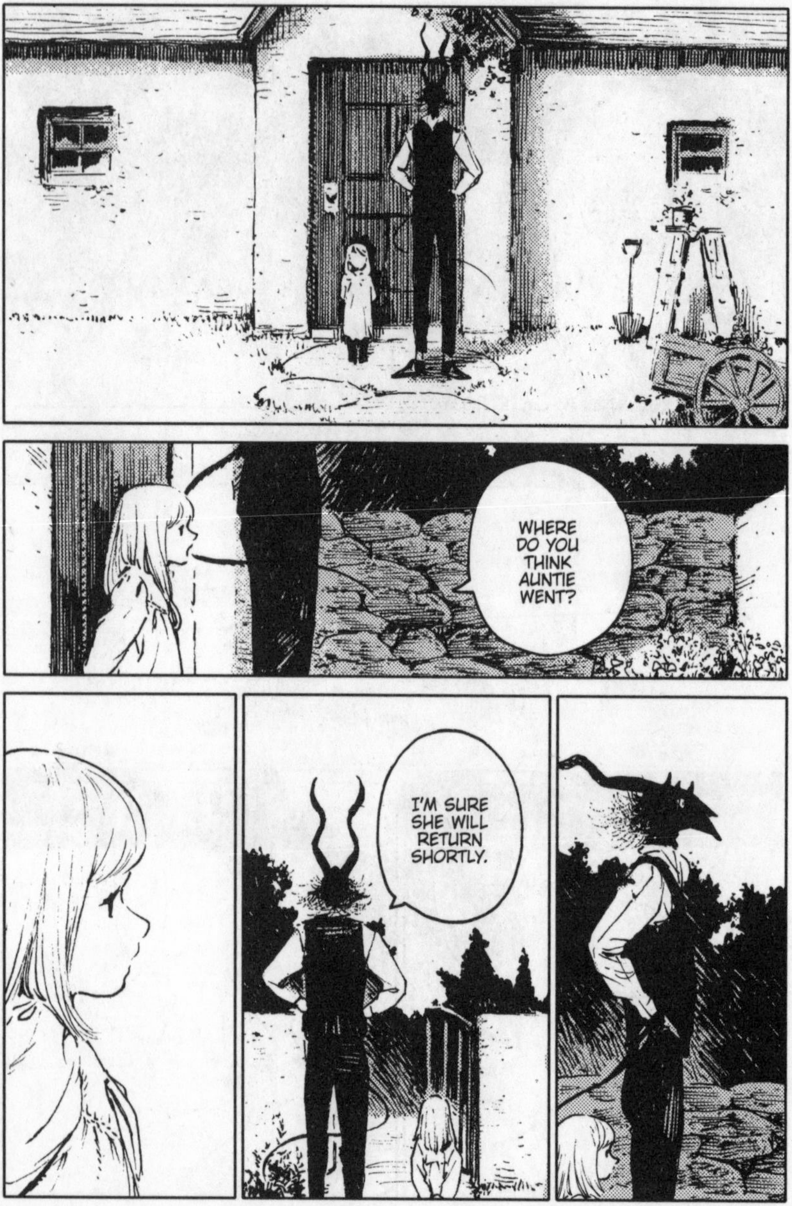
WHERE DO YOU THINK AUNTIE WENT?
I'M SURE SHE WILL RETURN SHORTLY.

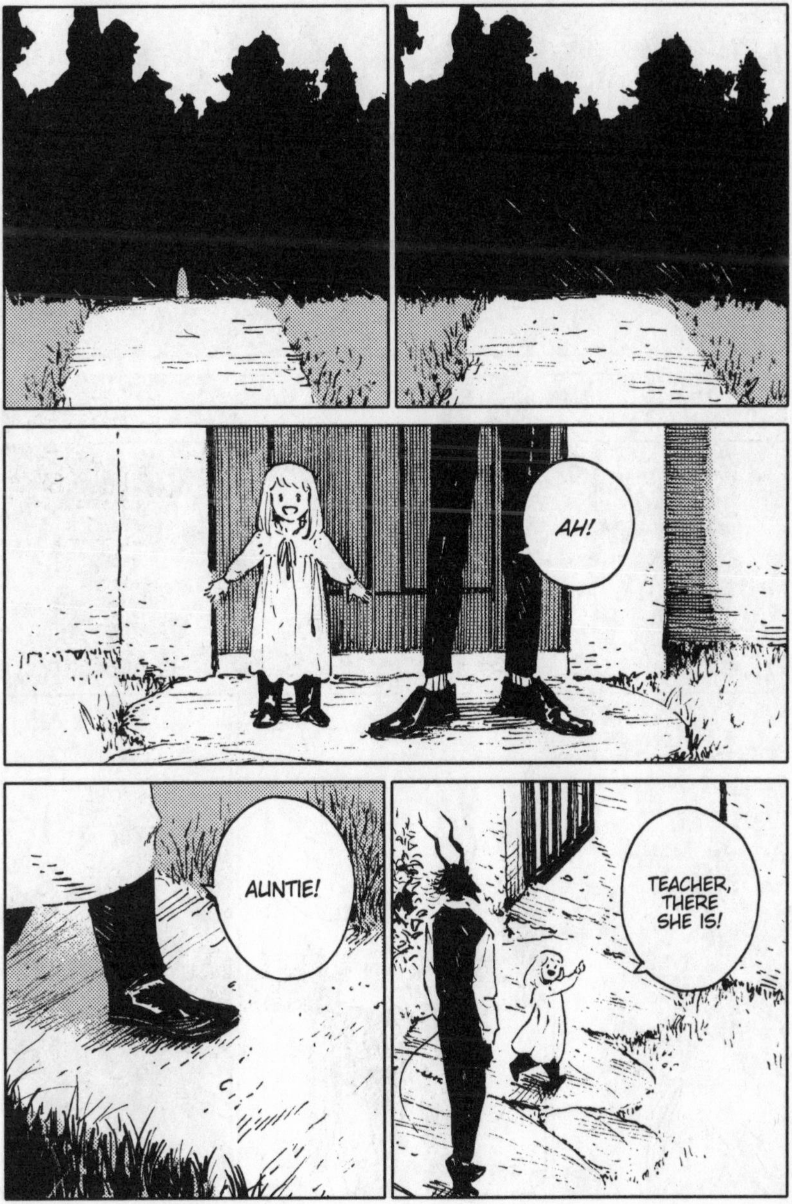
AH!
AUNTIE!
TEACHER, THERE SHE IS!

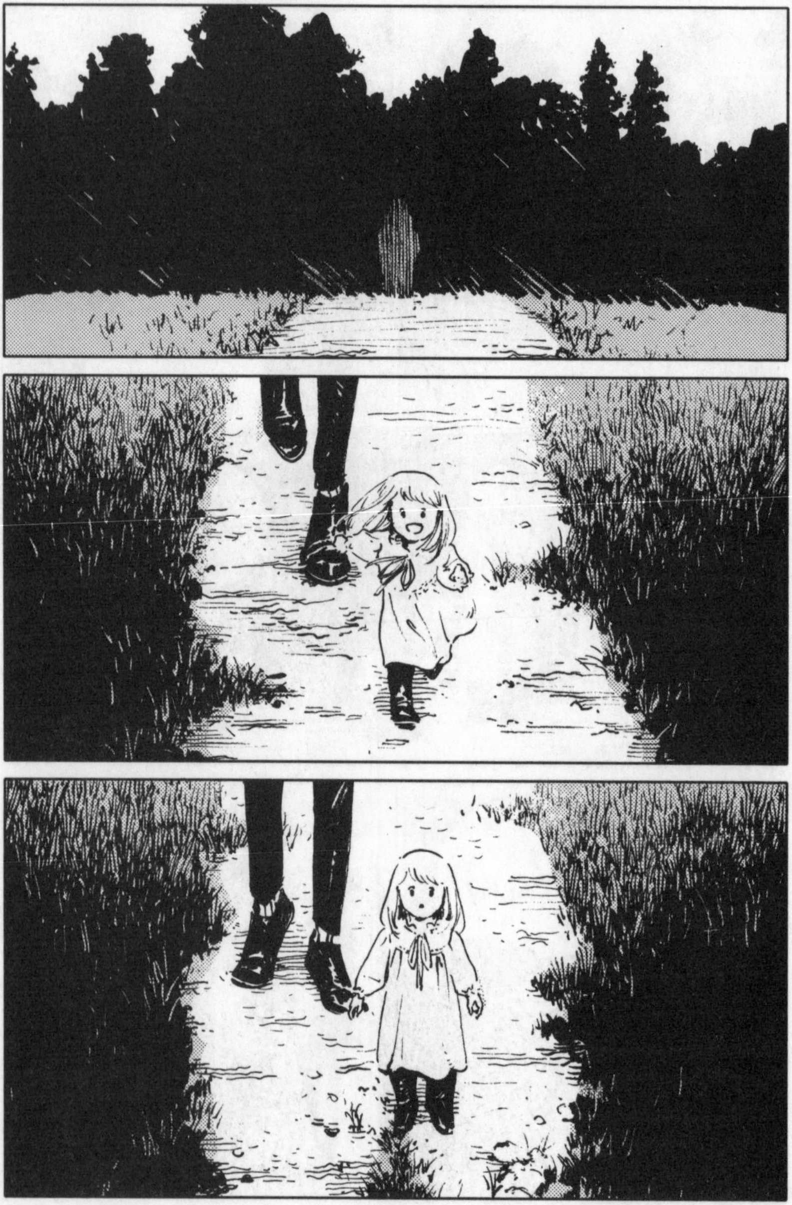

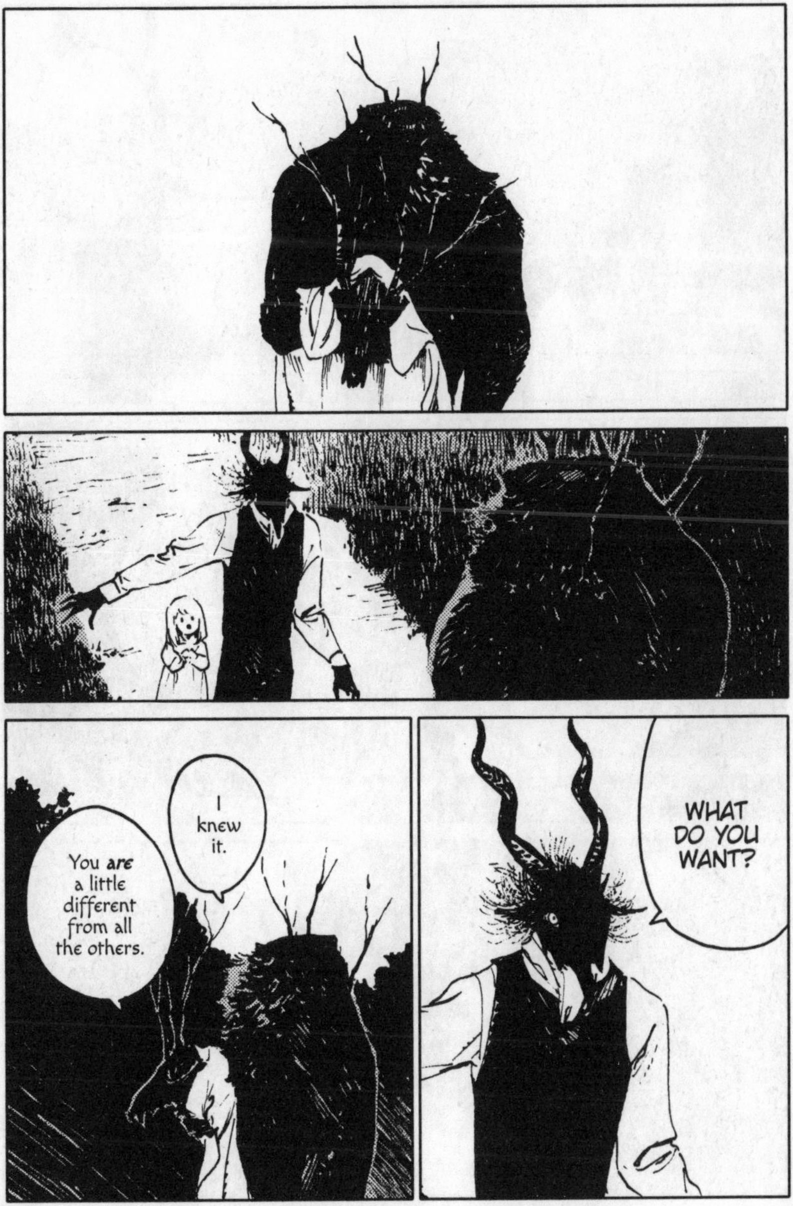
WHAT DO YOU WANT?
I knew it.
You *are* a little different from all the others.

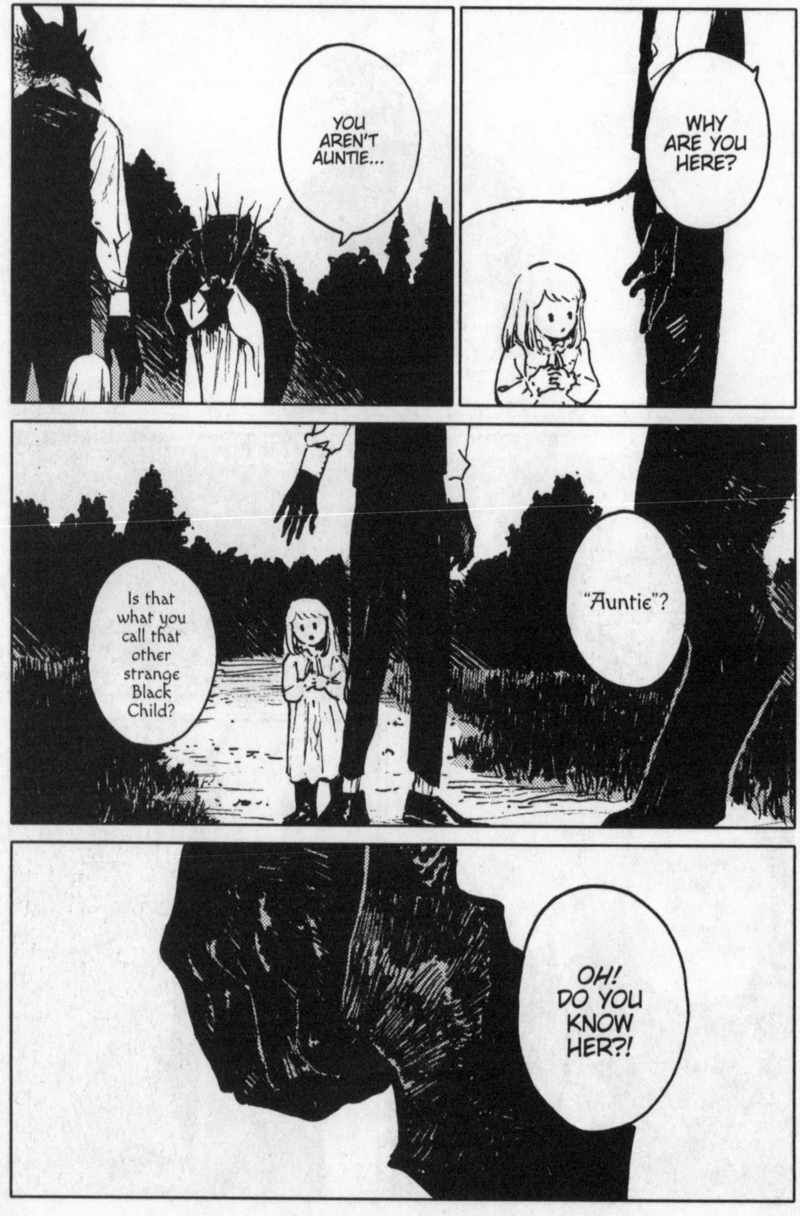
WHY ARE YOU HERE?
YOU AREN'T AUNTIE...
"Auntie"?
Is that what you call that other strange Black Child?
OH! DO YOU KNOW HER?!

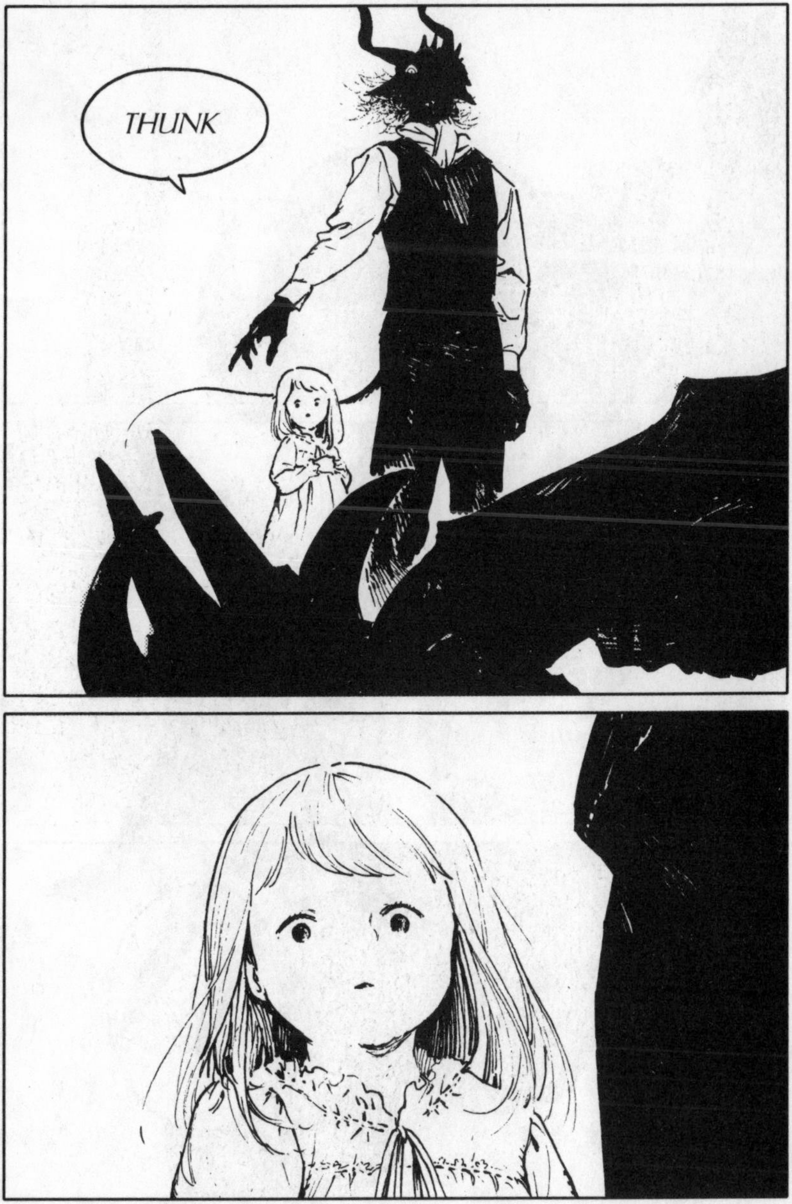
THUNK

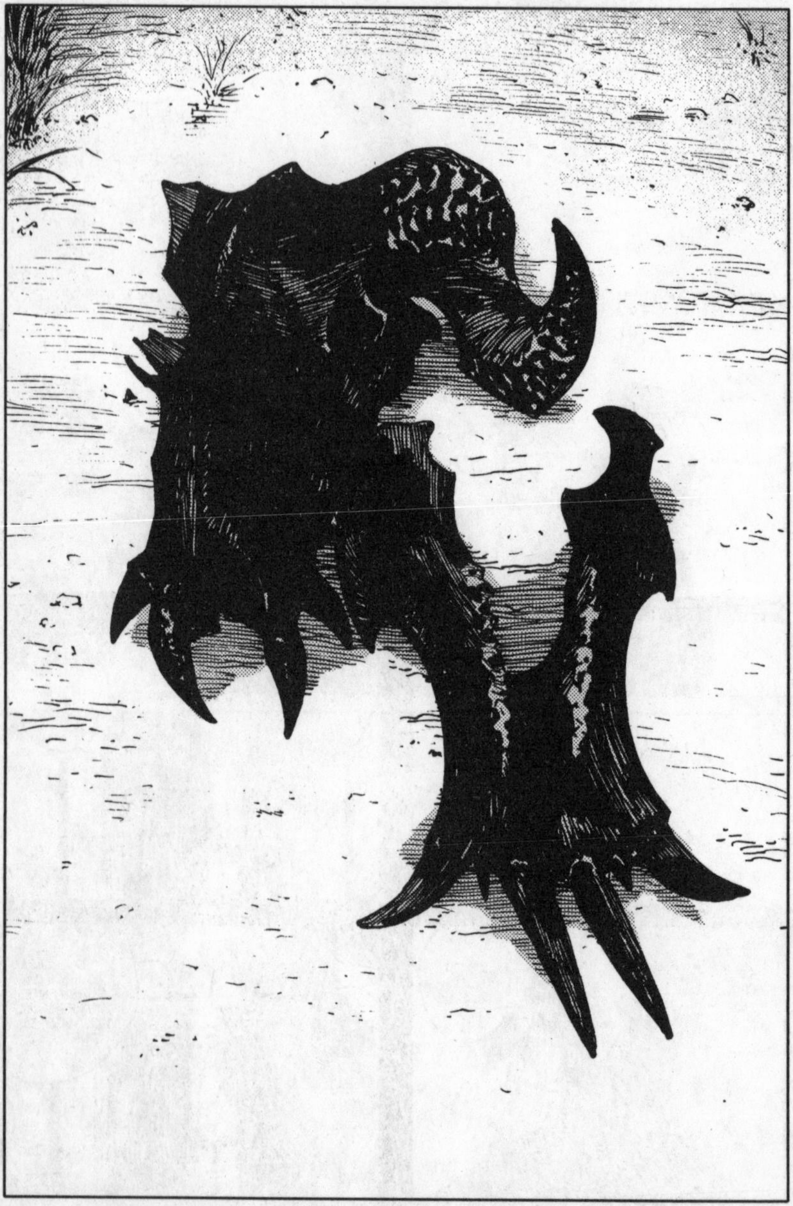

The Girl from the Other Side: Siúil a Rún Vol. 4 – END